SOUTHWEST INDIAN SILVER
FROM THE DONEGHY COLLECTION

The Navajo warrior "Many Arrows" photographed by
A. C. Vroman in 1903. (Courtesy of the Natural History
Museum of Los Angeles County)

SOUTHWEST INDIAN SILVER
FROM THE DONEGHY COLLECTION

Edited by Louise Lincoln

The Minneapolis Institute of Arts
University of Texas Press, Austin

This book was produced in conjunction with the exhibition
*Finished in Beauty: Southwest Indian Silver from the
Doneghy Collection.*

The Minneapolis Institute of Arts
15 July–31 October 1982

The Wheelwright Museum of the American Indian, Sante Fe
13 March–4 June 1983

Natural History Museum of Los Angeles County
7 December 1983–26 February 1984

Cooper-Hewitt Museum, New York
17 April–8 July 1984

Copy edited by Elisabeth Sövik
Designed by Ruth Dean
Catalogue photographs by Gary Mortensen
with the assistance of Petronella Ytsma

©1982 by The Minneapolis Institute of Arts
2400 Third Avenue South
Minneapolis, Minnesota 55404
All rights reserved
Printed in the United States of America

Library of Congress Catalog Card Number 82-80799
ISBN 0-292-72440-3 (hardcover)
ISBN 0-292-72441-1 (paperback)

This exhibition and catalogue have been made possible
through a generous grant from the National Endowment for
the Humanities, a federal agency. Additional support has
been received from the Minnesota Humanities Commission
and from Mr. and Mrs. John M. Musser.

Foreword

Virginia Doneghy was the sort of collector museum directors dream about. She possessed the knowledge, tenacity, and sense of purpose necessary to form a singularly comprehensive collection in the area of her specialty, and she simply appeared one day, miraculously, on the museum's doorstep, inquiring if we might be interested in "seeing her things." We, who never knew of her activities, were confronted with her staggering accomplishment fully grown—a *fait accompli*—and it had all happened in our backyard.

Her subsequent association with the museum was delightful. Over storage tables laden with her collection, and over lunch tables, she entertained us with tales of her adventures in the Southwest, at the same time providing valuable insights into the formation of her collection. Miss Doneghy's knowledge of her silver was nothing short of astounding. If we had a question about a piece we could telephone her, and from our brief description she could recall where and when she bought it and what was known of its history, all without reference to her notes. Her notes, too, are extraordinary; filling three oversized notebooks and several file card drawers, they are orderly and complete, as befits the work of a professional librarian. They are also, like Miss Doneghy, disarmingly direct and filled with anecdote and humor. She noted down

the discovery of a fake in her collection with as much relish as she recorded the purchase of a wonderful old Navajo necklace on the Ponte Vecchio in Florence. She held strong opinions about her pieces, as her recollections at the end of this book attest; she disagreed unhesitatingly with experts and frequently held her own.

Asked once if she had intended to create such a major assemblage of Indian jewelry, she replied: "Oh no. It just happened. It just grew like Topsy. I couldn't control myself. It was an obsession. I would go out to the Southwest. I knew I didn't need anything more, didn't want anything more. But what I would come back with! I was just helpless. It is like drink really. It really is. You see these things and you feel you've got to have them. Why? God only knows. You don't." A Collector's collector.

Her death in November 1981 left the museum staff and her many friends with a deep sense of personal loss. With characteristic generosity she bequeathed her entire collection of Southwest Indian silver to The Minneapolis Institute of Arts. We can think of no more appropriate tribute to Virginia Doneghy than this exhibition and catalogue.

Samuel Sachs II
Director

5

Acknowledgments

Any museum exhibition is a cooperative endeavor, drawing on the specialized knowledge of dozens of experts in widely divergent fields. This project is no exception; it could not have come about without the hard work and the advice of many collaborators. Among them we must acknowledge with special thanks the consultants to the project: John Adair, Professor Emeritus of San Francisco State College; LaRayne Parrish, Curator of the Wheelwright Museum of the American Indian, Santa Fe; and Joe Ben Wheat, Curator of the University of Colorado Museum. These scholars not only contributed essays to the catalogue, but also patiently sifted through the nearly 1,200 objects in the Doneghy collection and commented on each of them. They were generous with their time and their expertise, and our debt of gratitude to them is large indeed. Al Packard, a Santa Fe trader, also examined each piece with particular reference to dates and turquoise mines, as did Marsha Lund, and they have made invaluable contributions to the catalogue. My predecessor, Ellen Bradbury, now Associate Director, Fine Arts, Museum of New Mexico, has taken a great interest in the collection since it was first offered to the Institute as a loan in 1977. It was she who recognized the importance of the collection and first proposed an exhibition. She has served as a consultant, and we have profited greatly from her knowledge and advice.

Other scholars have offered much assistance with various aspects of the exhibition and catalogue. Barbara Tedlock, Associate Professor of Anthropology at Tufts University, freely shared her extensive knowledge of Zuni materials. Harold Blau, of the Community College of New York; Seymour Freed, Curator of North American Ethnology at the American Museum of Natural History in New York; William Merrill, Associate Curator of North American Ethnology at the Smithsonian Institution; and James G. E. Smith, Curator of North American Ethnology at the Museum of the American Indian in New York, all provided advice and assistance in the early phases of the project. Research was greatly facilitated by Phyllis Rabinow, Curator of Collections, and Lillian Novak, Archivist, at the Field Museum in Chicago; Laurie Davis of the Wheelwright Museum; and the staffs at the Archives of Anthropology at the Smithsonian Institution and the National Archives. Harold Edwards, of the Department of Geology at the University of Minnesota, kindly examined and identified many stones. Ron Libertus, of the Minnesota Department of Natural Resources, and Evan Maurer, Director of the University of Michigan Museum of Art, made numerous helpful suggestions. The exhibition was designed by Dextra Frankel and Thomas Hartman of LAX Studios, Los Angeles.

Many colleagues on the staff of The Minneapolis Institute of Arts have played major roles in the organization of the exhibition and catalogue. Todd Maitland, Cataloguer in the Registrar's Office, has been involved with the collection for more than four years. Her knowledge and judgment have made possible the awesome task of organizing and describing 1,200 objects, and she has contributed in countless other ways as well. Nancy Gunderson, Research Assistant, and Sharon Scott and Jeffrey Stoks, interns, have worked on various parts of the project with great intelligence and extraordinary devotion. Esther Nelson, Maintenance Technician, lovingly cleaned each of the objects to be exhibited. Gary Mortensen, Photographer, and Petronella Ytsma, Assistant Photographer, are responsible for the excellent catalogue photographs.

Assistance with photographic research came from Carroll T. Hartwell, Curator of Photography. The catalogue has been designed by Ruth Dean and edited with great skill and patience by Elisabeth Sövik. Funding for the exhibition was organized by DeCourcey McIntosh, Vice President for Development, Society of Fine Arts. Charles Skrief, Capital Gifts Counsel for the Society, has assisted with numerous details. Samuel Sachs II, Director of the Institute, provided much valued advice in both planning and execution. Michael Conforti, Bell Memorial Curator of Decorative Arts and Sculpture and Chairman of the Curatorial Division, has been involved in every aspect of the project and has provided direction, momentum, and inspiration. His guidance and his criticism, his support and encouragement, have been invaluable and greatly appreciated.

The exhibition and catalogue could not have come about without the assistance of a grant from the National Endowment for the Humanities, a federal agency. Further support for specific programs has been given by the Minnesota Humanities Commission and by Mr. and Mrs. John M. Musser. Finally, we wish to express our deep gratitude to Virginia Doneghy for her perception and skill in forming a collection, her meticulous recording of information, her enthusiasm for the subject and for this exhibition, and her extraordinary generosity in bequeathing her accumulated treasures to The Minneapolis Institute of Arts.

Louise Lincoln
Assistant Curator
African, Oceanic, and
New World Cultures

Contents

9

Introduction

Louise Lincoln

To those unfamiliar with the history of the Southwest peoples and their art, it is surprising to learn that Indian silverwork is a fairly new art form. The Navajo, the first to acquire the craft, did not begin to work silver until the middle of the nineteenth century; yet the forms of their jewelry are so familiar and so well established that it is easy to assume an earlier beginning. Perhaps equally remarkable is the fact that the Navajo themselves are relatively new to the Southwest compared with their Pueblo neighbors, having migrated from their homeland in southern Canada shortly before the Spanish conquistadors pushed northward from Mexico. Within the context of Navajo culture, however, such rapid adaptation is not surprising. It has often been suggested that the Navajo as a group are particularly successful at adapting to new conditions and borrowing skills and ideas from outside cultures, and their use of silver is among the best known of these assimilated practices. To understand the relationship of Southwest silver to the history of the region, and also how the art matured so quickly, one must know something of Navajo history.

The American Southwest is one of the oldest continuously inhabited regions in the Western Hemisphere. Archaeological evidence suggests that human habitation of the area goes back at least 10,000 years and perhaps longer. Through the millennia various groups have settled there, obtaining their subsistence according to the climate of the time and the technology available to them. Some of these groups were relatively transient, while others occupied established sites over long periods of time.

The ancestors of the Navajo people were among the later arrivals to the Southwest. It has been established, largely through a comparative study of language, that the Navajo belong to a group known as Athapaskans, whose original homeland lay in what is now roughly Manitoba, Canada. At some time after the tenth century A.D., perhaps because of climatic changes, some of those people began to migrate southward and eventually reached the Southwest. Their descendants are the modern Apache and Navajo peoples.

The recently arrived Athapaskans may have been the "Querecho" encountered by the Spanish explorer Francisco Vásquez de Coronado in 1541, when he ventured northward onto the Plains, and described by him as bison hunters. To be sure, the first Athapaskan immigrants to the Puebloan Southwest were small bands of hunters. By the late sixteenth century, when the Spanish began their colonization efforts in New Mexico, the Athapaskans had begun to engage in trade with the agricultural Pueblo settlements. The Spanish focused their attempts on the Pueblo farmers, since there were never enough Spanish militia, horses, or guns to control the roving Athapaskans.

The arrival of the Spanish disrupted the emerging trade networks of the Athapaskan and Pueblo peoples, forcing the Navajo into remote areas and causing them to rely on periodic raids on Spanish and Indian villages to obtain goods previously available through exchange. Both the Navajo and the Pueblos proved difficult for the Spanish to control. In the late seventeenth century the Europeans

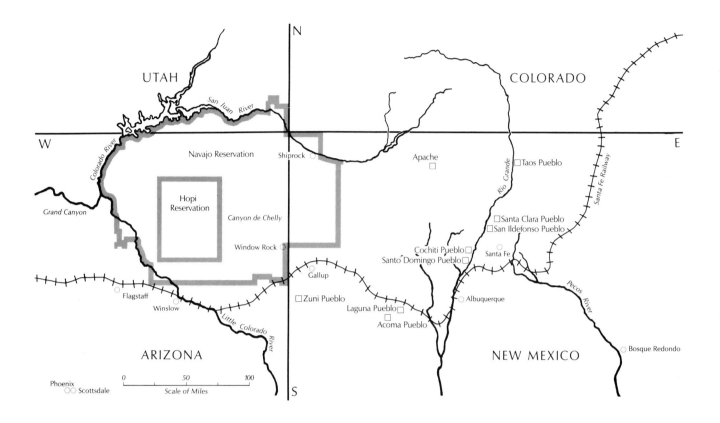

were drawn into repeated military campaigns against the Pueblo villages, suffered heavy losses at times, and were temporarily driven back. By the eighteenth century, however, the Spanish had achieved an uneasy social and political control as well as partial conversion of the Pueblo peoples to Christianity. The Navajo, who were more widely dispersed and perhaps had less to gain from peace with the Spanish, were not so tractable. Although some Navajo groups made peace with the Spanish governor, most did not accept colonial jurisdiction and some continued to raid for subsistence.

Relations between the Navajo and their Pueblo neighbors were no less complex. Exchange of goods continued in some places, while in others the Pueblo peoples were subject to Navajo raids. At times during the

Spanish occupation the two groups lived in proximity and intermarried. The period of the Navajo arrival in the Southwest, closely coincident with that of the Spanish, was clearly one of great stress and conflict. Nevertheless, under conditions of extreme adversity, the Navajo developed over the course of several centuries a distinctive and complex culture, different in significant ways from that of their Athapaskan forebears. They borrowed extensively but selectively from the Pueblo peoples in the areas of agricultural and craft techniques, hunting, herding, and certain aspects of religious ideology and practice; but they resisted Pueblo influence in the equally important areas of language, domestic architecture, and social organization.

The situation of the Navajo remained unchanged in the early years of American rule after the annexation of New Mexico as a territory in 1846, but the westward expansion of white settlement required suppression of Indian raids. A U.S. Army campaign against the Navajo was begun in 1863 under the leadership of Kit Carson. Navajo livestock and crops were systematically destroyed, and by the following year groups of Navajo, driven to starvation, were surrendering. The captives were marched more than three hundred miles to a newly established reservation in eastern New Mexico known as Bosque Redondo. The plan of American military authorities was to resettle them in an isolated and tightly controlled location where they could be kept under surveillance. At the same time they would be taught Euro-American farming techniques, introduced to Christianity, and in general separated as much as possible from their former way of life. Such control of the "Indian problem" would open the territory to Euro-American farmers, ranchers, and miners.

Weakened by exposure and disease, many Navajo died en route to Bosque Redondo. Conditions at the reservation were no better. The army did in fact attempt to teach them agricultural and herding methods and to provide them with some means of future subsistence. But heavy-handed paternalism, combined with the government's insensitivity to Navajo wishes and customs regarding food, housing, and religion, made the Navajo distrustful of their captors. Furthermore, the land was arid and unproductive, the supply of rations and equipment inadequate, and the Navajo so beset by epidemic disease and hunger that they no longer constituted an impediment to white expansion. In 1868, their numbers decimated, they were permitted to return west to a new reservation in the region of their homeland.

The internment at Bosque Redondo brought vast changes to Navajo culture, among them greater interaction with Euro-Americans. In the 1870s, when the U.S. government permitted white traders to open trading posts on Indian reservations, contact with the outside culture increased and so did dependence on goods from that culture. Through the barter system that developed, the Indians could exchange goods like wool, sheep pelts, and agricultural produce for credit with which to obtain tools, cloth, canned food, and other manufactured items. They could also get credit by pawning personal articles, and in this arrangement silver jewelry played a highly important role.

The latter part of the nineteenth century saw a steady increase in the Navajo population and some improvement in their economic situation. By 1880 the Atchison, Topeka, and Santa Fe Railroad had reached the Southwest, and by the turn of the century the tourist trade was established and thriving. "Indian goods" became fashionable as curios and souvenirs, and traders encouraged artists to make textiles, baskets, pottery, and silver specifically for this market. Hotels sprang up, guided tours to the reservation became common, and artisans displayed their goods at every train stop. The automobile permitted further penetration of the reservation, and serious collectors of Indian art were thus able to acquire dead pawn from remote trading posts.

In the twentieth century the Navajo have encountered new problems. Their growing population and the declining productivity of the arid reservation lands have meant an insufficiency of crops and livestock forage. The federal government has intervened in numerous areas, from public health to control of soil erosion, with mixed results. Government-established boarding schools took children away from the traditional way of life and taught them skills not necessarily useful on the reservation but inadequate for employment in the outside culture. During World War II many Navajo men were drafted into military service and sent abroad; when they returned, readjustment was often difficult. Thus, for the Navajo, living on the reservation has become less a matter of course, and some have settled in urban areas of the Southwest, even though it is often hard for them to find jobs. Each year fewer Navajo maintain the "traditional" way of life of the late nineteenth and early twentieth centuries. At the same time, however, many aspects of that life are carried on, and there is a general interest, among the young especially, in preserving their heritage.

Early Southwest Metalwork

Joe Ben Wheat

The desire for personal adornment seems to be a universal trait. Thousands of years ago, people began searching their surroundings for natural objects with which to beautify themselves—bits of wood, colorful berries, insect wings, feathers, furs, bones, teeth, claws, horns, and shells from ocean and stream all found their way into ornaments. Molded clay and pottery, as well as ordinary, semiprecious, and precious stones, also were used for decorative effect. Metals occurring free in nature could simply be hammered to shape, and as metallurgy became more advanced, the mining and smelting of formerly unknown metals brought new material under the smith's hand. Ornaments unobtainable from the immediate environment were sought through trade, often passing hundreds of miles through exchange networks of astonishing complexity. Long before commerce in necessities had developed, the exchange of exotic goods for personal adornment flourished.

The native Indians of the American Southwest were not exceptions to this desire for self-adornment. What they could not find at home, they imported from Mexico or from the shores of the Pacific Ocean or the Gulf of Mexico. Long before the coming of the Spanish in the sixteenth century, prehistoric southwesterners wore necklaces, pendants, bracelets, anklets, rings, headbands, combs and hairpins, earrings, buttons, and plaques. Some even wore plugs in ears, lips, and nose.[1] It is likely that the Navajo, who arrived in the Southwest shortly before the Spanish, shared in this native heritage.

A great variety of materials found their way into these ornaments. Often, they were combined with each other in composite forms, for example, necklaces of juniper berries, acorn caps, ephedra seeds, and walnuts strung on hand-spun cord; carved and painted wood, or wood overlaid with mosaics of turquoise, jet, and shell stuck on with pine gum; and combs made from polished sticks of hardwood bound together and often embellished with feathers. Stones such as selenite, mica, and quartz crystals were drilled, carved, polished, and suspended as beads or pendants. Common stones like travertine, shale, and argilite were treated in the same manner, and hematite and jet (the organic stone) were shaped and polished for use as pendants, buttons, and plaques, either alone or combined with turquoise. Turquoise, the most sought-after stone, became surrounded with myths and even religious beliefs, some of which have come down to modern times.

Artistry in shell combined a few local species of freshwater snails and mussels with many imported varieties. From the Pacific Coast or the Gulf of California came abalone, olivella, olive, pecten, glycymeris, and spiny oyster, as well as conus, turritella, and vermetus. Some came as raw materials to be worked locally into disk or tubular beads, pendants, and tesserae for mosaics, but others were traded as finished products. A huge shell manufactory in northern Sonora, Mexico, produced bracelets cut from glycymeris, which were traded through the Hohokam to the Mogollon and Anasazi—the prehistoric ancestors of the modern Pueblo and other Indians of the Southwest. Sometimes the umbo of these shell bracelets was carved to resemble a frog. Other bracelets were engraved or even etched with complex geometric designs, and some were inlaid with turquoise. Rings made of conus shell were treated in the same way as the bracelets. As early as the time of Christ, abalone was worked into pendants of various forms, and by A.D. 1000, abalone pendants were frequently carved in the forms

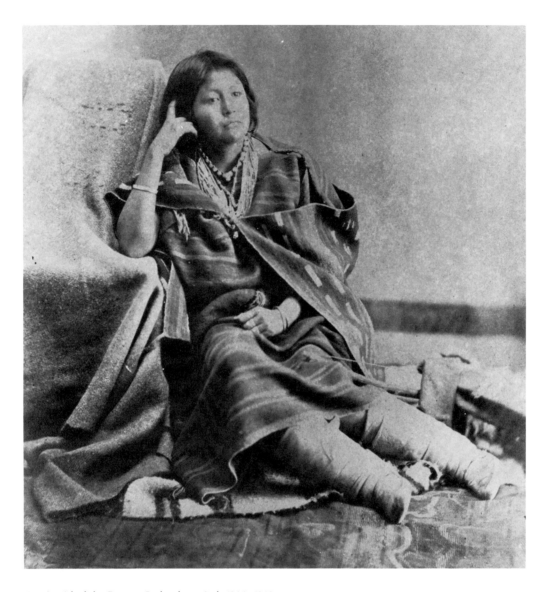

Navajo girl of the Bosque Redondo period, 1864–1868.
She is wearing three narrow band bracelets, three rings,
numerous strands of shell or coral and turquoise beads,
and a necklace of silver buttons strung on a thong.
(Photograph courtesy of the Museum of New Mexico)

of birds, lizards, turtles, and even humans.
Other shells, such as olives and olivellas,
were strung as necklaces.

Perhaps the most common prehistoric jewelry
of this region was the necklace made from
disk beads of shell and turquoise. It is a
style that remains popular today. Although
some free metal—mostly copper—occurred
in the Southwest, few native-hammered
ornaments have been found. However, a

number of cast copper bells and other copper
objects came by trade from Mexico into all
parts of the Southwest, lending an exotic
touch to the native jewelry.

It was into this rich heritage of native
ornament that the Spanish introduced
European jewelry. No exploring expedition
venturing for the first time into unknown
territory would set out without a stock of cloth
and ribbons and beads and baubles with which

to please the native population by gift or trade. No doubt Coronado and subsequent explorers carried such items, but we do not know what they were.

When Oñate came in 1598 to settle what is now New Mexico, he was prepared to gratify the Indians he found living in pueblos there and such of the roving tribes as might wish to deal with the Spanish colonists. His inventory of items intended for barter included 56 bunches of glass beads, with 1,000 to 10,000 beads per bunch, in blue, black, white, red, and green; 900 beads called aquamarines; 4,500 small glass beads called half-aquamarines; and enough wooden beads, painted like coral, for seven rosaries. There were 54 rosaries, together with 56 Tlascala rosary tassels, and 63 necklaces of glass beads. Glass beads were also made into 44 throatbands, while there were "some" beads of an alloy intended for the same ornament. Sixteen medals of tin, 680 medals of an alloy, and 238 smaller medals were listed along with 54 amulets made of badger bone. All would serve as pendants. The ears were not neglected, for there were 82½ dozen glass earrings, as well as 6 small gourd-shaped earrings of colored glass. Six dozen jet rings, 25 rings of an alloy, and 22 finger rings of bone were listed. Miscellaneous ornamental objects included 10 or 12 small glass buttons, 25 ordinary combs, 19 small Flemish mirrors, 1 jet headpiece, and 19½ dozen hawksbells. An earlier inventory had also "barley corals, since artificial glass beads are not available" and amber beads large and small.[2]

The ornaments brought for the Indian trade in 1598 were just a beginning; the supply continued throughout the Spanish regime. Itinerant traders carried beads, metal ornaments, and other such things with them to trade fairs for the different tribes, and missionaries and government officials commonly gave ornaments to the Indians. In 1706, Governor Cuervo y Valdez gave a visiting delegation "ribbons, hats, needles, beads, and many other trifles."[3] Beads and other trifles from sites in the traditional Navajo homeland, Gobernador Canyon in New Mexico, give us a picture of Navajo

ornamentation about 1750.[4] Native-made ornaments consisted of about 1,000 shell disk beads, 550 olivella beads, shell ear pendants, tubular bone beads, a bead of jet, and an elk-tooth pendant. These native products were vastly outnumbered by Spanish goods—copper bells, metal crosses, bronze jinglers or pendants, a lead disk, an iron and copper bridle-bit, a gold-washed copper-button bridle ornament, engraved hollow copper buttons, and a hand-wrought copper buckle very similar in design to the silver belt conchas of later times. One necklace was strung with units of 3 red glass beads alternating with units of about 20 white shell disk beads. Found unstrung were an astounding number of trade beads. There were more than 15,000 glass beads—large and small, faceted, globular, flattened, spherical, tubular, petaloid, knobbed, and annular—of 21 basic types. Most of the beads were translucent, in crystal, milky white, two shades of amber, three of blue, three of green, yellow, red, and dark garnet. Opaque beads were white, black, yellow, blue, and turquoise. Some beads of dark blue glass had been painted with gold. Several large opaque beads were inlaid with floral or geometric patterns in glasses of different colors. Finally, there were about 20 beads of Mediterranean coral, a bead material exceedingly popular to this day among the southwestern Indians.

The practice of rewarding the good Indian became a standard element of Spanish Indian policy, and money was appropriated to secure the needed items. In 1786, Governor Anza was instructed to spend the money "economically for supplies for the militia, settlers, and Navajos . . . and for presents for the latter who may merit it because of good conduct, in scarlet cloth, colored bayetta, long sheathed knives, and bridles." One charge against the fund in 1787 included "lazos [ornaments] to recompense the Navajos"—ornaments that included glass beads (coquinillos). A year later, Vicinte Troncoso reported that the Navajo women were decorated with coral, small glass beads, and shells, and by 1795 Governor Chacon had noted that Navajo men as well as women "go decently clothed; and their Captains are rarely seen without silver jewelry." The jewelry probably was made by

Navajo delegation to Washington, D.C., 1874. Articles of jewelry and clothing worn by the Navajo include concha belts, necklaces (some with jaclas), bracelets, rings, earrings, ketohs, and shoulder pouches with beaded or silver-mounted straps. One man has a silver powder-charger and tweezers, and one is wearing a leather shirt with beadwork panels. (Photograph courtesy of the Smithsonian Institution, National Anthropological Archives)

Spanish silversmiths working near Silver City, New Mexico, who regularly made silver ornaments to supply tribes of the Southern Plains, such as the Kiowa, and also the Pueblos and the Navajo.[5]

In the early 1800s, ornaments such as glass and coral beads, scarf pins, combs, rings, and eardrops were imported from Mexico.[6] But shortly after Mexico won its independence from Spain in 1821, the borders of New Mexico were opened to American traders, who soon came to dominate the trade of northern Mexico. Along with cloth, medicines, hardware, liquors, and fine foods, they imported quantities of beads and other ornaments.[7] In 1824, Nathaniel Patten described a slain Navajo chief who "wore . . . small clothes [pants] connected at the sides by silver buttons . . . and a scarlet cloth cap, the folds of which were also seamed by silver buttons" and remarked that the Navajo bridles were "made of tanned leather, and often embellished with silver ornaments."[8]

The year 1846 was a turning point in the history of the Southwest, for in that year of the Mexican War the Americans took over New Mexico, Arizona, California, and other lands claimed by Mexico. Along with the territory, the Americans inherited the "Indian problem," and like the Spanish and Mexicans before them, they sought to buy peace by "gratifying" the Indians with gifts. Agents to each of the tribes were appointed, and among their duties were the purchase and distribution of trade goods. Ornaments, or the materials for making ornaments, always constituted a part of the gifts.

One of the journalists of the 1846 Mexican War observed Navajo women wearing "brass rings upon their arms, the larger the better."[9] It is almost certain that the brass bracelets were made by the Navajo themselves, for they required only a length of brass wire and files to produce decorative grooves or to engrave bracelets that were flattened by hammering. Sometimes two or three of these bands of wire would be twisted together to form a larger bracelet. The Navajo and other southwestern tribes continued to make and wear brass wire bracelets for a very long time. A trader to the Navajo in 1852 carried 197 pounds of brass wire, along with brass kettles which could be cut into pieces for jewelry after their use as camp utensils.[10] Between 1854 and 1871, when its issue was discontinued, the Navajo were given over 2,000 pounds of brass wire to be made into bracelets or wire loop earrings. Over 7,000 pounds of brass kettles and 500 pounds of copper kettles were issued during the same period. The Navajo received more than 250 gross of flat, ball, or bell brass buttons and about half a million brass-headed tacks used to ornament saddles, cradles, gun stocks, and other items.[11]

All of this time, southwestern Indian tribes continued to receive glass and coral beads. In 1850, at least ten bunches of silver beads were given to the Navajo, along with some finger rings, earbobs, mirrors, and hawksbells.[12] Most of these beads they made up into necklaces. However, the beading of leather goods, such as shirts, shoulder pouches, and straps, was fairly common among the Navajo. Beads issued to the Navajo included black, white, blue, red, imitation coral, ruby, pink, gold, and agate. One Navajo war shirt dating to about 1840 has leather sleeve and shoulder panels beaded with white and blue pony beads. The shirt is made of red and blue trade cloth and is further ornamented with flat brass buttons.[13]

Despite the profusion of glass beads, neither the Pueblos nor the Navajo lost their love for necklaces of shell, turquoise, and coral.[14] While some coral necklaces were issued to the Navajo, most were acquired by trade from the Pueblos. The pueblos of Santo Domingo and Zuni were, and are, great centers for the manufacturing of shell and turquoise necklaces, which were traded to the Hopi for woven ceremonial clothing and to the Navajo for their finest blankets. During the 1800s and early 1900s, these necklaces consisted of white shell disk beads interspersed with disk beads of turquoise or polished tablike pendants, many of which had seen earlier service as ear pendants. Jaclas (ear pendants) made of loops of turquoise beads were frequently hung on the necklace as pendants when they were not in the ears. Subsequently,

the jacla became a standard part of the turquoise and coral necklaces. Necklaces of brown shell heishi disk beads and rough nugget pendants became popular in the 1920s.

Although the Navajo are known to have had silver ornaments since the late sixteenth century, we do not know when they began to work silver themselves. Most scholars place the time around 1850. In working brass, it was only necessary to bend the lengths of brass wire to the desired shape and to file grooves for decoration, but before iron or silver could be hammered to shape, the metal had to be heated, or annealed, to make it tougher and less brittle. Silver sometimes had to be melted and cast into suitable forms before it could be made into ornaments. While a few Navajo may have learned some elements of the craft earlier, in 1854 Agent Dodge hired George Carter, a blacksmith, to teach smithing to the Navajo at Fort Defiance. Juan Anaya, a Mexican silversmith, was hired as Carter's assistant.[15] The next year, Dodge requested 1,000 pounds of iron and four sets of blacksmith tools to supply "eighteen native blacksmiths who work with the hand-bellows and the primitive tools used by the Mexicans with which they make all of the bridle bits, rings, buckles, & etc."[16] Silver, as such, is not mentioned, but the presence of the silversmith should not be overlooked. At any rate, silver jewelry formed a regular part of Navajo costume at this time.

Several drawings of the early 1850s show Pueblos and Navajo wearing silver-buttoned pantaloons and button-bedecked straps. The Navajo are depicted with leather belts mounted with oval silver plates.[17] In 1854, Dr. Letherman mentioned that the Navajo man covered himself with "a blanket, under and sometimes over which is worn a belt to which are attached oval pieces of silver, plain or variously wrought."[18] Perhaps the best description was given in 1855 by W. W. H. Davis.

The Nabajo . . . dress with greater comfort than any other tribe, and wear woolen and well-tanned buckskin. The skin breeches come down to the knee, where they are met by blue stockings that cover the lower half of the leg; the breeches fit tight to the limb, and the outer seams are adorned with silver or brass buttons. The coat reaches below the hips, with a hole at the top to thrust the head through, and open at the sides; it is made of wool, woven of bright colors, and is fastened around the waist by a leather belt, highly ornamented with silver when the wearer can afford it. They wear numerous strings of fine coral, and many valuable belts of silver, and generally appear with a handsome blanket thrown over the shoulder in the style of a mantle.[19]

That not every Navajo was so adorned is made clear by the report of a skirmish in 1858 in which a Zuni scout captured from a woman "a silver belt worth $50 or $75—also $100 or $200 worth of coral necklace, precious stones [probably turquoises], and other articles greatly prized by the Indians and possessed only by the rich."[20]

By the early 1860s, the Navajo were clearly making their own silver. The almost continuous raiding of the Rio Grande valley, which had in the past rewarded the Navajo with livestock and slaves as well as many ornaments, finally resulted in the Navajo campaign of 1863–1864, led by Kit Carson. In a classic guerilla war, the Americans defeated the Navajo and forced them into an internment at Bosque Redondo on the Pecos River in eastern New Mexico, an internment that lasted until 1868, when they were allowed to return to a reservation established in their old homeland. Early in 1864, a war correspondent wrote to the *Rio Abajo Weekly Press* of Albuquerque, "The warriors themselves fabricate saddles, and bridles, and buckles, buttons, and clasps of silver which are tasteful ornaments to their finely fitting cloth and buckskin dresses." Later the same year, another correspondent informed the *Army and Navy Journal* that the Navajo at Bosque Redondo "also manufacture silver ornaments of a very creditable style of workmanship."[21]

During the Navajo campaign, in 1864, one Mexican raid on the Navajo resulted in the capture of "over $200 of silver plate for belts," and even the Navajo chief, Delgadito,

had his silver "belt worth one hundred dollars . . . stolen from him, and the theft was traced to some American soldiers."[22]

At Bosque Redondo the Navajo soon added new metalworking skills to those they had brought with them. In 1864, some of the Navajo being instructed in metalworking learned to produce copies of the government stamps and dies used to fabricate the metal ration tickets that regulated distribution of food and other items to the Navajo internees. They counterfeited over 3,000 of these metal tickets, causing the government to substitute tickets of cardboard with an engraved design so intricate that it could not be duplicated locally.[23] The skills they acquired in making their own metal stamps and dies were put to good use later when they began decorating their silver with stamped designs copied from Mexican leatherworking stamps.

When they returned to their reservation in 1868, the Navajo brought with them a small but growing craft in silverwork. Throughout the 1870s they improved their skills and considerably increased the kinds of objects they could make. By 1880 they were so involved in the silver craft that Indians working for the government demanded their pay in silver. Agent Galen Eastman reported, "They all want silver (Mexican preferred in that it is softer to work into their uses than American . . .)." In August, Eastman paid out $2,488.75 in Mexican silver for various services. This was not universally appreciated, for a complaint to the solicitor of the U.S. Treasury accused Eastman of paying Indians in debased coins ("Mexicalli dollars purchased for 80–90 cents") and appropriating the difference to personal use.[24]

Nevertheless, the Navajo desired the silver. According to the report of special inspector John McNeil in late 1880:

Nearly all the young Navajos are good blacksmiths. Many work in silver . . . driving sheep, making blankets or silver ornaments pays better [than being on the police force] and that determines the choice for the young men. . . . These Indians [need] blacksmith tools of light sort that they can use in their silver manufactures. Out of the latter industry and the Blanket weaving they derive a profitable trade with other tribes as well as the white people. . . .[25]

To this, the Navajo chief Ganado Mucho added "files hammers and anvils, and small iron [silver]."[26] Thus it would appear that the Navajo at Fort Defiance were further advanced in silver craft than those at Fort Wingate reported on by Washington Matthews in 1884, who were, apparently, still relative novices in silverwork.[27]

Except for their homemade brass wire bracelets and earrings, most of the metal jewelry possessed by the Navajo before and during the 1850s came from the Spanish, Mexicans, and Americans and consisted of silver buttons, concha belts, and silver-mounted bridles. When they began to make their own jewelry, they continued making these items but added many more.

It is safe to say that between the return from Bosque Redondo in 1868 and the beginning of the 1880s the basic techniques of annealing, hammering, and soldering became well established throughout the reservation area. This occurred in a surprisingly short time, considering the isolated life-style and the difficulty of communication on Navajo lands during the nineteenth century. There was, of course, encouragement from outsiders. Federal agents, seeking to establish a sound economic base for the repatriated Navajo people, supplied smiths with tools and materials. Later this role was taken over by the traders, who stocked dies and anvils beside canned goods and cotton fabrics. It is also clear that even before the 1880s fairly consistent styles were emerging for standard items such as necklaces, belts, bracelets, and earrings. The common use of these designs (which were borrowed from diverse sources) and the quickness with which innovations were adopted suggest that there was a great deal of interest in the appearance of jewelry and some agreement about how it should look, as well as a willingness among the smiths to share their knowledge and technique.

Bear hunters at Chinle Trading Post, Arizona, about 1900. The men's clothing is a mixture of commercial pants and shirts and old-style pantaloons and blouses; the women are wearing calico skirts with velveteen blouses. Much silver jewelry is in evidence. (Photograph by Ben Wittick, courtesy of the Museum of New Mexico)

NOTES

1. A detailed study of prehistoric ornament in the Southwest can be found in Wesley E. Jernigan, *Jewelry of the Prehistoric Southwest* (Albuquerque: University of New Mexico Press, 1978).

2. George Peter Hammond and Agapito Rey, *Don Juan de Oñate: Colonizer of New Mexico, 1598–1628* (Albuquerque: University of New Mexico Press, 1953), pp. 220–223; ibid., p. 107.

3. Charles Wilson Hackett, *Historical Documents Relating to New Mexico, Nueva Vizcaya, and Approaches Thereto, to 1773*, 3 vols. (Washington, D.C.: Carnegie Institution of Washington, 1937), 3:368.

4. Roy L. Carlson, *Eighteenth Century Navajo Fortresses of Gobernador District*, University of Colorado Series in Anthropology, no. 10 (Boulder, 1965), pp. 10–40, 91–96.

5. Alfred Barnaby Thomas, *Forgotten Frontiers: A Study of the Spanish Indian Policy of Don Juan Bautista de Anza, Governor of New Mexico, 1777–1787* (Norman: University of Oklahoma Press, 1932), p. 269; Spanish Archives of New Mexico (SANM), 1600–1821, microfilm rolls 11, 13, New Mexico State Records Center and Archives, Santa Fe, 11:1173–1204; p. 5 of David Brugge's translation (MS, n.d.) of Vicinte Troncoso, "Report of Escorting Antonio El Pinto to His Home, 1788," Internal Provinces, vol. 65, 26 June 1788, General Archives, Seville, Spain; SANM, 13:735; James Mooney, "Calendar History of the Kiowa Indian," in Bureau of American Ethnology, Annual Report no. 17 (Washington, D.C., 1898), p. 319.

6. Ortiz Papers (1818) and Marques y Melos Papers (1819), New Mexico State Records Center and Archives, Santa Fe.

7. Mexican Archives of New Mexico (MANM), 1821–1846, microfilm rolls 4–34, New Mexico State Records Center and Archives, Santa Fe, 4:1226, 25:1420, 5–34 passim.

8. Arthur Woodward, *A Brief History of Navajo Silversmithing*, Museum of Northern Arizona, Bulletin no. 14 (Flagstaff, 1938), p. 51.

9. Jacob S. Robinson, *A Journal of the Santa Fe Expedition under Colonel Doniphan* (Princeton, N.J.: Princeton University Press, 1932), p. 51.

10. National Archives, Record Group 75 (NA RG-75), Letters Received by the Office of Indian Affairs, New Mexico Superintendency, 1846–1880, microfilm copy M234, rolls 546–580, and Records of the New Mexico Superintendency, 1849–1880, micro-film copy T21, rolls 1–30, Washington, D.C., M234:546, and T21:1.

11. NA RG-75, M234:546, and T21:1–12 passim.

12. NA RG-75, T21:1, 19 September 1850.

13. University of Colorado Museum, specimen no. 25132. See also Frank S. Edwards, *A Campaign in New Mexico with Colonel Doniphan* (1847; reprint ed., Philadelphia: Readex Microprint, 1966), p. 61.

14. NA RG-75, T21:2, 31 March 1856, and M234:548, November 1856.

15. L. R. Bailey, *The Long Walk* (Los Angeles: Westernlore Press, 1964), p. 57.

16. NA RG-75, M234:548, 30 September 1855.

17. A. W. Whipple, Thomas Ewbank, and William W. Turner, "Report on the Indian Tribes," in *Explorations and Surveys for a Railroad Route* (Washington, D.C.: U.S. War Department, 1855), plate 21; James H. Simpson, *Navajo Expedition: Journal of a Military Reconnaissance from Santa Fe, New Mexico, to the Navajo Country, Made in 1849*, edited by Frank McNitt (Norman: University of Oklahoma Press, 1964), plate facing p. 112; Joseph C. Ives, *Report upon the Colorado River of the West Explored in 1857 and 1858* (Washington, D.C.: U.S. Government Printing Office, 1861).

18. Jonathan Letherman (Letterman), *Sketch of the Navajo Tribe of Indians, Territory of New Mexico*, Smithsonian Institution, Annual Report no. 10 (Washington, D.C., 1856), pp. 283–297.

19. W. W. H. Davis, *El Gringo; or, New Mexico and Her People* (1857; reprint ed., Chicago: Rio Grande Press, 1962), p. 239.

20. Woodward, p. 16.

21. Ibid., pp. 16–17; ibid, p. 17.

22. NA RG-75, T21:6, 19 May 1864; Lawrence C. Kelly, *Navajo Roundup* (Boulder, Colo.: Pruett Publishing Company, 1970), p. 109.

23. Bailey, p. 205.

24. NA RG-75, M234:579, 24 January 1880; NA RG-75, M234:580, 2 February 1880.

25. NA RG-75, M234: 580, 23 December 1880.

26. Ibid.

27. Washington Matthews, "Navajo Silversmiths," in Bureau of American Ethnology, Annual Report no. 2 (Washington, D.C., 1884).

The Cultural and Economic Context of Navajo Jewelry

John Adair

The Navajo and Pueblo Indians live primarily in northern New Mexico and Arizona and in southern Utah. Today the Navajo number close to 150,000—much the largest Indian tribe in the United States—and spread with their sheep, horses, and cattle over an area the size of West Virginia. By contrast, the Hopi and Zuni tribes each number under 10,000 persons and live in small towns surrounded by fields where they grow crops of corn, beans, and squash. The Navajo's residence in the Southwest goes back only to around 1500, while the Pueblo Indians can be traced to Basket Maker ancestors who lived there before the time of Christ. The Pueblos' history as silver craftsmen, however, is even more recent than the Navajo's.

The Navajo did not learn to work silver until 1868, after they were released from Bosque Redondo, New Mexico, where they had been prisoners of the United States. They learned the art of silversmithing from Mexican *plateros* who had come up the Rio Grande valley from the south and whose technique and designs were derived from the Old World, from the art of the Moorish craftsmen in Spain and North Africa. In 1870 a Navajo named Atsidi Chon taught the craft of silversmithing to Lanyade, a Zuni, who in turn taught the Hopi to work silver around 1900.

Each of these tribes—Navajo, Zuni, and Hopi—has developed its own style of jewelry. In Navajo work there is a balance between silver and turquoise; heavy metalwork and large turquoise set off and balance each other. The early work of Zuni craftsmen resembled that of the Navajo. But when turquoise became more readily available, Zuni smiths used the silver as a means of holding a myriad of small stones in place, and since World War II they have produced complex lapidary work. The Hopi were for many years influenced by Navajo and Zuni work. In the 1940s, however, they developed what is called overlay design, in which curvilinear designs, often copied from pottery motifs, are cut in a stencil fashion and stand out against an oxidized silver background.

The Navajo and Pueblo Indians do not regard art as the creation of people outside the mainstream of the community. Artists are greatly respected, but to a large degree everyone is an artist. Art is the very substance of their lives. As the anthropologist Gary Witherspoon said of the Navajo, "Art is not divorced from everyday life, for the creation of beauty and the incorporation of oneself in beauty represent the highest attainment and ultimate destiny of man."[1] This is equally true of the Zuni and other Pueblo cultures, where, at least traditionally, all is art and art is not separated from the business of living. And it is true even today for those who work in silver and turquoise, for Pueblo painters working on canvas rather than on the *kiva* walls, for experts in the ritual art of the dance, for storytellers who hand down ancient myths and invent new tales, and for the ritual clowns in the summer rain dances. For them, art is naturally an integral, inseparable part of life.

Jewelry is valued both for its aesthetic qualities and as a sign of wealth. The Navajo and the Pueblo peoples do not hide their money in pockets and banks but invest it in silver and turquoise and display it on their persons. Prestige is gained by possessing and displaying jewelry as well as by owning sheep, goats,

Lorenzo Hubbell's trading post in Ganado, Arizona, as it appeared in the 1890s. Hubbell stands beneath the tree. (Photograph courtesy of Sharlot Hall Historical Society, Prescott, Arizona)

cattle, and horses. Jewelry is essentially family property, and spouses often exchange wearing the same necklace or concha belt.

Before the development of trading posts in the 1870s, and long before the opening of outside markets for Navajo jewelry, the silversmiths fashioned their pieces for kinsmen and fellow Navajo or traded them to strangers for other goods and services. For instance, a ketoh (a leather wristband with a silver mounting) might be traded to a neighbor for several sheep. The Rio Grande Pueblo Indians exchanged turquoise and shell beads, as well as garden produce, for Navajo silver jewelry. Among the Navajo themselves, the skill of a silversmith would often be traded for the curative skills of the medicine man. A concha belt might be the fee for a curing rite that would extend over several days, or the smith might make a pouch to hold the medicine man's supplies.

Silversmiths learned their craft in their late teens or early twenties from kinsmen, most often their fathers but sometimes an older brother or mother's brother. This apprenticeship was of mutual value. The skilled smith needed help performing the less exacting work of his craft—pounding out silver, filing and sanding the jewelry—and the apprentice, over the years, learned silversmithing. Strangers to the family and the community were not welcome as onlookers, because it was feared they might steal the methods of the senior craftsmen.

In 1937 I made a field study of the Navajo trading post economy at Ramah, New Mexico, some forty-five miles south of Gallup. At that time the Navajo were not part of a cash economy. Theirs was a subsistence livelihood based on agriculture (corn, beans, and squash were the main crops) and on their livestock, of which sheep and goats were the most important. Lambs and wool were bartered at the trading post for food, clothing, tools, and household goods. Very little cash was available, and silversmiths and weavers were paid for the most part in store goods. The small amounts of cash handed out to them came from traders who "farmed out" the raw silver and turquoise to silversmiths and then paid them for each ounce of silver that they

made into jewelry and returned to the trading post. As late as 1940 the going rate was fifty cents an ounce, plus a small amount for each turquoise set.

Since cash was scarce at the trading posts, coins did not jingle in the pockets of the Indians. What silver they had they wore on their wrists (ketohs and bracelets), around their necks (necklaces and bandoliers), encircling their waists (concha belts), or sewn onto garments and necklaces as buttons. They began wearing silver in this way in the decades following their return from Bosque Redondo. During the late nineteenth century and the first decades of the twentieth, the Navajo and Pueblo smiths fashioned all their silver jewelry from American and Mexican coins. By 1938, however, pesos had been replaced by slugs of silver about one inch square and a quarter inch thick, each weighing just one ounce, which the traders acquired from silver refineries in the East and on the West Coast.

Jewelry was often used as collateral on the trader's pawn rack.[2] Usually it was pawned to obtain additional credit at the trading post to tide the customers over to the spring or fall, when they would bring in their wool crop or their lambs. If the customer was a good one and the trader wanted to keep his business, he would not foreclose on the pawn for a long time—often a year or more—although government regulations required him to hold the pawn for only thirty days. Pawned jewelry was frequently redeemed before public events and ceremonial occasions, when the Navajo wanted to look their finest. In 1938, at Pine Springs, Arizona, I noted the amount one silversmith had on pawn racks in four different trading posts. John Burnsides had pawned over twenty-five pieces of jewelry in addition to a rifle, a buckskin, and a wagon. He valued all these belongings at $877 but had received a total of only $215 in credit for them. Sometimes the trader would extend cash for pawned jewelry, but he would allow considerably less value than for trade.

The first systematic exploitation of outside markets for Indian jewelry goes back to 1899, when Herman Schweizer, head of the curio department of the Fred Harvey Company, ordered turquoise cut to square and oblong shapes from a mine owner in Nevada. He took the turquoise, and silver purchased from a refinery, to a trading post near Thoreau, New Mexico, about thirty miles east of Gallup, and asked the trader to have them made into lighter weight jewelry for the tourist market. The finished jewelry was sold in curio stores in the Harvey hotels or by "butchers," who carried it on trays up and down the aisles of the Santa Fe Railroad passenger cars. As more and more tourists traveled to the Grand Canyon and California, the commercialization of Indian silverwork spread from Thoreau to surrounding areas as far as Gallup, where the principal wholesale traders were located. They too began entering the jewelry market as middlemen between the individual trading posts and the outside world. Zuni also saw commercialization of the craft through the four trading posts in the community.

By 1950 the subsistence economy of the Navajo had changed to a wage-work, cash economy, and this had a marked effect on silversmithing. While in 1938 most silversmiths worked at anvils placed on the floors of their hogans or on rough tables, by 1950 many were commuting to production shops, where they made jewelry almost entirely for tourists and others in outside markets. The tourist industry, which had slumped during the war, was reviving by the late 1940s. This growing market for inexpensive souvenirs encouraged commercial production of silverwork off the reservation, a trend that had begun some decades earlier in Albuquerque and other towns along the railroad line. In Albuquerque drop presses and other mechanical devices were used to speed up production; however, jewelry from Gallup, Phoenix, Scottsdale, and Tucson, although mass-produced by benchworkers, was made by hand rather than machine. The well-known Sun Bell in Albuquerque was one of the largest production shops, hiring Indians from Isleta and Santo Domingo, as well as urban Navajo, to turn out small-scale pieces for tourists—a far cry from the family- and community-centered craft of only a few decades earlier.

Interior of Volz's trading post, Oraibi, Arizona, 1901. Bolts of calico and skeins of yarn can be seen on the shelves; above the counter, in front of the large plaque basket, is a chain of hammered silver bracelets. (Photograph by A.C. Vroman, courtesy of the Southwest Museum, Los Angeles, California)

27

Pawn vault at the Pinon Mercantile Company, Pinon,
Arizona, 1975. (Photograph by Jerry D. Jacka)

The inexpensive and widely available Southwest jewelry has appealed to markets outside the Southwest. During periods when it is especially popular, the price of traditional or antique pieces rises dramatically, while the bottom end of the market is flooded with mass-produced items and nonsilver imitations. In recent years the market has been large enough and lucrative enough to attract non-Indian producers of jewelry. The renamed town of Reservation, Japan, is well known for the Navajo-style jewelry made there. The so-called hippie jewelers (Euro-American silversmiths working in Southwest styles) have been accused of sloppy workmanship, but they can turn out beautifully crafted pieces, as a remarkable necklace in the Doneghy collection clearly shows (no. 482).

Despite machine production and competitive prices, traditional craftsmen have not been driven out of the market, and the number of silversmiths has continued to increase. In 1940 I made an economic survey for the Indian Arts and Crafts Board of the Department of the Interior which included a census of silversmiths. Approximately 600 Navajo smiths were working for traders on or near the reservation. Of these, 10 percent were women, a change from earlier decades when silversmithing was done almost entirely by men. (Many women have given up weaving in favor of silversmithing because it is more profitable.) I estimate that today there are at least 2,000 Navajo smiths, half of whom are women. In Zuni, my 1940 census showed 134 smiths, including 26 women. In 1978 there were 303 men and 669 women silversmiths in Zuni.

Silversmiths' incomes also were accounted for in the 1940 survey. Navajo who could be called professional silversmiths—as distinguished from those who worked only occasionally—earned between $500 and $1,500 a year from their craft. Current figures are not available for the Navajo, but at Zuni many silversmiths today take in more than $10,000 a year and a few earn as much as $50,000 annually.

Silver has played a complex and changing role in the Navajo economy. At first it was a luxury, a means of displaying wealth and gaining prestige. After trading posts were established on the reservation, the Indians began pawning their silver jewelry for credit against later sales of animals and blankets. And silverwork also became a source of income for smiths who made tourist items on a cottage industry basis. Since World War II, urban production shops have provided many jobs, and yet there is enough interest in fine Southwest jewelry to support a number of silversmiths who work more or less in the traditional way.

To some degree the shifting role of silver reflects the changes in Navajo culture as a whole—the steady and inevitable process of acculturation. These changes also have a visual counterpart in the stylistic development of Navajo silverwork described in LaRayne Parrish's article. The move from a subsistence to a barter economy parallels the evolution from early jewelry design to the first tourist pieces. Both were a partial accommodation to the surrounding culture: they brought additional goods or cash into Navajo society, with the white trader acting as middleman. Likewise, the shift from barter to cash, which took place in the years after I made my early studies at Ramah, can be compared with the present trend toward extreme diversity. On the one hand is large-scale commercial manufacturing, and on the other, the revival of certain traditions of the craft in the last fifty years, the recognition of the smith as an individual artist, and the genuine stylistic synthesis of outside influences with old forms.

NOTES

1. Gary Witherspoon, Language and Art in the Navajo Universe (Ann Arbor: University of Michigan Press, 1977), p. 151.

2. The pawn racks in the early days, and even up to the 1940s, were in full view of the customers but behind the counter, with necklaces and belts suspended from a horizontal bar. But as time passed, trading posts installed steel vaults as a measure of security, especially as a protection from fire.

Zuni silversmith at work, before 1898. (Photograph courtesy of the Smithsonian Institution, National Anthropological Archives)

The Stylistic Development of Navajo Jewelry

LaRayne Parrish

From its earliest period, Navajo silverwork has been admired by non-Navajo for its aesthetic qualities. A profound appreciation of Navajo art, however, requires an awareness of its significance in the Navajo cosmos. To the Navajo, beauty is a quality not a form, a content not an arrangement. Their metalwork expresses a philosophy in which harmony, order, and beauty are paramount and which is summarized in the words and practice of the Blessingway, a religious ceremony of central importance.

The Blessingway may be performed for various occasions: the building of a new home, a girl's initiation, a wedding, and other times when wishes for protection, long life, and happiness are appropriate. At the beginning of the ceremony the singer introduces the surroundings—the hogan where the ceremony is taking place and the terrain outside. Then he describes the origin of the Navajo people and traces their mythic history, explaining how the world and the Navajo way of life came to be, and returning gradually to the present surroundings. The Blessingway structure thus emphasizes the cyclical nature of Navajo thought and mythology and the integration of all aspects of existence into a harmonious whole. This structure informs my own art and writing, and I believe that by looking at silver from the perspective of the Blessingway we can more readily see the metaphysical, cosmological, sociological, psychological, and aesthetic dimensions of the art form.

The technical, stylistic, and artistic development of Navajo metalwork reflects both the accessibility of materials and technology and the economic pressures exerted by the outside world. The discontinuities apparent in traditional Navajo art forms indicate three periods of Navajo silverwork. The first (1860–1910) is distinguished by vigorous technical achievement and simple classical design. Silverwork of the second period (1910–1940) shows the influence of unrestrained commercial exploitation. And in the third period (1940–present), the revival of traditional principles, combined with original design of the highest order, has produced work that is both splendid and sophisticated.

First Period (1860–1910)

No written record tells us exactly when Navajo metalsmithing began. It is generally assumed, however, that before 1850 the Navajo obtained their metal jewelry through trade with the Plains, Pueblo, and Mexican peoples and that the incarceration at Bosque Redondo (1864–1868) greatly influenced the development of Navajo metalsmithing. Despite the deplorable conditions at Bosque Redondo, the Navajo people acquired there a knowledge of metalsmithing techniques that gave them another vehicle of cultural expression. Particular importance has been assigned to the Navajo silversmiths Atsidi Sani ("Old Smith") and Atsidi Chon ("Ugly Smith"). Atsidi Sani was generally recognized as the first Navajo to have mastered metalsmithing techniques. As a student of Nakai Tsosi ("Slender Mexican"), Atsidi Sani worked solely with iron, forging bridles and bits for trade; not until his return from Bosque Redondo did he begin working with silver.[1]

The Navajo obtained materials for metalwork through trade. Long-established trade systems with neighboring tribes and Mexican smiths provided them not only with necessary metals—iron, brass, copper, and silver—but also with an array of metal forms and designs. The naja, concha, pomegranate ("squash blossom"), button, cross, canteen, and motifs for bridle decoration were not unique inventions of the Navajo; they were borrowed from the Plains and Mexican cultures by Navajo smiths whose keen powers of observation and concentration enabled them to reproduce such designs in detail. In exchange for their iron and silver ornaments, livestock, fruit, and textiles, the Navajo received turquoise and

shells from the Pueblos; beadwork, baskets, jewelry, and animal hides from the Plains tribes; and sheep, horses, metals, tools, and technical expertise from the Mexicans.

Despite their crude tools, the early silversmiths developed and perfected their limited metalworking techniques and invented new ones. They acquired tools through trade or ingeniously constructed them, fashioning bellows from goatskin and wood, molding forges from sticks and mud, and shaping crucibles from clay and sherds. They also forged blowpipes from brass wires, chisels and stamps from railroad spikes and nails, and anvils from scrap iron and wood. By 1870 Navajo silversmiths had mastered basic metalworking techniques such as annealing and soldering and had learned how to embellish their designs with stones. Most important of all, they had invented the tufa-casting technique, in which melted silver coins and slugs were poured from crucibles into intricately carved sandstone molds. With tufa-casting they could produce a wider range of shapes and designs than had been possible before.

Early silverwork is distinguished by utter simplicity of both composition and technique, due partly to the smiths' preference and partly to the scarcity of tools and materials. Most of the conchas and buttons from this period are round, and the bracelets are wide and heavy. Early artisans applied surface design by chasing, filing, and engraving, and they attempted to add diversity and three-dimensionality by stamping with simple crescent, round, and sunburst-pattern dies. As new tools and techniques became more accessible and familiar to them, they redefined borrowed motifs to reflect their own culture. From their work a vital silversmithing tradition emerged, expressing Navajo cultural values and aesthetic principles.

During the classic period, the form of silver pieces and also their decoration came to have iconographic significance. The colors of certain stones, such as turquoise and coral, and the use of four decorative elements in a design became associated with the cardinal directions. Double or paired forms suggested the relationship of earth and sky; six elements,

Navajo smith at work in a brush shelter, 1880–1890.
(Photograph courtesy of the Smithsonian Institution,
National Anthropological Archives)

for example a row of six stones, echoed the six inner forms of the sacred mountains. In this way a variety of silver objects, from necklaces and belts to tobacco canteens and bridles, articulated a distinctively Navajo aesthetic ideal.

By the early 1900s the availability of new tools and the mastery of new techniques allowed silversmiths a greater range of artistic expression in design and form. Applying the techniques of repoussé, chasing, filing, stamping, and embossing, they created elegant and more sophisticated pieces. Simple round conchas evolved into scallop-edged ovals with delicate sunburst patterns executed in repoussé and stamping. Cast or wrought ketohs and bracelets developed into compositions that displayed an aesthetic appreciation of the relationship between geometric patterns and curved lines. The overall effect was enhanced by set stones—usually turquoises—surrounded by stamped designs.

Second Period (1910–1940)

The second period in the development of Navajo metalsmithing was characterized by economic intervention, exploitation, and commercialization that almost extinguished the native tradition. These complex forces exerted unrelenting pressure on the Navajo to comply with prevailing aesthetic and economic standards.

The white trader's appearance on the reservation during the 1870s had provided a new means of exchange and communication. As the traditional system of trade gradually shifted in the direction of the external economy, the Navajo's bargaining position became dependent on the trader's cash flow and line of credit and on supply and demand in the outside market. When the demand for wool, sheep, jewelry, and textiles declined elsewhere, so did the prices traders offered for Navajo goods and livestock. The result was a diminished cash flow for the trader and a decreasing line of credit for the Navajo consumer.

Changes that linked the Navajo economy

more closely to that of the surrounding culture also affected Navajo metalsmithing. The rising commercial tourist trade demanded inexpensive Indian-made curios, and by 1915 Albuquerque, Gallup, Flagstaff, and other cities along the Santa Fe Railroad had become bustling centers of commerce and trade in the Indian arts. Local businesses that catered to the growing tourist market furnished native artisans with an array of new tools, materials, and techniques. Although in the past increased access to tools and materials had inspired silversmiths to cultivate Navajo designs and techniques, during this period commercialization and economic exploitation discouraged authentic Navajo expression.

The need for financial security forced native artisans to accept work in commercial jewelry businesses that mass-produced curios for tourists. Native craftsmen were coerced into adopting nontraditional motifs (swastikas, bows and arrows, and thunderbirds) and nontraditional forms (boxes, letter openers, ashtrays, combs, and beetle pins). These benchwork pieces are characterized by their redundant form, repetitive design, and unrestrained decoration. The traditional regard for proportion and simplicity gave way to the lower standards of commercial mass production, resulting in an era of technically and artistically inferior silverwork.

The significance of this "railroad curio" period should not be underestimated. Deliberate commercial misrepresentation of the traditional metal art-form promoted false stereotypes based upon the questionable quality, style, and artistic merit of mass-produced items. Between 1910 and 1940 the profusion of curios overshadowed traditional jewelry. The majority of traditional pieces made during this time were fashioned by silversmiths who lived away from the important trade centers, and most of those bracelets, buckles, ketohs, concha belts, and necklaces testify to the Navajo sense of harmony and order. Relatively few such pieces were made, however, because the tourists seemed to prefer commercial products. Then, as the tourist demand for souvenirs dwindled during the depression, silver production diminished and the metal-working tradition was nearly lost.[2]

Silversmithing was not the only aspect of Navajo life adversely affected by economic conditions. A scarcity of jobs on the reservation, combined with the reduction of sheep herds forced by the government, imperiled the very nature of the traditional Navajo culture and economy. More than ever, both personal and newly fashioned jewelry was used as collateral at the trading post so the Navajo could purchase the requisite blankets, baskets, food, and fabrics for their ritual curing and blessing ceremonies. As more and more Navajo lacked the means to redeem their pawned jewelry, the increasing quantity of dead pawn ornaments in trading post vaults facilitated the acquisition of Navajo jewelry by tourists, collectors, and museums.

Cultural and economic disruption continued until Congress passed the Indian Reorganization Act in 1934. By legally sanctioning the right of tribal nations to incorporate, to govern themselves, and to hold land, the act halted further efforts to acculturate tribal peoples and helped restore tribal identity and purpose. In 1935 the Indian Arts and Crafts Board was organized to improve the status of silversmiths and to open new markets. Jewelry meeting the standards established by the board was stamped with the words *U.S. Navajo* and a number indicating where the piece was made. The formation of guilds to teach apprentices traditional designs and techniques, as well as encouragement and financial support from public institutions and museums, further contributed to making silversmithing an economically feasible occupation.

Third Period (1940–present)

In the years following World War II the Navajo enjoyed a wider range of educational opportunities. They requested and received classroom instruction in Navajo art, culture, and history, and Navajo artisans participated in a variety of programs such as the Wingate Guild. The Wingate Guild, started in 1939/40 by the educational division of the Bureau of Indian Affairs, employed well-known silversmiths like Ambrose Roanhorse to teach their craft at Fort Wingate Vocational High School. The Navajo Arts and Crafts Guild, created in 1941,

grew out of the Wingate Guild. In addition, public institutions and patrons of Indian art established competitions that encouraged excellence in design and craftsmanship. Even today, artists continue to enter these competitive shows in order to achieve individual recognition and thereby increase the marketability of their works. In this way they are encouraged to develop their own creative spirit.

Navajo silversmiths have learned to appreciate the importance of both tradition and originality. In many cases tribal styles have become the basis for distinctive individual styles. By incorporating the color and charm of gold, silver, brass, and precious and semiprecious stones in their work, Navajo smiths have effectively combined contemporary designs with the principles of the early styles. Their work is vigorous, sophisticated, and often splendid.

The work produced by Fred Peshlakai during the 1940s is notable for eloquent curved forms accented with spiderweb turquoise stones and decorated with sunburst and corn designs in fine repoussé. He characteristically placed delicate twisted wires and small round drops around stones set in serrated bezels, often surrounded by alternating stamped designs.

Kenneth Begay's designs of the 1950s combine elegant forms and graceful rhythms. Fine chiseled and filed lines separate wide expanses of silver, contrasting with subtle curvilinear and geometric forms. Restrained stamping highlights turquoises of rare color and shape on ornaments, flatware, and hollowware. Begay's bold sculptural compositions show the self-confidence that only a long-established tradition can boast.

Contemporary Navajo smiths, although drawing on traditional forms, are more individualistic in their approach. My own interest in art was whetted by college courses in Southwest anthropology and art, and my creative direction has been influenced by my friendships with Kenneth Begay and Hopi artist Charles Loloma. As Kenneth Begay's silversmithing student, I discovered the intrinsic vitality of traditional Navajo designs and techniques. As a respectful admirer of Charles Loloma's

Silversmith Ambrose Roanhorse teaching students at Fort Wingate Vocational High School. (Photograph by Laura Gilpin, courtesy of the Amon Carter Museum, ©1981)

genius, I learned the meaning of "essential intrepidity" from the bold multidimensional metal forms with which he expresses traditional cultural values. As an apprentice to the properties of my own metals, and after many long hours of trial and error, I became expert at tufa-casting.

I am particularly fond of the intrinsic textural qualities of tufa-cast metals. The texture of tufa-cast pieces derives from the tufa mold's density, not the silversmith's skill—the softer the tufa, the grainier the texture; the harder the tufa, the finer the texture. By contrasting rough cast surfaces with smooth burnished ones in my tufa pieces I emphasize their sculptural character, and I use semiprecious and precious stones to enhance the metal forms. As an artisan, I maintain my creative tensions by exploring new avenues of expression in metal; in recent years I have begun using lost-wax casting and more intricate stone techniques in my work. I find excitement and challenge in creating jewelry that expresses my conscious effort to blend the traditional with the distinctively original.

In keeping with the Navajo Blessingway chant form, where an ending returns to the begin-

ning, I add my own refrain. My formative years were influenced by watching my parents exchange food, clothing, blankets, and services for pieces of jewelry. These necklaces, bracelets, belts, and buttons embellished the collars, yokes, sleeves, and waistlines on the velvet blouses, skirts, and shirts my mother had sewn for each of her children. Although I understood these clothes to be "special" I appreciated them more after one of my buttons (which I had deliberately removed) brought me a bag of candy at the Kayenta Trading Post.

NOTES

1. John Adair, *The Navajo and Pueblo Silversmiths* (Norman: University of Oklahoma Press, 1944). Adair relates the silversmith Grey Moustache's account of Atsidi Sani teaching five early smiths (p. 4). It was Atsidi Chon who freely shared his metalsmithing expertise with Lanyade, a Zuni, who in turn taught the Hopi (pp. 122–123, 173).

2. Secretary of the Interior Harold L. Ickes's order that only handmade jewelry could be sold in the National Parks helped keep the craft alive during the depression years. See Ruth Falkenburg, "Navajo Silversmithing," *El Palacio* 52, no. 3 (1945):44.

Navajo Silver, Navajo Aesthetics

Louise Lincoln

In principle, works of art originating in a foreign culture are best approached on their own terms: through the eyes of their makers, their users, and their first admirers. Such an approach hardly seems revolutionary, and yet it is difficult to look at the art of unfamiliar, often distant, cultures in such a way. This method requires extensive background knowledge on the viewer's part; injudiciously applied, it may degenerate into what anthropologists have called the "if I were a horse" mode of interpretation. As a result, less demanding and more comfortable methods often prevail—for example, looking at an individual artist's work and attempting to unravel his or her personal style and imagery. Alternatively, one can study the artistic products of other cultures for what they reveal about the art of one's own culture, looking for stylistic parallels, conscious borrowing of motifs, and the like. Or one may search for some mystic level at which cultural differences become irrelevant and "universal" themes, sentiments, or standards of beauty seem to emerge.

With specific reference to Navajo art, all of these approaches hold certain promise. Recently, scholars of Southwest art have begun to pay attention to personal styles, artistic schools, and the influences of one master upon another, and have recovered the names of previously anonymous artisans—all methods for treating the artist as an individual. The influence of indigenous southwestern artists upon certain trends and individuals in contemporary American and European art is widely acknowledged but rarely treated in any depth, the influence of Navajo sand painting on the work of Jackson Pollock being the best-known example. Finally, the strong and immediate appeal of Navajo blankets, sand painting, and silver for even the viewer least familiar with other aspects of Navajo life and thought is evidence of their "universal" qualities. Such methods as these, however, tend to treat non-Western art in terms developed for and appropriate to European and American art. While useful in ways, they ignore completely the Navajo-ness of Navajo art and tell us nothing about the Navajo mind and hands that gave visual expression to Navajo values.

Such a problem does not arise when we look at a work of art that originates in our own culture, for then we share knowledge, attitudes, and assumptions with the artist. One of the functions of art within any society is to give visual expression to the values central to members of that society, producing an unconscious resonance in the "initiated" viewer. The artist thus speaks on behalf of the culture, informing or reminding others of beliefs held in common. Although modern industrialized, national societies have often cultivated other functions of art (art as a form of social criticism, for instance), in traditional societies such as the Navajo—more homogeneous, smaller, and more tightly integrated—it is the model of artist as portrayer of cultural values that prevails. Within a tightly integrated society, values and beliefs are broadly shared and permeate all spheres of activity—religion and law no more or less than cooking and dress. For art, a still stronger point can be made: not only is it permeated by cultural values, it consciously and intentionally articulates them. Looking at objects of art without the presuppositions of our own culture, we can begin to appreciate the values of the culture in which they were made. Having begun to appreciate those values, we can then appreciate the works of art more fully. The process is a continuous one, in which we can move back and forth from art to culture, learning more at each step of the way.

In Navajo thought it is a given that fundamental societal values order and pervade all activities. To take but one example of how these values influence every aspect of life, we might consider agriculture. The Navajo learned to plant relatively late in their history, having been hunters and gatherers in Canada until the time of their migration to the Southwest with other Athapaskan groups. Once settled in their present locale, they rapidly acquired knowledge of crops and planting techniques from their Pueblo neighbors. However, while the crops and much of the technique remained constant, the intellectual dimension of agriculture—what is thought and said about what is done—was transformed by Navajo values and patterns of reflection, as evidenced by an agricultural terminology and ritual different from those of the Pueblo peoples.[1] In both language and action, traditional Navajo farmers made conscious and explicit daily reference to the supporting structures of their lives and to cosmology and mythology, which can be regarded as metaphors or elaborations of those structures.

Special preparation of seeds before planting, for example, was a common practice in traditional Navajo agriculture. Watermelon seeds were soaked in the juice of a sweet red berry so that upon fruition they would produce melons that were themselves red, juicy, and sweet.[2] While such treatment has occasionally been dismissed as nothing more than sympathetic magic, it is much more than that. The practice rests on a deep understanding that any process is continuous from beginning to end, all final results of the process being fully present at its inception. The berry syrup is thus a coded checklist of ideal watermelon-ness,

and its application ensures that this specific watermelon will attain that ideal of perfection. Were the seeds not soaked in this syrup, they would be deficient, imperfect; the process of growth would be flawed from the outset, and the resulting watermelon would be equally flawed. One could press the analysis still further, for the watermelon seed is placed in the syrup only by a farmer who is knowledgeable and caring, having become a proper farmer through a process of development from seed to maturity.

The same concern for process is evident in the rich set of Navajo terms to denote the various stages of growth through which plant species pass. Germination of seeds is traditionally welcomed by a song: "It grows in both directions" (i.e., up and down, having developed a shoot and a root). When sprouts begin to show leaves, these are always counted in pairs to designate stages of growth—thus, "beans with two ears," "beans with four ears," and so forth.[3] This elaborate terminology holds great interest, for it marks symmetry and axiality as the characteristics of proper development and order. From the possible ways of marking growth stages—simple measurement of the length of the vine, for instance—traditional Navajo farmers chose to count matched pairs of leaves and to note simultaneous growth in two opposite directions. The first stage of plant life is defined as the motion up and the motion down, which can be graphically expressed thus:

The second stage extends the motion to the right and left, balancing the earlier paired motion and producing a graphic form in which pairs of pairs are captured:

Similar concerns with form and symmetry occur elsewhere in agricultural practice, especially in the frequent appearance of cruciform or quadrantal arrangements. Thus, for example, harvested stalks of corn were

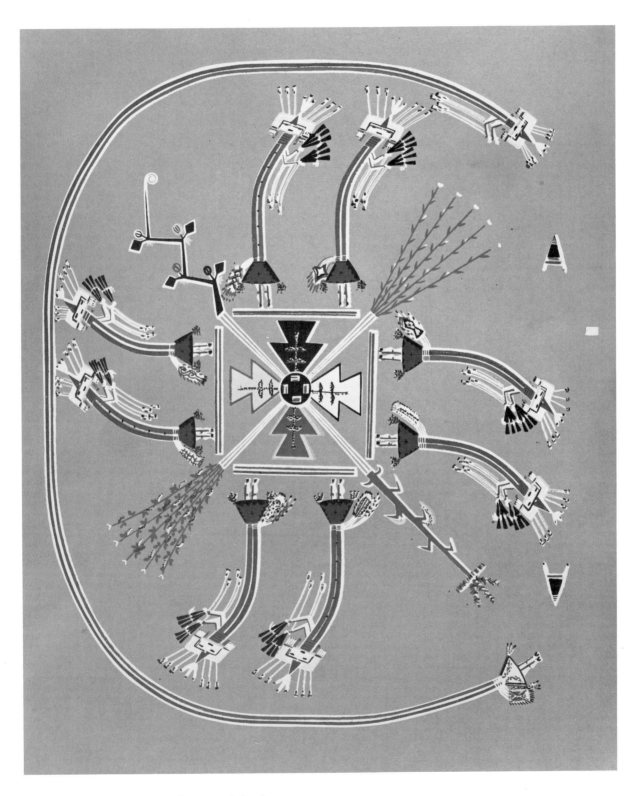

Figure 1. "Rainbow people," sand painting design from
the Beautyway ceremony. (From Leland C. Wyman, ed.,
Beautyway: A Navaho Ceremonial, Bollingen Series 53,
pl. 11. Copyright © 1957 by Princeton University Press.
Reprinted by permission.)

always stacked in crosses, rather than being bundled or stacked at random. Similarly, the appropriate size of a field to be cultivated by one man was determined by his standing in the center and shooting arrows to the cardinal directions, thereby establishing the location of the sides.[4]

Examination of these and other details of Navajo agricultural practice suggests a certain set of values—values that transcend the specifics of agriculture and the practical desire for abundant and nourishing crops. Among these are an emphasis on process, rather than on end product alone, and on ordered, formal activity. Symmetry and cardinal orientation are also prominent, as expressions of a formally ordered, balanced state. The same values embodied in agricultural practice are to be found in all other aspects of Navajo culture, and ritual healing provides a convenient supporting example.

Traditional Navajo medicine is consciously based on the perception of what we would term "illness" as dis-order. Although illness may be caused by many factors, it is always an indication that the victim has in some way become removed from the normal course of life. For our purposes, however, perhaps the most interesting etiology of illness is that of excess. Too much of any activity—weaving, for example—or an obsession, such as avarice, produces a state of imbalance that manifests itself as physical or mental illness. These and other diseases, once identified and diagnosed, are cured by a ceremony conducted by a medical practitioner—a singer. Through song, through ritual activity, through administration of various plant-derived drugs, and through sand paintings, the patient is restored to normal, "normal" here suggesting health, happiness, and productiveness.[5]

Sand painting designs, although numerous, are to a large degree standardized and specific to the chant being performed; thus, a person suffering from a malady of one sort or another may be treated by exposure to a particular sand painting from the Beautyway chant series, for example (Figure 1). The sand painting serves to recall episodes of Navajo

mythology and to attract benevolent force to the patient. Most importantly, however, it restores balance, health, and happiness through ordered designs that depict the ideal state of things.

The concerns we have observed in agriculture and healing, taken together, suggest a coherent and elegant set of values: order, stability, harmony, and the interaction and interrelatedness of all things. These values are all contained in the concept of hózhǫ́, which is perhaps the central principle of Navajo religion, philosophy, and aesthetics. The term is roughly and inadequately translated as "beauty," but its broad meaning has no precise English equivalent. As the anthropologist Gary Witherspoon has noted, "Hózhǫ́ expresses the intellectual concept of order, the emotional state of happiness, the moral notion of good, the biological condition of health and well-being, and the aesthetic dimensions of balance, harmony, and beauty."[6] And it is through this complex and carefully articulated principle that every aspect of Navajo life, from the mundane to the sublime, is lent focus, purpose, and form.

The relationship of art to the concept of hózhǫ́ is particularly interesting. Not only must a finished work of art exhibit hózhǫ́—that is, embody or be permeated by hózhǫ́, be governed by principles of hózhǫ́ in its form, materials, etc.—it must also discuss hózhǫ́, relfect on hózhǫ́, communicate to the viewer just what it is to achieve the condition of hózhǫ́. Moreover, it is not enough to speak only of the finished work of art; one must also take into account the process whereby the work was created, the artist who created it, the use to which it will be put upon completion, and the person who will use it. All of these are linked together by the finished piece—within European and American culture the only important concern, but for the Navajo something quite different. From the Navajo perspective, the piece is merely the vehicle whereby beauty, hózhǫ́, is transmitted from an artist, who is himself or herself in a state of beauty, to a recipient or audience, who will in some measure be brought into a state of beauty through viewing, wearing, or appreciating what the artist has done and made. For this process to succeed, the artist, whether weaver, silversmith, potter, or singer, must be in a state of harmony, balance, health, beauty, or the process and the end product will fail. All who engage in creative action must thus be in a state of *hózhǫ́*. A hogan, the traditional Navajo dwelling, must be properly built and properly blessed in order to be habitable, just as a watermelon seed cannot carry out the usual course of growth into a proper watermelon unless it is brought into a state of harmony with its own proper nature and made beautiful at the very start. The hogan, made in beauty, becomes beautiful to live in. The seed, made in beauty, becomes beautiful to eat. The sand painting, made in beauty, has the power to restore one who has fallen from a state of beauty to his or her proper, beautiful existence.

Silverwork, no less than other elements of Navajo culture, is permeated by this central value. And no less than other forms of Navajo art, it articulates the nature of that value. To be sure, silverwork is a relatively recently acquired art among the Navajo, and its general forms are largely derived from European sources. But just as Navajo thought and values restructured the agriculture learned from Pueblo neighbors, so too Navajo thought and values restructured the silverwork learned from Mexican smiths, making it into a distinctly Navajo product. And although the development of the art form has been greatly influenced by the surrounding culture, perhaps most notably by white traders attempting to obtain goods for the tourist trade, this only suggests that silver is an especially accurate mirror of Navajo culture as a whole.

Some have argued that because silver, unlike weaving, pottery, sand painting, or basketry, is a nonutilitarian art form among the Navajo, it may be dismissed as purely ornamental. To this there are two replies. First, this observation rests on a European notion of what utility is and ignores the patterns of jewelry use among contemporary Navajo. We may note that the Navajo continue to make and wear distinctive silver jewelry even though other traditional elements of dress and hairstyle have almost entirely disappeared. Further-

more, silver jewelry plays an important role in Navajo ceremonial life. This is evident, for example, in the girls' initiation ceremony, in which the initiate wears much jewelry, the chanter or singer is regularly paid in jewelry, and the participants in the ceremony often receive gifts of jewelry from the girl's family. In other ceremonies the patient for whom the ritual is performed may receive a bead or shell upon completion of the ceremony to symbolize its success, and this token is commonly worn thereafter on a necklace.[7] The persistence of jewelry in everyday and ceremonial life suggests that it contributes in an external way to group identity and cultural cohesiveness and implies a degree of resistance to external influences. In other words, there is something essentially Navajo about Navajo jewelry in the minds of its wearers.

More importantly, there is no such thing as mere ornament; ornament always expresses numerous aspects of its mother culture. When beauty is a central cultural value, as it is for the Navajo, the attempt to capture beauty is nothing less than a conscious expression of crucial values. This implies that there must be a more or less clear set of standards for what beauty is and for which things are or are not beautiful, although the existence of such aesthetic canons has been questioned.[8] An anecdote told by Virginia Doneghy, the collector of the objects exhibited here, provides support for the idea that such standards do in fact exist. On one of her many trips to the Southwest, she bought a silver necklace and immediately put it on. As she walked down the street in Albuquerque, proudly exhibiting her new acquisition, an elderly Navajo man approached her. Studying the necklace intently, he indicated his disapproval and remarked "Too long." "I realized at once," she later said, "that he was perfectly right—the necklace was awkward." More than awkward, it was un-balanced, and thus, un-beautiful. Like the sick individual, it was dis-ordered, out of conformity with *hózhǫ́*, as the Navajo observer recognized.

Indeed, just by looking closely at individual pieces of jewelry and at jewelry in groups, we can discern a number of characteristics of style related to the concept of *hózhǫ́*. In a cast

Figure 2. Cast Navajo bracelets from the Doneghy collection. *Left,* bracelet with cast leaf ornaments and stamping, 1930s (no. 80). *Right,* a similar form with contrasting unpolished areas, 1970s (no. 334).

bracelet from the 1930s, for example, aesthetic and philosophic values are manifest on numerous levels (Figure 2, left). Perhaps the most striking feature of this piece is the contrast between the elegantly curved side elements and the blocky, rectangular center. Although such contrast can easily be read as a "balance" between two linear forms, the philosophic implications of that balance are rather more subtle. The idea of contrast as balance rests on the assumption that balance is completeness, is the presence of all components. The curve of a curved line is, in effect, meaningless without reference to a straight line. The Navajo see a similar "balance" between activity, which is explicitly associated with the curve, and stasis, which is associated with straight lines. In turn, activity is considered a trait of the female, both human and divine, while stasis is connected to gods and men.[9] Thus, (curve = activity = female) + (straight = stasis = male) = whole. In the ideal sand

painting the curved and the straight complement each other, just as in ideal social relations the male and female complement one another. All are necessary parts of the whole.

There is balance of another kind between the more traditional external curved forms and the "leaves," the latter being a naturalistic, Anglo-inspired innovation which was a relative novelty in the 1930s. The combining of old and new in this way is entirely consistent with Navajo interest in the past and respect for tradition, on the one hand, and interest in creative innovation on the other. The Navajo recognize the value of both, but draw on neither too heavily. These balances imply an avoidance of excess; the weaver who weaves too much will become ill and must be cured through a restoration of balance, of *hózhǫ.*

Returning to the bracelet at hand, we should note also its careful quadrantal symmetry.

Obviously this is in some ways related to balance, but it is also connected to another, no less complex, set of ideas. Quadrantal symmetry is simply another way of describing cardinal orientation, which, as we saw above, is important in various traditional farming practices. And it is emphasized in traditional hogan architecture, too. The house frame consists of five long poles interlocked at the top, of which two, closer together and facing eastward, form the door frame (Figure 3). So insistent are the Navajo on the importance of the cardinal directions that they consider the two doorposts to be only one, so that it may be said that four poles support the hogan—an example, as we shall see, of mythic truth prevailing over reality.[10]

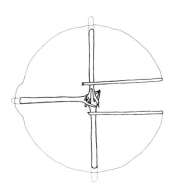

Figure 3. Supporting structure for a conical hogan, seen from above. The four (five) poles are interlocked at the top; the eastern pole(s) forming the doorway is visible at the right.

But why are the Navajo so insistent on the importance of the four directions? First, the cardinal directions are prominent features of Navajo myths about the creation of the world and the origin of the Navajo people. Division of the world into quadrants, each associated with a specific mountain on the periphery of Navajo territory, brought order out of chaos. With this in mind, we may look again at the hogan framework, in particular at the elaborate terminology and set of associations for each of the four (or five) poles. The eastern pole(s) is called *Nahasdzáán bijáadii*, "earth world's leg"; the southern pole, "mountain world's leg"; the western, "water world's leg"; the northern, "corn world's leg." Earth and mountain world refer to the sources of the

wood and dirt used in the hogan's construction, and hence to its origins; water and corn, the basic elements of human sustenance, may be seen as a coded reference to the hogan's intended purpose as the center of family life.[11] Literally and figuratively, then, the hogan stands at the center of all things. It is the axis mundi: its poles mark off the four directions, the sacred mountains, and the origins and mythic structure of the people as well as their past and present (Figure 4).

Cardinal orientation, or division into quadrants, naturally implies a center point at which north-south and east-west axes intersect and which is a part of both axes and all four directions, or alternatively, a point which transcends all distinctions and dualities, partaking of perfect harmony and totality. Just so, the midpoint of the central bar in the bracelet under consideration is the point on which all lines and forms converge, or from which they all radiate, as in agriculture all labor—planting, weeding, harvesting, and even the singing of farming songs—begins at the center of the field.[12] Also reminiscent of agriculture are the two "leaves" that form one of the axes. When considered together with the straight central bar, they strongly suggest the "beans with two ears" stage of plant growth, when a plant first acquires all its distinguishing features. Far more important than this possible iconography, however, is the general pattern of focal center and axes leading to the cardinal points. This pattern permeates all of Navajo art and thought and is emphasized in creation mythology, wherein the first Navajo people are said to have come out of the earth's depths at Emergence Rim, the spot where the axes described by the four sacred mountains intersect.

Even the treatment of the bracelet's surface may be seen to result in large measure from the precept of *hózhǫ́*. Like all cast ornaments of that period, this bracelet was made in a stone mold; when a silver piece is removed from the mold it is dull gray, and the surface is rough and pitted. The bright luster of this piece, and all cast pieces, is the result of days of sanding and polishing by the smith. The effect of this part of the manufacturing process is to eradicate all signs of the previous

Figure 4. Ceremonial hogan under construction, 1905. The doorway is at the right; a small boy sits atop the interlocked poles. (Photograph by Simon Schweinberger, courtesy of the Smithsonian Institution, National Anthropological Archives)

step. By polishing away the marks of melting and casting, one returns the metal to its ideal, beautiful state; the process leads to a state of *hózhǫ́*. But, perhaps because the uninterrupted shiny surface is too neutral, Navajo smiths commonly use a restrained, delicate stamping to enhance their work, thereby returning to it the mark of the maker's hand. The process is exactly analogous to the finishing of Southwest pottery, in which the pot is burnished at length to produce a smooth, lustrous surface. (The famous Hopi potter Fannie Nampeyo complained that nowadays girls are not patient enough to burnish their pots for the amount of time required to produce the proper sheen.) When the pot is smoothed and no longer bears the prints of its maker's hands, designs are painted on and the maker is again in evidence.

On this particular bracelet, a single V-shaped stamp has been used repeatedly along the ridge or apex, echoing the acute angle of the bracelet in section. The arrow is well known in sand painting, where it has the same directional connotation that it has acquired in wider culture. Thus, it is easy to see the line of stamped Vs as implied motion, converging on the curved elements toward the center and radiating outward on the rectangular bar. The regular spacing of the stamps suggests rhythmic progression, the same steady beat that accentuates Navajo music. The silversmith Ambrose Roanhorse has recorded a smith's song about making beautiful silver, in which the rhythm is tapped out by a metallic hammering sound.[13] Listening to the song, one can easily envision a piece like this one.

Necklaces require the smith to address the same question—How can the values implicit in *hózhǫ́* be translated into silver?—but because of their different form they require a different set of solutions. Unlike the fixed, rigid form of bracelets, necklaces are mobile and fluid. They offer little flat surface for stamped decoration, nor do they permit the kind of exploration of cardinal orientation that

Figure 5. Necklaces from the Doneghy collection. *Left,* Navajo squash blossom necklace, double naja with turquoise sets and pendant, about 1910 (no. 371). *Right,*

Santo Domingo necklace of turquoise and shell nuggets interspersed with heishi, jaclas of discoidal turquoise and white shell beads, about 1920 (no. 884).

we saw so clearly in bracelets. The symmetry of their design revolves about one axis, not two. Necklaces are perhaps the most complex of Southwest jewelry forms and the most eclectic in their design sources. At the same time, they show relatively little variation from the typical forms, perhaps because the typical forms are highly satisfactory.

Looking at a necklace from the early period (Figure 5, left), in which the type is already well established, we may describe that typical form as being composed of graduated spherical beads flanking a crescent-shaped pendant and interspersed with so-called squash blossom beads on shanks. Although the outline of the form is different, the necklace is centered on

the naja, or pendant, as surely as the bracelet mentioned above was centered on the rectangular bar. The naja is not just a visual center, however, but a center of weight as well. Without the pendant, the necklace would lack a focus, lack a way of maintaining its alignment, lack a way of defining its axis. The naja serves to break the curve of the necklace, changing the curved line of a simple bead necklace into a more or less straight and orderly progression toward the center. The same broken curve is apparent in jaclas, early earrings consisting of a string of small tubular beads, usually of turquoise. At the center of each jacla strand were threaded several wedge-shaped beads, sometimes of coral or white shell, forcing the string to double back abruptly and the two sides to hang closely parallel (Figure 5, right). Although there are doubtless functional considerations influencing this arrangement,[14] there can be no doubt that there are aesthetic ones as well, for the use of beads of a contrasting color is obviously intended to give emphasis and weight to the center. We may note in passing that jaclas are now seldom worn as earrings; since the late nineteenth century or earlier it has been customary to tie them to turquoise or turquoise-and-shell bead necklaces as a center pendant, thus giving them the same role as najas on silver necklaces.

Beads on early necklaces like this one are often graduated, the largest being placed toward the middle of the strand; there are even examples of necklaces in which the squash blossom beads are graduated in size. Like the pendant, graduation serves to define the center, both visually and by the weight of the larger, heavier beads. A simple strand of beads, graduated or not, suggests a rhythmic progression, and until about 1880 silver necklaces made by the Navajo consisted of plain beads hung with a pendant in naja form. Photographic evidence indicates that in about that year smiths began to make what are commonly termed squash blossom beads (the Navajo word describing the type means "bead that spreads out")[15] and to intersperse them after every third, or in this case fourth, plain bead. Because they were mounted by means of a shank rather than strung directly on the necklace cord,[16] both the bead and the blossom extended beyond the body of the necklace, setting up a more complex visual rhythm. Similar rhythmic structures exist in music. Navajo song has been described as making creative use of repetition by introducing subtle patterns of alternation and progression.[17] The evolved formal arrangement of necklace beads suggests a similar interest in repetition with variation.

We have already discussed the role of the naja in defining the axis and center of the necklace. But the form of the naja itself, as inherited from Spanish sources, seems to have presented an interesting set of problems to early smiths. Because it revolves on one axis, not two, the naja cannot be said to have a center as such. Smiths apparently felt this as a lack of focus, for in naja designs from the early period to the present they have tried various ways of adding weight and emphasis to the basic form. Early najas usually thicken at the top into a true crescentic form or else echo the same shape in a double naja held together at the top by a vertical strip, as in this example. When stone settings came into use, the most common site for a setting on a naja was the apex of the curve, where the piece is joined to the necklace. Slightly later the more direct solution of extending the design into the void came into use. On the necklace we are considering, for example, a turquoise pendant has been tied to the small silver tab protruding into the open space. Turquoise or silver pendants and cast or soldered ornaments descending into the open space of the naja remain extremely common variants on the basic form.

Looking at Navajo art forms other than silver for parallel examples of this centering device within an open circle, we find them readily in sand paintings (Figure 1). Many sand painting designs are enclosed by a greatly elongated figure of the rainbow god bent into a C shape or sometimes into a three-sided square. This figure serves as the guardian of the painting and, by analogy, of the ceremony and the patient for whom the painting is made. Sand paintings, no less than bracelets, focus strongly on the center, where the patient will sit to be restored to health, and thus the form of a typical sand painting at its most basic level is an open circle with a dot in the middle.

Not surprisingly, we can argue for the same pattern in architecture, for the ground plan of a traditional hogan is a C-shaped outer wall. The hogan walls perform in concrete fashion the protective function of the rainbow god "frame" of sand paintings. The parallel is reinforced when we consider that sand paintings are traditionally made within hogans, the open side of the sand painting oriented toward the hogan door, which faces east—another example of form organized along an axis. The only fixed feature of interior hogan arrangement is the location of the hearth in the middle. The hearth is literally the center of family life and activity; a hogan without a hearth is incomplete, uninhabitable. Given the apparent need to fill the void of the naja, it seems that without a focus this form is also in some measure unsatisfactory. It is clear, however, that the open circle—especially the open circle with a central device, be it pendant, fireplace, or pattern in colored sand—is a prominent feature of Navajo design. (Even bracelets may be regarded as C forms; the Navajo almost never make closed hoop bracelets.) The opening has been related to the supposed cultural trait of independence and fear of encirclement.[18] If the form is put into the third dimension, however, a new set of associations and a more satisfactory interpretation may result. In terms of Navajo material culture, the spheroid with a single opening calls to mind gourd containers and storage pits hollowed out of the ground. If the open side of the hogan is the door, and the opening in a storage pit gives access and means of withdrawing, we can find a mythological parallel in the hole in Emergence Rim through which the First People in the Navajo creation myth came out of the earth into the world (the analogy to the womb is explicit in creation accounts). The first hogan was built at Emergence Rim at the time of the creation.

Much more remains to be said about the motif of the open circle and its various manifestations in Navajo art and thought. For present purposes it is sufficient to suggest that in nonsilver media the form has connotations of both protection and the creative process. We might speculate that, by extension, the naja also carries these associations; the occasional addition of hands as terminals, seeming to suggest encircling arms, has led some scholars to argue for the motif as a protective device, but there is no clear testimony to support the interpretation.

Necklaces, then, echo the same preoccupations we encountered in bracelets—the same interest in order, in stability, in harmony—but the approach and the form are more complex. The evolution of the basic form shows an interest in imparting stability to a mobile structure, in balance and rhythm, and in the problem of creating a center or focus. All of these aesthetic concerns are entirely consistent with the ideal of hózhǫ́. The Navajo are often cited for their ability to adopt aspects of other cultures and make these traits their own; they are said to be, in the anthropologist Evon Vogt's term, incorporative. There can be no better visual example of this ability than the squash blossom necklace, in which disparate elements have been brought together into a harmonious whole.

Having observed characteristics of Navajo style in silverwork that seem strongly related to Navajo ideology, we may now find it useful to examine silverwork from another Southwest group. The Zuni are perhaps the most instructive example in this regard, for they are as well known as the Navajo for their skill but are vastly different from their neighbors both in culture and in artistic style. They belong to a different language group, and their social, religious, and kinship systems, and the values derived from these, are quite different also. Whereas Navajo cultural expressions, as we have seen, emphasize harmony, simplicity, and focus, the Zuni stress complexity, multiplicity, fragmentation, and elaboration. The anthropologist Barbara Tedlock has elucidated the meaning of the Zuni term coʔya, a word corresponding in some ways to the Navajo hózhǫ́ but describing an aesthetic of multiplicity and dynamic asymmetry.[19]

The Zuni learned to work silver from the Navajo about 1872, and we know from period photographs that their early pieces resembled those of the Navajo. But using the same elements of turquoise and silver, they quickly developed a style based on a different aesthetic and an entirely different way of looking at their materials. Their jewelry gives primacy to turquoise, and the stones are often cut in small pieces of roughly equal size which are then set in radiating or grid designs. The silver so lovingly worked by the Navajo serves chiefly as a medium to set stones, although the ability to set dozens of "needlepoint" turquoises attests to the Zuni's skill in smithing. Diework is largely absent from Zuni silver, the rhythmic quality it imparts being supplied by multiple sets.

The essential stylistic differences between Zuni and Navajo silver may be most clearly seen in the differing treatment of stones and squash blossoms. The Zuni, covering the surface of the squash blossom with turquoises, expand the form to occupy the entire necklace; the beads become an invisible supporting structure, and the necklace seems to consist of closely set, unvaried squash blossom units, far different from the alternation present in the classic Navajo arrangement. Similarly, Zuni rowwork bracelets display closely set small turquoises—dozens of tiny identical units, in contrast to the Navajo preference for a single large set. It is tempting to suggest here an architectural analogy, relating the Navajo interest in centrality and focus (and hence use of one large center stone) to their pattern of living in single hogans, isolated from other family groups. The Zuni, who rather display a preference for multiplicity, for dividing a visual field into numerous similar elements, have for centuries lived in large multiunit "apartment" complexes. Given the integrative nature of both cultures, it does not seem excessively daring to posit a relationship of this kind.

Despite the separation and distinctiveness of the two styles, and the identification with cultural values that we have suggested, there has always been some overlapping of the styles. Members of one group have always worn the other's jewelry, whether through geographic proximity to silversmiths working in that style, patterns of intermarriage, or "aberrant" aesthetic preference. Some smiths have worked in the style of a neighboring group for commercial or personal reasons. Stylistic influence, or even a synthesis of styles, might be expected to result from such contact, but in fact the opposite is true. In many ways the styles seem to be becoming further differentiated: Zuni lapidary work is becoming ever tinier, and Navajo silverwork is becoming more and more sculptural. Among Navajo smiths a conscious revival of older traditions can be seen, for example, in the new use of graduated beads in squash blossom and other necklaces.

It is clear that Navajo smiths, recognizing the close relationship between their art and the concept of *hózhǫ́*, are seeking and finding new ways to express that ideal, as a recently made cast bracelet in the Doneghy collection

demonstrates (Figure 2, right). The smith has deliberately left various planes of the center motif rough and unfiled after the casting process. Like stamping, it is a way of drawing notice to the smoothness of the other surfaces. The strong contrast between light and dark that the method produces is an explicit reminder of the importance of balance and of resolution into a harmonious state. By suggesting the process of its manufacture, the piece reflects and comments on its own origin in the same way that the names of hogan structural supports recall their sources.

In mainstream American and European culture it is considered appropriate and necessary to compartmentalize various fields of thought and activity. Medicine and religion are not allowed to permeate each other's borders; the raising of crops and the education of children are considered separate endeavors. For this reason, trying to learn about silver jewelry by examining how houses are built, how the sick are healed, or how farming is made productive may at first seem an improbable technique. Fundamentally, however, we have attempted to come to an understanding of Navajo art and aesthetics through the concept of *hózhǫ́*. Navajo life and thought are informed at every level by this central idea; in turn, all aspects of Navajo culture are interconnected through their association to *hózhǫ́*. A study of any idea or object inevitably leads first to *hózhǫ́*, then to all its other manifestations.

Thus far we have pursued meanings and implications of *hózhǫ́* other than its usual English equivalent, "beauty." That Navajo jewelry is beautiful, in the English sense, is surely beyond debate. I have attempted to demonstrate that it is also beautiful in the Navajo sense. That is to say, it is ordered, balanced, harmonious; it reflects and comments on the condition of its maker, on the process by which it was made, and on the past and present of the Navajo people; it suggests the ideal state of existence. All of these are preconditions necessary to the manifestation of *hózhǫ́*. In fulfilling them, silverwork is in every sense *hózhǫ́ nahastlín*, "finished in beauty."

NOTES

1. W. W. Hill, *The Agricultural and Hunting Methods of the Navaho Indians,* Yale University Publications in Anthropology, no. 18 (New Haven, Conn.: Yale University Press, 1938), pp. 182–190.

2. Ibid, pp. 57–58.

3. Ibid., pp. 35, 63.

4. Ibid., pp. 20, 40.

5. See Gladys A. Reichard, *Navaho Religion: A Study of Symbolism,* 2nd ed. (Princeton, N.J.: Princeton University Press, 1974), pp. 80–122.

6. Gary Witherspoon, *Language and Art in the Navajo Universe* (Ann Arbor: University of Michigan Press, 1977), p. 154.

7. Reichard, pp. 524–525.

8. For a summary of this position see Daniel J. Crowley, "An African Aesthetic," *Journal of Aesthetics and Art Criticism* 24 (summer 1966):523.

9. Witherspoon, p. 160.

10. Leland C. Wyman, *Blessingway* (Tucson: University of Arizona Press, 1970), p. 13.

11. Stephen C. Jett and Virginia E. Spencer, *Navajo Architecture* (Tucson: University of Arizona Press, 1981), p. 22.

12. Hill, pp. 29–30, 39–40, 68.

13. Ambrose Roanhorse, "Silversmith's Song," in *Folk Music of the United States — Navajo,* recorded and edited by Willard Rhodes, Library of Congress Division Recording Lab AFS L41, Washington, D.C.

14. The wedge-shaped beads prevent the earrings from forming a stiff curve, thus avoiding stress on the inner edges of the beads. If the beads were strung loosely enough to "break" on their own, the angled beads at the bottom would quickly wear through the string.

15. John Adair, *The Navajo and Pueblo Silversmiths* (Norman: University of Oklahoma Press, 1944), p. 44.

16. Attachment of the bead by means of a shank is explained by historical antecedents as well as functional and aesthetic considerations. The form is most likely derived from the ornate silver buttons in the shape of pomegranates used to decorate Hispano-Mexican men's trousers in the late eighteenth and early nineteenth centuries. This ornamental form, with shank attached, is essentially identical to the Navajo type. Although one might expect that in necklaces the bead would be strung directly on the cord, this adaptation would require soldering the blossom on at the seam, a weak point in the bead's structure. (A few necklaces are nevertheless made this way; of particular interest in the Doneghy collection is no. 482, made by the Euro-American smith Wolf Reed.) Furthermore, beads without shanks would not extend so far from the body of the necklace and thus would not produce the same uninterrupted external outline that incorporates the naja into a smooth exterior curve.

17. David McAllester, cited in Witherspoon, p. 156.

18. Reichard, p. 89.

19. Barbara Tedlock, personal communication, June 1981; see also her "Songs of the Zuni Kachina Society," in Charlotte J. Frisbie, ed., *Southwestern Indian Ritual Drama,* School of American Research Advanced Seminar Series (Albuquerque: University of New Mexico Press, 1980), p. 18.

Catalogue and Photographs

The following catalogue lists all of the southwestern silver objects in the collection of Virginia Doneghy. Not included are objects of stone or shell (which are numerous and beautiful), a small group of so-called peyote jewelry from contemporary Plains silversmiths, and a very few objects made as intentional fakes. Because Virginia Doneghy kept detailed records of her collection, we know the provenance and date of purchase of most pieces and in some cases the name of the maker.

In the catalogue descriptions of the jewelry it is assumed that the primary material is silver. We have not differentiated hand-wrought silver from machine-produced. Clearly objects made before the introduction of machine-rolled sheet silver in 1929 are almost without exception fabricated by hand; those made after that date frequently include commercially produced sheet metal, wire, and bezel wire. Similarly, we have not attempted to distinguish between tufa-cast pieces, sand-cast pieces, and their modern spin-cast descendants. For the most part traces of the spin-casting process are polished away, and the technique can be difficult to identify by sight, although the existence of nearly identical modern cast pieces within the collection suggests the use of this method.

Turquoise mines are named where they can be identified from the stone. It is important to remember that old jewelry was sometimes set with new stones, and for this reason some older pieces display turquoises that are incompatible in size or cut with the age of the piece or that come from mines not yet in operation when the silver was worked.

Dimensions are given in inches, with centimeters in parentheses. The dimensions measured for each category of object are described separately for each section. Complete sets, groups, or pairs of objects are not always pictured; for example, a photograph may show only one button of a pair or one bracelet of a set. References cited are listed in the Bibliography.

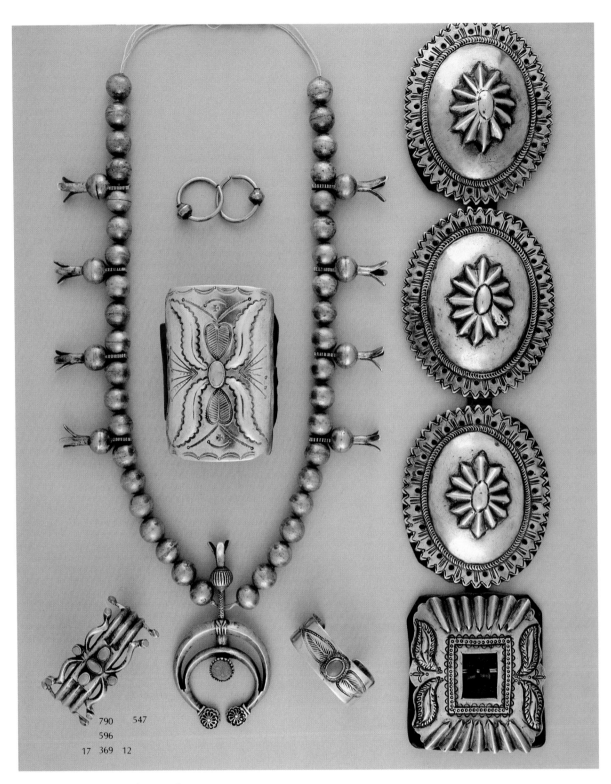

790   547
596
17 369 12

Navajo jewelry of the early period (1860–1910)

603
609   110
81   389
822   718
557

Navajo jewelry of the middle period (1910–1940)

452 794 570
234
328 616

Navajo jewelry of the modern period (1940–present)

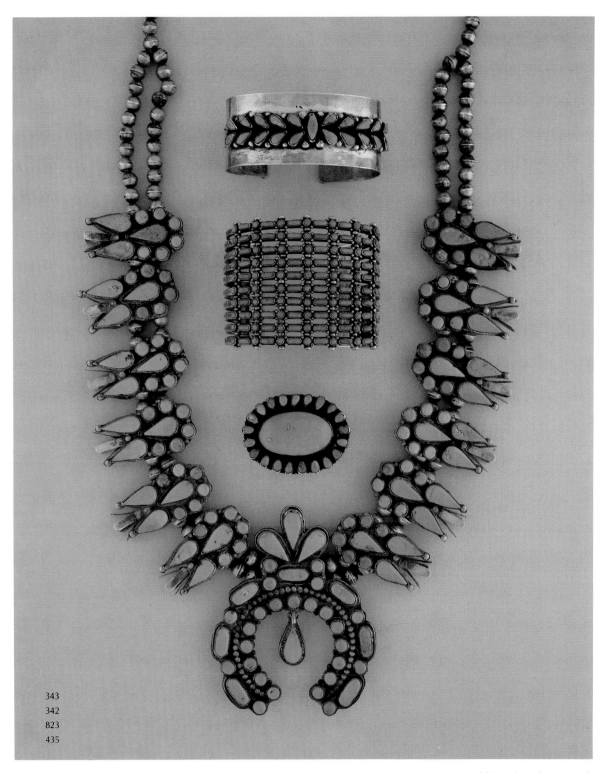

343
342
823
435

Zuni jewelry of the middle and modern periods

639
637
200
163
383
822

Hopi and other Pueblo jewelry

Bracelets

There is nothing in the historical records to indicate that metal bracelets were a significant form of Southwest Indian jewelry before the introduction of brass wire by Euro-American traders. Early in the nineteenth century wire was imported to the region by the spool and had only to be cut to the appropriate length, decorated with filing or stamping, and bent to fit the arm. Bracelets from the earliest period of silverworking duplicated this form in hand-hammered wire, but as the skill of smiths increased, they made many types of bracelets.

Elaborate variations of the wire bracelet included bracelets composed of several strands of twisted square wire, which were popular through the early years of the twentieth century. Two or three round wires soldered together at the ends and splayed at the center were used as mountings for stones, and double round wires twisted together were often used in the same way. Hammered carinated (triangular) wire bracelets also appeared early. These elaborated wires were combined in various ways in the splayed form mentioned above, and by the 1920s this type of bracelet was firmly established as a basic model. After 1940 bracelets of looped wire appeared briefly, but the older forms continued in use.

Narrow, flat band bracelets decorated by filing and chasing were another early form, and as the supply of silver increased they grew wider and more complex. Many bracelets of the late nineteenth century combined stamping with repoussé. By the turn of the century, bands were sometimes split into strips with a cold chisel and spread apart. These split bands resembled the splayed wire bracelets already mentioned and were also frequently set with stones.

The development of casting permitted smiths to create free-form designs. Early cast bracelets were composed of delicate, thin straight and curvilinear elements in openwork patterns. Cast openwork, like split bands and wire bracelets, allowed the smith to produce a wide bracelet without the cost or the weight of a great amount of silver. Later cast pieces were thicker and frequently more curvilinear. Cast bracelets are typically triangular in cross section, like carinated wire, and some cast bracelets echo the design of carinated pieces. Twentieth-century casts often provide space for setting stones. In the early 1970s smiths began to leave some areas unpolished to show the texture of the mold.

The setting of stones began about 1880 with the use of crude hand-hammered bezels, some with deep serrations to help the metal fit around the stone. Bracelets, more than other jewelry forms, permit the use of large or multiple stones, and so from the turn of the century turquoise and other stone sets have been of primary importance in bracelet design. For the most part early sets were small and flat and set flush to the bezel. In the teens and early twenties, however, cabochon cuts became prevalent, and although in the thirties and forties many stones were finished flat, or flat with a slightly beveled edge, cabochons reasserted themselves in the following decades. In the thirties and forties especially, some bracelets were made to display one or several enormous stones. The type of bracelet delightfully described by Margery Bedinger as "stones all around" came into use in the early twentieth century and remains basic. Sometimes cast, sometimes of wire, these bracelets required multiple stones that were at least roughly matched or graduated. Precut stones came into use in the first decade of

the twentieth century, and after 1940
machine-cut stones became nearly universal,
with the result that sets are of uniformly
regular shape and size.

The use of added decorative elements on
bracelets and other articles is a good indicator
of the date of the piece. Fine double twisted
wire embellished jewelry, especially bracelets,
from the teens on. The twenties and thirties
saw elaborate designs of fine twisted and
spiral wire, and in the 1930s bead wire,
imitating rows of teardrops, was frequently
added. Patterns composed of small segments
of bent wire, and appliqué ornaments,
appeared at about the same time.

The work of Zuni smiths began to be distin-
guishable from that of their Navajo teachers
by 1910, and by the 1920s the stylistic
differences were clear. Setting many small
pieces of turquoise in clusters or in rows,
they used just enough silver to hold the stones
together. Often several narrow row-set bands
would be soldered together to make a wide
band. The effect is one of delicacy and
fragmentation, quite different from the
sculptural manner and larger sets characteristic of Navajo work. Nevertheless, Navajo
smiths appreciated and borrowed elements of
the Zuni style, and cluster or row sets from
the two groups are often indistinguishable.

The dimensions given are width and height
(including stone); width precedes height.

J.B.W.
L.L.

1 BRACELET, about 1910
Navajo
Four twisted square wires; set
with nine elliptical cabochon
Battle Mountain turquoises in
serrated bezels; teardrop
decoration; 3 × ½ (7.6 × 1.3).
Provenance: Navajo Indian
Trading Post, Tucson, Arizona,
1965.

2 BRACELET, about 1910
Navajo
Two carinated bands enclosing a
filed round wire; set with one
oval turquoise and two small
round turquoises at terminals;
stamped decoration; 2⅝ × ¾
(6.7 × 1.9).
Provenance: Packard's Trading
Post, Santa Fe, New Mexico, 1960.

3 BRACELET, about 1900
Navajo
Three twisted square wires
enclosing two square wires; set
with eight round turquoises;
appliqué decoration; 3⅛ × ½
(7.9 × 1.3).
Provenance: Tom Bahti, Tucson,
Arizona, 1965.

4 BRACELET, about 1915
Navajo
Two square twisted wires; set
with three round turquoises
on hammered sheet backing;
teardrop decoration; 2½ × ⁷⁄₁₆
(6.4 × 1.1).
Provenance: Hubbell's Trading
Post, Winslow, Arizona, 1953.

5 BRACELET, 1915 or later
Navajo
Three twisted square wires; set
with three oval drilled turquoises;
appliqué and stamped decoration;
2½ × ¾ (6.4 × 1.9).
Provenance: unknown, about
1961.

6 7
8 9

6 BRACELET, about 1910
Navajo
Hammered band; set with one
square and two triangular
turquoises; repoussé and stamped
decoration; 2⁵⁄₁₆ × 1½ (5.9 × 3.8).
Provenance: W. S. Dutton,
Santa Fe, New Mexico, 1957.

7 BRACELET, about 1900 or before
Navajo
Scratched inscription inside:
P E S [−] E April 12, 1921
Heavy band with two filed
grooves; set with single square
turquoise on appliqué; stamped
decoration; 2⁹⁄₁₆ × ⅝ (6.5 × 1.6).
Provenance: Maisel's, Albu-
querque, New Mexico, 1965.
Cf. Bedinger, p. 45, fig. 17.

8 BRACELET, about 1900
Navajo
Hammered band; set with single
square turquoise; stamped
decoration; 2⁵⁄₁₆ × ½ (5.9 × 1.3).
Provenance: Packard's Trading
Post, Santa Fe, New Mexico, 1960.

9 BRACELET, 1890s or later
Navajo
Hammered band; set with three
elliptical turquoises; repoussé
and stamped decoration; 2¼ ×
1¹⁄₁₆ (5.7 × 2.7).
Provenance: Clay Lockett, Gallup,
New Mexico, 1953.

10 11
12 13

10 BRACELET, 1900–1910
    Navajo
    Annealed band; set with single
    elliptical cabochon turquoise;
    repoussé and stamped decoration;
    2½ × 1 (6.4 × 2.5).
    Provenance: Chester Copman,
    Santa Fe Gift Shop, Santa Fe,
    New Mexico, 1952.
    Cracked and repaired.

11 BRACELET, about 1890
    Navajo
    Annealed band; set with single
    oval cabochon turquoise; chased
    and stamped decoration; 2⅝ ×
    ⅞ (6.7 × 2.2).
    Provenance: Hubbell's Trading
    Post, Winslow, Arizona, 1954.
    Bought as pawn.

12 BRACELET, about 1910
    Navajo
    Hammered band; set with single
    elliptical cabochon turquoise;
    stamped decoration; 2¹⁄₁₆ × ¾
    (5.2 × 1.9).
    Provenance: Tom Bahti, Tucson,
    Arizona, 1965.

13 BRACELET, about 1920
    Navajo
    Annealed dapped band; set with
    single trapezoidal turquoise;
    stamped decoration; 2½ × ⅝
    (6.4 × 1.6).
    Provenance: Quivira Shop,
    Santa Fe, New Mexico, 1957.

Not shown:

14 BRACELET, about 1910
    Navajo
    Annealed band; set with single
    oval green Nevada turquoise
    in serrated bezel; stamped
    decoration; 2¾ × ¹⁵⁄₁₆ (7 × 2.4).
    Provenance: Santa Fe Indian
    School, Santa Fe, New Mexico,
    1955.

15 17
16
18 19

15 BRACELET, before 1925
Navajo
Cast openwork band; set with
one square and six round Nevada
turquoises; 2¾ × 1⅞ (7 × 4.8).
Provenance: Turpen Trading Post,
Gallup, New Mexico, 1950s.

16 BRACELET, about 1900
Navajo
Hammered carinated band; set
with two round turquoises (third
missing, bezel filed off); 2³⁄₁₆ ×
⁵⁄₁₆ (5.6 × 0.8).
Provenance: Fred Harvey Co.,
Albuquerque, New Mexico, 1954.
Bought as pawn.

17 BRACELET, about 1900
Navajo
Cast openwork band; set with
thirteen small round and oval
Nevada turquoises (possibly
Burnham); 1½ × 2⅝ (3.8 × 6.7).
Provenance: Tom Moore, Gallup,
New Mexico, 1955.

18 BRACELET, about 1915
Navajo
Split band; set with single
rectangular cabochon turquoise
mounted on filed plate; 2½ × 1⁵⁄₁₆
(6.4 × 2.4).
Provenance: Hubbell's Trading
Post, Winslow, Arizona, 1956.
Bought as pawn.
Stone and setting probably
predate band.

19 BRACELET, 1920 or before
Navajo
Annealed band; stamped and
filed decoration; 2⁵⁄₁₆ × ⁹⁄₁₆
(5.9 × 1.4).
Provenance: Fred Harvey Co.,
Albuquerque, New Mexico, 1953.
Bought as pawn.

20
21 22

20 BRACELET, 1930s
Navajo
Annealed band; set with seven
round cabochon turquoises; 2⅞ ×
¹³⁄₁₆ (7.3 × 2.1).
Provenance: Fred Harvey Co.,
Albuquerque, New Mexico, 1960.
Cf. Bedinger, p. 95, fig. 46.

21 BRACELET, about 1900
Navajo
Two round wires enclosing square
wire; set with six elliptical
turquoises (seventh missing);
2½ × ⅝ (6.4 × 1.6).
Provenance: Reese Vaughn,
Scottsdale, Arizona, 1960.
Said to have been purchased by
the seller's mother in 1919 exactly
as is.

22 BRACELET, 1900–1919
Navajo
Hammered band; set with three
elliptical glass sets in worn
serrated bezels; teardrop and
stamped decoration; 2¹³⁄₁₆ × ½
(7.1 × 1.3).
Provenance: Quivira Shop,
Santa Fe, New Mexico, 1960.
Cf. Bedinger, p. 49, fig. 19.

23 25
    24
26 27

23 BRACELET, 1930s
Navajo
Four double twisted wires
enclosing one square wire; set
with five large elliptical Persian
and Number 8 turquoises;
teardrop decoration; 2⅞ × 1
(7.3 × 2.5).
Provenance: Fred Harvey Co.,
Albuquerque, New Mexico, 1955.
Said to have been obtained by
the seller from pawn, Turpen
Trading Post, Gallup, New Mexico.

24 BRACELET, about 1930
Navajo
Three double twisted wires; set
with single heart-shaped
cabochon Burnham turquoise;
2⅝ × ½ (6.7 × 1.3).
Provenance: George Rummage,
Gallup, New Mexico, 1956.

25 BRACELET, about 1925
Navajo
Three double twisted wires; set
with five elliptical cabochon
turquoises in serrated bezels;
bent wire and stamped decoration
on terminals; 2¾ × ⅞ (7 × 2.2).
Provenance: Quivira Shop,
Santa Fe, New Mexico, 1955.

26 BRACELET, 1930s
Navajo
Two double twisted wires
enclosing round wire; set with
three round flat turquoises;
teardrop decoration; 2¹³⁄₁₆ × ¹⁵⁄₁₆
(7.1 × 2.4).
Provenance: Fred Harvey Co.,
Albuquerque, New Mexico,
before 1952.
Bought as pawn.

27 BRACELET, about 1930
Navajo
Two double twisted wires; set
with three elliptical flat Blue Gem
turquoises; stamped decoration;
2¾ × 1⁵⁄₁₆ (7 × 3.3).
Provenance: Fred Harvey Co.,
Albuquerque, New Mexico, 1955.

Not shown:

28 BRACELET, 1920s or possibly
later copy
Navajo
Four double twisted wires; set
with one square and two oval
turquoises in serrated bezels;
2⅞ × ¹³⁄₁₆ (7.3 × 2.1).
Provenance: Chester Copman,
Santa Fe Gift Shop, Santa Fe,
New Mexico, 1957.
Said to be from Seligman
collection.
Cf. Mera, p. 41, pl. 10.

29
30 31
32

29 BRACELET, about 1935
Navajo
Two round wires enclosing double
twisted wire; set with large
triangular malachite; flattened
teardrop and twisted wire
decoration; 2¹¹⁄₁₆ × 1¾
(6.8 × 4.4).
Provenance: Fred Harvey Co.,
Albuquerque, New Mexico, 1952.
Bought as pawn.

30 BRACELET, 1920s
Navajo
Ten double twisted wires; set
with single triangular turquoise;
twisted wire and bead wire
decoration; 2⅝ × ¾ (6.7 × 1.9).
Provenance: George Rummage,
Gallup, New Mexico, 1956.
Bought as pawn.

31 BRACELET, 1930s
Navajo, with possible later
additions in Zuni style
Three double twisted wires; set
with single flat elliptical
turquoise; overlay bands set with
eight small turquoises each and
terminating in bowknot; stamped
decoration; 2¾ × ⁹⁄₁₆ (7 × 1.4).
Provenance: Turpen Trading Post,
Gallup, New Mexico, 1955.
Bowknot is probably a later
addition.
Cf. Frank and Holbrook, p. 115.

32 BRACELET, 1930s
Navajo
Possible maker's mark: A L
Two flattened undulating wires
enclosing flattened double
twisted wire; stamped decoration;
2⅝ × ¹¹⁄₁₆ (6.7 × 1.7).
Provenance: Santa Fe, New
Mexico, 1964.

33 BRACELET, about 1925
Navajo
Hammered band; set with single
round Cerrillos turquoise;
stamped decoration; 2½ × ¾
(6.4 × 1.9).
Provenance: unknown.
Cracked and repaired.

34 BRACELET, about 1925
Navajo
Ingot-cast band; set with single
elliptical Cerrillos turquoise;
teardrop and stamped decoration;
2⅜ × 11⁄16 (6 × 1.7).
Provenance: Mrs. Richardson,
Gallup, New Mexico, 1953
or 1954.

35 BRACELET, 1910–1920
Navajo
Hammered band; set with single
elliptical Stennich turquoise;
teardrop and stamped decoration;
2⁹⁄16 × ⅝ (6.5 × 1.6).
Provenance: Chief Joe Secakuku,
Winslow, Arizona, 1952 or 1953.
Repaired at center back; formerly
had larger stone.

36 BRACELET, about 1930
Navajo
Hammered band; set with single
elliptical flat turquoise; twisted
wire and stamped decoration;
2½ × 11⁄16 (6.4 × 1.7).
Provenance: unknown.

Not shown:

37 BRACELET, 1890s or later
    Navajo
    Annealed band; set with three
    small turquoises; repoussé and
    stamped decoration; 2⅝ × 1¼
    (6.7 × 3.1).
    Provenance: Clay Lockett, Gallup,
    New Mexico, 1953.
    Stones may be later replacements.

38 BRACELET, 1920s
    Navajo
    Hammered band; set with single
    elliptical cabochon turquoise in
    serrated bezel; stamped and
    perforated decoration; 2⁹⁄₁₆ × ⁵⁄₁₆
    (6.5 × 0.8).
    Provenance: Fred Harvey Co.,
    Albuquerque, New Mexico, 1954.
    Bought as pawn.
    Band cracked and repaired;
    stone cracked.

39 BRACELET, about 1925
    Navajo
    Scallop-edged band; set with
    elliptical Cerrillos turquoise;
    stamped decoration; 2⅜ × 1
    (6 × 2.5).
    Provenance: Charlotte Goodrich,
    Albuquerque, New Mexico, 1961.

40 BRACELET, about 1930
    Navajo
    Sheet band; set with single round
    flat Battle Mountain turquoise;
    chased and stamped decoration;
    2½ × ½ (6.4 × 2.5).
    Provenance: Fred Harvey Co.,
    Albuquerque, New Mexico, 1952.
    Bought as pawn.

41 BRACELET, 1930s
    Navajo
    Hammered band; set with one
    round Lone Mountain spiderweb
    turquoise and two triangular
    Cerrillos turquoises; appliqué and
    filed decoration; 2½ × 1 (6.4 × 2.5).
    Provenance: Albuquerque,
    New Mexico.

42 BRACELET, 1930s
    Navajo
    Scallop-edged band; set with
    three small round turquoises;
    twisted wire and stamped
    decoration; 2½ × ⅞ (6.4 × 2.2).
    Provenance: Tesuque Trading
    Post, Santa Fe, New Mexico, 1954.

43 44 45
46 47
48

43 BRACELET, 1930s or later
    Navajo
    Heavy split band; set with single
    large elliptical turquoise;
    stamped, appliqué, teardrop, and
    twisted wire decoration; 1½ × 1⅝
    (3.8 × 4.1).
    Provenance: Original Curio Store,
    Santa Fe, New Mexico, 1954.

44 BRACELET, 1930s
    Navajo
    Split band; set with large
    triangular turquoise; teardrop
    and stamped decoration; 2¾ ×
    1⅞ (7 × 4.8).
    Provenance: Gallup, New Mexico,
    1962.

45 BRACELET, about 1930
    Navajo
    Split band; set with one square
    and two triangular Nevada
    turquoises; teardrop decoration;
    2¾ × ⅞ (7 × 2.2).
    Provenance: Fred Harvey Co.,
    Albuquerque, New Mexico, 1957.
    Bought as pawn.

46 BRACELET, 1920s
    Navajo
    Split band; set with single
    elliptical Number 8 spiderweb
    turquoise; appliqué and stamped
    decoration; 2⅜ × ⅞ (6 × 2.2).
    Provenance: Chief Joe Secakuku,
    Winslow, Arizona, 1953.
    Cracked and repaired.

47 BRACELET, 1930s
    Navajo
    Split band; set with single
    elliptical turquoise; appliqué,
    stamped, twisted wire, and
    teardrop decoration; 2½ × 15⁄16
    (6.4 × 2.4).
    Provenance: Fred Harvey Co.,
    Albuquerque, New Mexico, 1956.
    Bought as pawn
    Cf. Heard Museum, p. 16.

48 CHILD'S BRACELET, about 1930
    Navajo
    Split band; set with single
    elliptical turquoise; appliqué and
    stamped decoration; 1 15⁄16 × ½
    (4.9 × 1.3).
    Provenance: Chief Joe Secakuku,
    Winslow, Arizona, 1953.

Not shown:

49 BRACELET, about 1925
Navajo
Wide hammered band; set with
center turquoise cluster flanked
by two half-clusters; chased and
stamped decoration; 2 × 1⅜
(5 × 3.5).
Provenance: Fred Harvey Co.,
Albuquerque, New Mexico, 1956.

50 BRACELET, 1920s–1930s
Navajo
Split band; set with three small
round turquoises; appliqué,
teardrop, and stamped decora-
tion; 2½ × ¾ (6.4 × 1.9).
Provenance: Fred Harvey Co.,
Albuquerque, New Mexico, 1956.

51 BRACELET, 1930s
Navajo
Split band; set with cluster of
three turquoises flanked by two
half-clusters; appliqué and
stamped decoration; 2½ × 1
(6.4 × 2.5).
Provenance: Price's All Indian
Shop, Albuquerque, New Mexico,
1968.

52 BRACELET, 1930s
Navajo
Split band; set with large
shield-shaped Stennich turquoise
surrounded by crimped bezel
wire; stamped decoration; 2⅝ ×
1⅜ (6.7 × 3.5).
Provenance: Fred Harvey Co.,
Albuquerque, New Mexico, 1952.
Bought as pawn.

53 BRACELET, 1930s
Navajo
Split band; set with three round
turquoises; twisted wire, bent
wire, and stamped decoration;
2¾ × 1½ (7 × 3.8).
Provenance: Fred Harvey Co.,
Albuquerque, New Mexico, 1956.
Bought as pawn.

54 BRACELET, about 1940
Navajo
Split band; set with elliptical
Lone Mountain turquoise;
horseshoe appliqué, twisted wire,
and bead wire decoration;
2⅜ × 1¼ (6 × 3.1).
Provenance: Tom Moore, Gallup,
New Mexico, 1955.
Crack in stone has been filled
with aluminum solder.

55 BRACELET, about 1950
Navajo
Split band; large elliptical
turquoise surrounded by six tiny
round turquoises, flanked by two
semicircular turquoises; stamped
decoration; 2½ × 11⁄16 (6.4 × 1.7).
Provenance: Turpen Trading Post,
Gallup, New Mexico, 1962.

56 58
57
59 60

56 BRACELET, 1930s
Navajo
Three square wires; set with large
shield-shaped turquoise; teardrop
and stamped decoration;
2¹⁵/₁₆ × 3 (7.5 × 7.6).
Provenance: Gans', Santa Fe,
New Mexico, 1953.
Bought as pawn.
Cf. Bedinger, p. 96, fig. 48.

57 BRACELET, about 1940
Navajo
Hammered band; set with large
elliptical turquoise; twisted
wire, teardrop, and stamped
decoration; 2⅝ × 1⅛ (6.7 × 2.9).
Provenance: Turpen Trading Post,
Gallup, New Mexico, 1955.
Crack in stone has been filled
with aluminum solder.

58 BRACELET, 1950s
Navajo
Maker's mark: SFS
Sheet band; set with large
triangular turquoise; stamped,
repoussé, and twisted wire
decoration; 2½ × 2½ (6.4 × 6.4).
Provenance: Original Curio Store,
Santa Fe, New Mexico, 1954.

59 BRACELET, about 1950
Santo Domingo Pueblo
Three carinated wires; set with
large elliptical Bisbee turquoise;
twisted wire and teardrop
decoration; 3 × 2⅜ (7.6 × 6).
Provenance: Irma Bailey,
Albuquerque, New Mexico, 1969.

60 BRACELET, 1930s
Navajo
Four square wires; set with single
large elliptical chalcedony; bead
wire and twisted wire decoration;
2½ × 2½ (6.4 × 6.4).
Provenance: Mary Bateman, Hot
Springs, Arkansas, about 1951.

Not shown:

61 BRACELET, 1930s
Navajo
Three flattened double twisted
wires enclosing two square wires;
set with large square Nevada
turquoise; stamped decoration;
2⅝ × 1⅞ (6.7 × 4.8).
Provenance: Turpen Trading Post,
Gallup, New Mexico, 1952.
Stone broken, one corner
replaced.

62 BRACELET, about 1935
Navajo
Split band; set with large
irregularly shaped turquoise in
serrated bezel; appliqué,
stamped, and filed decoration;
2½ × 1¾ (6.4 × 4.4).
Provenance: Turpen Trading Post,
Gallup, New Mexico, 1963.
Bought as pawn.

63 BRACELET, about 1940
Navajo
Three carinated wires; set with
large round chalcedony; appliqué,
twisted wire, and stamped
decoration; 2½ × 1¹¹⁄₁₆ (6.4 × 4.3).
Provenance: Hubbell's Trading
Post, Winslow, Arizona, 1954.

64 BRACELET, 1945
Navajo
Two undulating half-round wires;
set with elliptical Lone Mountain
turquoise in serrated bezel
mounted on rectangular block;
2⁷⁄₁₆ × 1⅛ (6.2 × 2.9).
Provenance: Turpen Trading Post,
Gallup, New Mexico, 1960.
Bought as pawn.

65 BRACELET, about 1950
Navajo
Three square wires; set with small
rectangular turquoises supporting
large round aggregate stone of
chalcedony and felsite; 2¹⁵⁄₁₆ × 2⅜
(7.5 × 6).
Provenance: Tom Moore, Gallup,
New Mexico, 1953.
Possibly a recombination of
elements.

66 BRACELET, 1950s
Navajo
Two carinated and two round
bands enclosing double twisted
wire; set with large shield-shaped
turquoise (possibly Royal Blue);
2¹³⁄₁₆ × 2¼ (7.1 × 5.7).
Provenance: Original Curio Store,
Santa Fe, New Mexico, 1954.

67 69
68
70 71

67 BRACELET, about 1980
Navajo
Made by Arthur Lujan, Taos,
New Mexico; maker's mark: ⒭
Half-round band; set with single
Royston turquoise of irregular
shape in serrated bezel; teardrop
and appliqué decoration;
2¹⁵⁄₁₆ × 1 (7.5 × 2.5).
Provenance: Sewell's, Scottsdale,
Arizona, 1981.

68 BRACELET, 1920s
Navajo
Split band; set with one square
and two triangular flat Arizona
turquoises; appliqué and stamped
decoration; 2¼ × ⅝ (5.7 × 1.6).
Provenance: Turpen Trading Post,
Gallup, New Mexico, 1953.

69 BRACELET, 1920s
Navajo
Two twisted square wires
enclosing carinated band; set
with one elliptical and two
pear-shaped cabochon sintered
glass sets in serrated bezels;
appliqué crescents; teardrop and
stamped decoration; 2¹³⁄₁₆ × 1⅝
(7.1 × 4.1).
Provenance: Mrs. Richardson,
Gallup, New Mexico, 1953.
Said to have been purchased by
Mrs. Richardson in 1925 in
Tuba City, Arizona.

70 BRACELET, about 1930
Navajo
Three double twisted wires; set
with seven flat elliptical
turquoises (possibly Blue Gem)
in cross formation; appliqué and
stamped decoration; 2⅜ × 1¼
(6 × 3.1).
Provenance: Turpen Trading Post,
Gallup, New Mexico, 1960.

71 BRACELET, about 1930
Navajo
Two round wires enclosing square
twisted wire; set with square
cabochon turquoise in serrated
bezel; appliqué and stamped
decoration; 2½ × ¾ (6.4 × 1.9).
Provenance: Turpen Trading Post,
Gallup, New Mexico, 1961.

72

Not shown:

72 BRACELET, about 1930
Navajo
Sheet band enclosing double
twisted wire; set with three small
elliptical turquoises in filed
appliqué collars; stamped
decoration; $2^{11}/_{16} \times \frac{5}{8}$ (6.8 × 1.6).
Provenance: Fred Harvey Co.,
Albuquerque, New Mexico, 1960.

73 BRACELET, about 1930
Navajo
Hammered band; set with three
small round turquoises; chased,
appliqué, and stamped
decoration; $2\frac{5}{8} \times \frac{3}{8}$ (6.7 × 1).
Provenance: Fred Harvey Co.,
Albuquerque, New Mexico, 1952.

74 Bracelet, 1930s
Navajo
Split band; set with five graduated
elliptical turquoises on sheet
backing; twisted wire and bent
wire decoration; $2\frac{3}{4} \times 1\frac{1}{4}$
(7 × 3.1).
Provenance: Fred Harvey Co.,
Albuquerque, New Mexico, 1956.
Bought as pawn.

75 BRACELET, 1930s
Navajo
Two round wires enclosing twisted
square wire; set with three round
cabochon turquoises in collars;
appliqué and stamped decoration;
$2\frac{5}{8} \times {}^{15}/_{16}$ (6.7 × 2.4).
Provenance: Turpen Trading Post,
Gallup, New Mexico, 1953.
Bought as pawn.

76 BRACELET, 1930s or later
Navajo
Two carinated wires enclosing
round wire; set with two drilled
pear-shaped Cerrillos turquoises;
teardrop and stamped decoration;
$2\frac{3}{4} \times {}^{15}/_{16}$ (7 × 2.4).
Provenance: Turpen Trading Post,
Gallup, New Mexico, 1954.

77 BRACELET, 1940s
Navajo
Triple carinated wire; set with one
elliptical Blue Gem turquoise and
six smaller round turquoises;
stamped decoration; $2\frac{5}{8} \times 1\frac{1}{8}$
(6.7 × 2.9).
Provenance: Mr. Hubbell, New
Oraibi, Arizona, 1945 or 1946.

78 BRACELET, about 1945
Navajo
Two carinated bands enclosing
double twisted wire; set with five
flat elliptical Blue Gem and Lone
Mountain turquoises; twisted
wire, appliqué, and stamped
decoration; $2\frac{5}{8} \times 1\frac{1}{8}$ (6.7 × 2.9).
Provenance: Turpen Trading Post,
Gallup, New Mexico, 1965.
Bought as pawn.

79
80
81
82 83

79 BRACELET, 1930s
Navajo
Cast band; set with ten
pear-shaped turquoises in serrated
bezels; stamped decoration;
2⅝ × 1⁹⁄₁₆ (6.7 × 4).
Provenance: Packard's Trading
Post, Santa Fe, New Mexico 1960.

80 BRACELET, 1930s
Navajo
Made by Walter Henry, Prescott,
New Mexico.
Scratched inscription: Tom
Katens[——]
Cast openwork band; stamped
decoration; 2⅞ × 1⅞ (7.3 × 4.8).
Provenance: C. G. Wallace,
Gallup, New Mexico, 1956; Kirk
Brothers, Gallup (pawn).

81 BRACELET, 1910–1920
Navajo
Cast openwork band; set with
thirteen round and oval cabochon
turquoises; 2⅞ × 2¹⁄₁₆ (7.3 × 5.2).
Provenance: Chief Joe Secakuku,
Winslow, Arizona, 1953.
Cf. Mera, p. 24, pl. 3.

82 BRACELET, 1930s
Navajo
Cast openwork band; set with
large chalcedony; 2¾ × 1¹⁵⁄₁₆
(7 × 4.9).
Provenance: Turpen Trading Post,
Gallup, New Mexico, 1952.

83 BRACELET, about 1950
Navajo
Cast openwork band; set with
small flat elliptical turquoise;
2⅜ × 1½ (6 × 3.8).
Provenance: Turpen Trading Post,
Gallup, New Mexico, 1956.
Bought as pawn.

85
84   86
87 88
89

84 BRACELET, about 1915
   Navajo
   Hammered band; set with eleven
   elliptical Nevada turquoises;
   stamped and appliqué decoration;
   2½ × ¾ (6.4 × 1.9).
   Provenance: Fred Harvey Co.,
   Albuquerque, New Mexico, 1955.

85 BRACELET, about 1930
   Navajo
   Two round wires; set with eleven
   elliptical turquoises and twelve
   small pear-shaped turquoises;
   teardrop and appliqué decoration;
   3¼ × ¾ (8.3 × 1.9).
   Provenance: Fred Harvey Co.,
   Albuquerque, New Mexico, 1954.

86 BRACELET, about 1925
   Navajo
   Split band; set with seven
   elliptical turquoises; appliqué
   and stamped decoration;
   2 9/16 × 1/16 (6.5 × 2.7).
   Provenance: Fred Harvey Co.,
   Albuquerque, New Mexico, 1960.

87 BRACELET, 1920s
   Navajo
   Annealed band; set with ten
   square turquoises; teardrop and
   stamped decoration; 2¾ × 7/16
   (7 × 1.1).
   Provenance: Tom Moore, Gallup,
   New Mexico, 1955.

88 BRACELET, 1930s
   Navajo
   Sheet band; set with seven flat
   square turquoises; 2 9/16 × 5/8
   (6.5 × 1.6).
   Provenance: Price's All Indian
   Shop, Albuquerque, New Mexico,
   1961.

89 BRACELET, about 1920
   Navajo
   Hammered band; set with ten
   round flat turquoises; teardrop
   and stamped decoration;
   2 5/8 × ½ (6.7 × 1.3).
   Provenance: unknown.
   Bought as pawn.
   Cf. Bedinger, p. 95, fig. 46.

Not shown:

90 BRACELET, 1920s or earlier
Navajo
Sheet band; set with eleven flat
round turquoises (nine drilled);
teardrop and stamped decoration;
$2\frac{5}{8} \times \frac{3}{8}$ (6.7 × 1).
Provenance: Hagberg's, Gallup,
New Mexico, 1956.

91 BRACELET, about 1920
Navajo
Hammered band; set with five
elliptical turquoises; teardrop
and stamped decoration;
$3 \times \frac{1}{2}$ (7.6 × 1.3).
Provenance: Chief Joe Secakuku,
Winslow, Arizona, 1963.

92 BRACELET, 1920s
Navajo
Sheet band; set with eleven
round graduated Lone Mountain
turquoises; teardrop and stamped
decoration; $2\frac{15}{16} \times \frac{3}{8}$ (7.5 × 1).
Provenance: Quivira Shop,
Santa Fe, New Mexico, 1960.

93 BRACELET, 1920s
Navajo
Two carinated wires enclosing
double twisted wire; set with
five oval cabochon turquoises;
stamped decoration; $2\frac{1}{2} \times \frac{5}{8}$
(6.4 × 1.6).
Provenance: Hubbell's Trading
Post, Winslow, Arizona, 1953.

94 BRACELET, 1925
Navajo
Hammered band; set with nine
graduated elliptical turquoises;
teardrop and stamped decora-
tion; $2\frac{1}{2} \times \frac{3}{4}$ (6.4 × 1.9).
Provenance: unknown, 1961.

95 BRACELET, about 1925
Navajo
Triple wire; set with eleven
graduated flat elliptical
turquoises; teardrop decoration;
$2\frac{3}{4} \times \frac{1}{2}$ (7 × 1.3).
Provenance: Fred Harvey Co.,
Albuquerque, New Mexico.
Bought as pawn.
Three stones replaced, all ground
flush to bezel.

96 BRACELET, about 1930
Navajo
Sheet band; set with nine
elliptical turquoises; teardrop
and stamped decoration; $2\frac{1}{2} \times \frac{3}{4}$
(6.4 × 1.9).
Provenance: Turpen Trading Post,
Gallup, New Mexico, 1955.
Bought as pawn.

97 BRACELET, about 1930
Navajo
Two carinated wires enclosing
two twisted square wires; set
with seven elliptical turquoises;
stamped decoration; $2\frac{1}{2} \times \frac{1}{2}$
(6.4 × 1.3).
Provenance: Tom Moore, Gallup,
New Mexico, 1955.
Bought as pawn.

98 BRACELET, 1930
Navajo
Sheet band; set with seven oval
turquoises; stamped decoration;
$2\frac{1}{4} \times 2\frac{3}{8}$ (5.7 × 1).
Provenance: Peggy Evans,
Albuquerque, New Mexico.

99 BRACELET, 1930
Navajo
Sheet band; set with nine round
turquoises; teardrop and stamped
decoration; $2\frac{1}{2} \times \frac{1}{2}$ (6.4 × 1.3).
Provenance: Peggy Evans,
Albuquerque, New Mexico.

100 BRACELET, 1930s
Navajo
Hammered band; set with seven
square Stennich turquoises;
twisted wire and stamped
decoration; $2\frac{1}{2} \times \frac{3}{4}$ (6.4 × 1.9).
Provenance: Chief Joe Secakuku,
Winslow, Arizona, 1953.

101 BRACELET, 1930s
Navajo
Sheet band; set with seven round
turquoises; teardrop and stamped
decoration; $2\frac{5}{8} \times \frac{1}{2}$ (6.7 × 1.3).
Provenance: Hanns Hogan,
Gallup, New Mexico, 1952.

102 BRACELET, about 1935
Navajo
Two carinated wires enclosing
two double twisted flattened
wires; set with nine graduated
elliptical Blue Gem turquoises
on sheet; teardrop, stamped, and
twisted wire decoration; $2\frac{1}{2} \times 1$
(6.4 × 2.5).
Provenance: George Rummage,
Gallup, New Mexico, 1954.
Bought as pawn.

103 BRACELET, 1930s or later
Navajo
Two round wires; set with nine
flat elliptical Arizona turquoises;
teardrop and twisted wire
decoration; $2\frac{7}{8} \times \frac{7}{8}$ (7.3 × 2.2).
Provenance: Fred Harvey Co.,
Albuquerque, New Mexico, 1960.

104 BRACELET, about 1940
Navajo
Two square wires; set with fifteen
Nevada turquoises of varied
shape; teardrop decoration;
$2\frac{15}{16} \times \frac{5}{8}$ (7.5 × 1.6).
Provenance: Fred Harvey Co.,
Albuquerque, New Mexico, 1957.

105 BRACELET, 1940s
Navajo
Two round wires; set with seven
elliptical turquoises; teardrop
decoration; $2\frac{1}{2} \times \frac{1}{2}$ (6.4 × 1.3).
Provenance: Turpen Trading Post,
Gallup, New Mexico, 1954.
Bought as pawn.

106 BRACELET, 1940s
Navajo
Two round wires; set with seven
elliptical turquoises; teardrop
and stamped decoration;
$2\frac{15}{16} \times \frac{15}{16}$ (7.5 × 2.4).
Provenance: Turpen Trading Post,
Gallup, New Mexico, 1953.
Bought as pawn.

107 BRACELET, 1940s
Navajo
Two round wires; set with six
elliptical Arizona turquoises;
teardrop decoration; $2\frac{1}{2} \times 2\frac{3}{8}$
(6.4 × 1).
Provenance: unknown, 1954.

108 BRACELET, after 1935
Navajo
Four round wires; set with three
round Arizona turquoises;
commercial bead wire and
twisted wire decoration;
2¹¹⁄₁₆ × 1⅜ (6.8 × 3.5).
Provenance: Turpen Trading Post,
Gallup, New Mexico, 1955.

109 BRACELET, about 1940
Navajo
Four round wires; set with one
elliptical and two semicircular
King turquoises separated by six
smaller oval cabochon turquoises;
commercial bead wire, teardrop,
and stamped decoration;
3¼ × 2¼ (8.3 × 5.7).
Provenance: Fred Harvey Co.,
Albuquerque, New Mexico, 1956.

110 BRACELET, 1920s or earlier
Navajo
Scallop-edged annealed band; set
with seven elliptical cabochon
turquoises (possibly Stennich);
2⅝ × 1⅜ (6.7 × 3.5).
Provenance: F. H. Griswold, Fort
Defiance, Arizona, 1953.
Bought as pawn.

111 BRACELET, about 1930
Navajo
Three carinated wires enclosing
two double twisted wire bands;
set with three large oval
turquoises; 2⅝ × 1¼ (6.7 × 3.2).
Provenance: Fred Harvey Co.,
Albuquerque, New Mexico, 1952.

112 BRACELET, 1930s
Navajo
Two round wires enclosing sheet
band; set with three large
elliptical Cerrillos turquoises;
stamped and wire appliqué
decoration; 2⅝ × 2⅝ (6.7 × 6.7).
Provenance: Armijo's Trading
Post, Gallup, New Mexico, 1955;
C. G. Wallace, Gallup.

113 BRACELET, about 1910
Navajo
Hammered band; set with two
large Cerrillos turquoises (third
one missing) and two large
bosses; 2½ × ¹⁵⁄₁₆ (6.4 × 2.4).
Provenance: Hubbell's Trading
Post, Winslow, Arizona, 1953.
Traces of decorative stamping on
the inside suggest bracelet may
be reworked from an older piece.

Not shown:

114 BRACELET, about 1920
Navajo
Scratched inscription on inside:
Samuel Morgan 10 × 12
Two carinated wires enclosing
double twisted wire; set with
three elliptical cabochon
turquoises in serrated bezels
(side stones are Battle Mountain
turquoises); teardrop and
stamped decoration; 3⅛ × ¾
(7.9 × 1.9).
Provenance: Fred Harvey Co.,
Albuquerque, New Mexico, 1951
or 1952.
Similar to no. 116.

115 BRACELET, about 1920
Navajo
Split band; set with one elliptical
and two trapezoidal Stennich
turquoises; twisted wire,
teardrop, appliqué, and stamped
decoration; 2⁹⁄₁₆ × 11⁄₁₆ (6.5 × 1.7).
Provenance: Hubbell's Trading
Post, Winslow, Arizona, 1953.

116 BRACELET, about 1920
Navajo
Two carinated wires enclosing
double twisted wire; set with
three elliptical cabochon
turquoises in sawtooth bezels;
teardrop and stamped decoration;
3 × 13⁄₁₆ (7.6 × 2.1).
Provenance: El Navajo, Gallup,
New Mexico, 1953.

117 BRACELET, 1920s
Navajo
Split band; set with three
elliptical flat turquoises; looped
wire decoration; 2½ × ¾
(6.4 × 1.9).
Provenance: Turpen Trading Post,
Gallup, New Mexico, 1956.

118 BRACELET, 1920s
Navajo
Repoussé band; set with two
small elliptical turquoises;
stamped decoration; 2½ × 1⁵⁄₁₆
(6.4 × 3.3).
Provenance: Brice and Judy
Sewell, Taos, New Mexico, 1956.

119 BRACELET, 1920s
Navajo
Hammered band; set with three
elliptical cabochon turquoises;
teardrop and filed decoration;
2⅝ × ⁷⁄₁₆ (6.7 × 1.1).
Provenance: Fred Harvey Co.,
Albuquerque, New Mexico, 1954.

120 BRACELET, about 1930
Navajo
Two carinated wires enclosing
square wire; set with single
elliptical turquoise; teardrop,
filed, and stamped decoration;
2¾ × ⅝ (7 × 1.6).
Provenance: Tesuque Trading
Post, Santa Fe, New Mexico, 1954.
Bought as pawn.

121 BRACELET, 1930s
Navajo
Two round wires; set with three
large square turquoises (one
Cerrillos); bead wire decoration;
2¹³⁄₁₆ × 1 (7.1 × 2.5).
Provenance: Turpen Trading Post,
Gallup, New Mexico, 1956.
Bought as pawn.

122 BRACELET, 1930s
Navajo
Three round wires; set with one
large round and four rectangular
Blue Gem turquoises; twisted
wire decoration; 2¾ × 1½
(7 × 3.8).
Provenance: Fred Harvey Co.,
Santa Fe, New Mexico, 1955.
Stones have been treated.

123 BRACELET, 1935–1940
Navajo
Four half-round bands; set with
three large elliptical turquoises;
twisted wire and looped wire
decoration; 2¾ × 4½ (7 × 11.4).
Provenance: Fred Harvey Co.,
Santa Fe, New Mexico, 1957.
Bought as pawn.

124 BRACELET, 1940s
Navajo
Maker's mark: ⌒
Hammered band; set with three
elliptical turquoises in serrated
bezels; stamped decoration;
2½ × 1½ (6.4 × 3.8).
Provenance: Taos Book Shop,
Taos, New Mexico, 1953.
Reproduction of an older piece.

125 BRACELET, 1940s
Navajo
Two square wires; set with three
flat square turquoises; appliqué
and stamped decoration;
2⁷⁄₁₆ × 13⁄₁₆ (6.2 × 2.1).
Provenance: Kemp's, Sante Fe,
New Mexico, 1957.

126 BRACELET, about 1950
Navajo
Two twisted square wires
enclosing round wire; set with
one large and two smaller
turquoises of irregular shape;
appliqué decoration; 2⅝ × 1½
(6.7 × 3.8).
Provenance: Turpen Trading Post,
Gallup, New Mexico, 1963.
Stones have been filled with
aluminum solder.

127 BRACELET, 1950s
Navajo
Two carinated bands enclosing
two twisted square wires; set
with three irregularly shaped
turquoises in serrated bezels;
teardrop decoration; 2⅞ × 1½
(7.3 × 3.8).
Provenance: Turpen Trading Post,
Gallup, New Mexico, 1963.

128 129
130 131

128 BRACELET, 1935
Navajo
Two carinated bands enclosing
two double twisted flattened
wires; set with elliptical turquoise
in center, surrounded by twelve
triangular and twenty-four round
turquoises, three oval turquoises
at either side; twisted wire, spiral
wire, and stamped decoration;
2¾ × 2½ (7 × 6.4).
Provenance: Gans', Santa Fe,
New Mexico, 1957.

129 BRACELET, about 1970
Navajo
Five half-round wires; set with
seventeen Morenci turquoises of
irregular shape; teardrop and
twisted wire decoration;
2½ × 1¹³⁄₁₆ (6.4 × 4.6).
Provenance: Ann Clark, Phoenix,
Arizona, 1973.

130 BRACELET, about 1930
Navajo
Two carinated wires enclosing
two twisted square wires; set
with three elliptical Battle
Mountain turquoise clusters;
teardrop and stamped decoration;
2⅝ × 1¼ (6.7 × 3.1).
Provenance: Price's All Indian
Shop, Albuquerque, New Mexico,
1968.

131 BRACELET, 1940s
Navajo
Two carinated wires enclosing
cluster of eleven square and
elliptical Nevada turquoises;
teardrop and stamped decoration;
2½ × 1⅜ (6.4 × 3.5).
Provenance: Tom Moore, Gallup,
New Mexico, 1955.

Not shown:

132 BRACELET, 1920s
Navajo
Split band; set with five clusters
of flat oval Nevada turquoises;
stamped decoration; 2⅞ × 1¾
(7.3 × 4.4).
Provenance: Fred Harvey Co.,
Albuquerque, New Mexico, 1952.

133 BRACELET, about 1930
Navajo
Two twisted square wires
enclosing round wire; set
with cluster of nine elliptical
turquoises (possibly Cerrillos),
two elliptical turquoises on
either side; 2⅞ × 12⅜ (7.3 × 3.5).
Provenance: Turpen Trading Post,
Gallup, New Mexico, 1960.

134 BRACELET, about 1930
Navajo
Three round wires; set with three
clusters of eleven small elliptical
Nevada turquoises each, two
small round turquoises
asymmetrically placed between
clusters; stamped decoration;
2¾ × ⅞ (7 × 2.2).
Provenance: Fred Harvey Co.,
Albuquerque, New Mexico, 1956.

135 BRACELET, about 1930 or later
Navajo
Two twisted square wires; set
with one rectangular turquoise
surrounded by eight round
turquoises; teardrop decoration;
2⅝ × 15/16 (6.7 × 2.4).
Provenance: Turpen Trading Post,
Gallup, New Mexico, 1961.

136 BRACELET, 1930s
Navajo
Two round wires enclosing two
twisted square wires; set with
triangular turquoise surrounded
by twelve elliptical turquoises in a
cluster, two triangular turquoises
on each side; 2¾ × 1¾ (7 × 4.4).
Provenance: Chief Joe Secakuku,
Winslow, Arizona, 1955 or 1956.
Bought as pawn.

137 BRACELET, 1930s
Navajo, in Zuni style
Split band; set with three clusters
of small round turquoises;
2½ × 13/16 (6.4 × 2.1).
Provenance: Hagberg's, Gallup,
New Mexico, 1956.

138 BRACELET, 1930s
Navajo
Two carinated bands enclosing
two round wires and one double
twisted wire; set with three square
turquoises, each surrounded by
twelve small round turquoises;
teardrop decoration; 2½ × 15/16
(6.4 × 2.4).
Provenance: Fred Harvey Co.,
Albuquerque, New Mexico, 1956.
Bought as pawn.

139 BRACELET, mid-1930s
Navajo
Three flattened wires; set with
central rectangular turquoise and
two round turquoises surrounded
by small turquoises at sides;
2 11/16 × 1 9/16 (6.8 × 4).
Provenance: Dewey-Kofron Gal-
lery, Santa Fe, New Mexico, 1979;
George Freylinghuysen collection.

140 BRACELET, about 1935
Navajo
Two round wires enclosing double
twisted wire; set with three
clusters of nine large round
turquoises each; twisted wire and
teardrop decoration; 2½ × 1½
(6.4 × 3.8).
Provenance: Nettie Wheeler,
Muskogee, Oklahoma, 1952.

141 BRACELET, 1930s or later
Navajo
Sheet band; set with nine small
round turquoises; teardrop and
stamped decoration; 2 1/16 × 5/16
(5.2 × 0.8).
Provenance: unknown.

142 BRACELET, 1930s or later
Navajo
Hammered band; set with one
row of fifteen elliptical and two
rows of fifteen round turquoises
each; 2 7/16 × 1 (6.2 × 2.5).
Provenance: Hubbell's Trading
Post, Winslow, Arizona, 1953.
Bought as pawn.
Possibly unfinished.

143 BRACELET, about 1940
Navajo
Three carinated wires; set with
three clusters of nine small round
turquoises each, on sheet
mounting; twisted wire decoration; 2 9/16 × 1 (6.5 × 2.5).
Provenance: Fred Harvey Co.,
Albuquerque, New Mexico, 1960.

144 BRACELET, about 1940
Navajo
Four round wires; set with
nineteen small round and
elliptical turquoises in three
clusters, on sheet mounting;
2½ × ⅞ (6.4 × 2.2).
Provenance: Turpen Trading Post,
Gallup, New Mexico, 1956.
Bought as pawn.

145 146
147   149
    148

145 BRACELET, 1930s
Zuni
Three carinated bands; sheet
mounting set with cluster of one
elliptical, sixteen small round,
and sixteen oval Blue Gem
turquoises, flanked by two
half-clusters of twelve Blue
Gem turquoises; finely serrated
bezels; twisted wire and teardrop
decoration; 3 × 3³⁄₁₆ (7.6 × 8).
Provenance: Chief Joe Secakuku,
Winslow, Arizona, 1953.
Cf. Bedinger, pl. 3.

146 BRACELET, 1920s–1930s
Zuni
Three carinated wires; set with
flat triangular turquoise
surrounded by twenty-three
round turquoises and flanked by
vertical rows of five stones each;
finely serrated bezels; teardrop
decoration; 2⁷⁄₈ × 2³⁄₈ (7.3 × 6).
Provenance: Hubbell's Trading
Post, Winslow, Arizona, 1955.

147 BRACELET, about 1925
Zuni or Navajo
Three square wires; set with
cluster of nine elliptical
turquoises and thirty-four small
round turquoises on wires;
2¹⁵⁄₁₆ × 1³⁄₁₆ (7.5 × 3).
Provenance: Fred Harvey Co.,
Albuquerque, New Mexico, 1961.

148 BRACELET, 1930s
Zuni
Three round wires; sheet
mounting set with forty-seven
small oval turquoises in three
rows; teardrop and stamped
decoration; 2⁵⁄₈ × 1 (6.7 × 2.5).
Provenance: Chief Joe Secakuku,
Winslow, Arizona, 1959.

149 BRACELET, about 1940
Zuni
Three square bands; set with
fifty-two oval and round
turquoises in three clusters;
twisted wire, teardrop, and
stamped decoration; 2¾ × 1⁵⁄₈
(7 × 4.1).
Provenance: Hanns Hogan,
Gallup, New Mexico, 1953.
Bought as pawn.

81

Not shown:

150 BRACELET, about 1920
Zuni
Two round wires enclosing square
wire; set with twenty-seven
Nevada turquoises in three
clusters, serrated bezels; twisted
wire decoration; $2\frac{5}{8} \times \frac{15}{16}$
(6.7 × 2.4).
Provenance: Chief Joe Secakuku,
Winslow, Arizona, 1953.

151 BRACELET, about 1930
Zuni
Three twisted square wires;
set with large oval turquoise
surrounded by small turquoises,
flanked by squared clusters of
turquoises; teardrop and twisted
wire decoration; $2\frac{1}{2} \times 2$
(6.4 × 5).
Provenance: Eric Kohlberg,
Denver, Colorado, 1956.
Bought as pawn.

152 BRACELET, about 1930
Zuni or Navajo
Two round wires enclosing two
twisted square wires and single
square wire; set with three
clusters of elliptical Burnham
turquoises (nine in central cluster,
three on either side); teardrop
and twisted wire decoration;
$2\frac{5}{8} \times 1\frac{1}{2}$ (6.7 × 3.8).
Provenance: Quivira Shop,
Santa Fe, New Mexico, 1960.

153 BRACELET, about 1930
Zuni
Split band; set with three clusters
of nine flat round turquoises
each; spiral wire decoration;
$2\frac{3}{8} \times 1$ (6 × 2.5).
Provenance: Nettie Wheeler,
Muskogee, Oklahoma, 1952.

154 BRACELET, 1930s
Zuni
Two round wires; set with three
clusters of flat oval and elliptical
turquoises; teardrop decoration;
$2\frac{11}{16} \times 1\frac{3}{8}$ (6.8 × 3.5).
Provenance: Chief Joe Secakuku,
Winslow, Arizona, 1960.

155 PAIR OF BRACELETS, 1930s
Zuni
Hammered band; set with three
clusters of round cabochon
turquoises; repoussé and stamped
decoration; $2\frac{3}{8} \times 1\frac{3}{16}$ (6 × 3).
Provenance: Original Curio Store,
Santa Fe, New Mexico, 1950s.
Said to have been made near
Ramah, New Mexico.

156 BRACELET, 1930s
Zuni
Two flat bands; each set with
row of small round turquoises;
teardrop and stamped decoration;
$2\frac{3}{16} \times \frac{5}{8}$ (5.6 × 1.6).
Provenance: Hagberg's, Gallup,
New Mexico, 1956.
Bought as pawn.

157 BRACELET, 1930s
Navajo, with Zuni influence
Three carinated bands; set with
one round and two triangular
clusters of turquoises on sheet
mounting; twisted wire decora-
tion; $2\frac{5}{8} \times 1\frac{1}{4}$ (6.7 × 3.1).
Provenance: Nettie Wheeler,
Muskogee, Oklahoma, 1953.

158 SET OF BRACELETS, about 1930s
Zuni
Flat band; set with single row of
fourteen small round turquoises;
twisted wire and stamped
decoration; $2\frac{3}{8} \times 1\frac{3}{16}$ (6 × 3).
Provenance: unknown.

159 BRACELET, about 1940
Zuni
Three flat bands; each set with
fifteen small square turquoises;
$2\frac{1}{2} \times \frac{3}{4}$ (6.4 × 1.9).
Provenance: Quivira Shop,
Santa Fe, New Mexico, 1952.

160 162
161
163 164

160 BRACELET, about 1930
Navajo or Zuni
Three wires; nineteen oval and elliptical Burnham turquoises in central clusters flanked by two half-clusters; teardrop decoration; 2⅝ × 1⅜ (6.7 × 3.5).
Provenance: George Rummage, Gallup, New Mexico, 1956.
Bought as pawn.

161 BRACELET, 1930s or earlier
Hopi
Hammered band; set with nine small round turquoises; stamped "snakeskin" decoration; 2⅝ × 5/16 (6.7 × 0.8).
Provenance: Chief Joe Secakuku, Winslow, Arizona, 1954.

162 BRACELET, about 1940
Hopi
Made by Roscoe Navasie, Walpi, Arizona.
Four round wires; set with thirty-three small elliptical turquoises in three rows; teardrop decoration; 2⅝ × 1 7/16 (6.7 × 3.7).
Provenance: Chief Joe Secakuku, Winslow, Arizona, 1959.

163 BRACELET, about 1950
Hopi
Three round wires; set with one large elliptical and six small round Arizona turquoises; bead, twisted, and looped wire decoration; 2⅝ × 1½ (6.7 × 3.8).
Provenance: Chief Joe Secakuku, Winslow, Arizona, 1953 or 1954.
Said to have been made by "Sah-noi-ye-ma," a Hopi smith ninety years old at the time.

164 BRACELET, about 1940
Navajo
Sheet band; set with ten turquoises of irregular shape; bent wire and stamped decoration; 2⅜ × 1 5/16 (6 × 3.3).
Provenance: Turpen Trading Post, Gallup, New Mexico, 1960.

Not shown:

165 BRACELET, 1930s or later
Pueblo style, possibly Navajo made
Two round wires; sheet mounting set with thirty-three graduated oval and elliptical Arizona turquoises in three rows; appliqué and teardrop decoration; 2¾ × 1¼ (7 × 3.1).
Provenance: Turpen Trading Post, Gallup, New Mexico, 1956.

166 BRACELET, 1930s or later
Possibly Tesuque Pueblo
Four thin wires; set with large lozenge-shaped turquoise; 2½ × ⅞ (6.4 × 2.2).
Provenance: Tesuque Trading Post, Sante Fe, New Mexico, 1954.
Bought as pawn.

167 BRACELET, about 1950
Hopi
Hammered band; set with seven round turquoises; teardrop and filed decoration; 2½ × ½ (6.4 × 1.3).
Provenance: Chief Joe Secakuku, Winslow, Arizona, 1954.

168 169 170
171 172
173

168 BRACELET, 1940s–1950s
Navajo
Two looped round wires enclosing
single round wire; set with single
round turquoise; teardrop and
bent wire decoration; 2¼ × ¹¹⁄₁₆
(5.7 × 1.7).
Provenance: unknown.

169 BRACELET, about 1950
Navajo
Four half-round wires enclosing
triple twisted wire; 2 × 1⅛
(5 × 2.9).
Provenance: Fred Harvey Co.,
Albuquerque, New Mexico, 1957.

170 BRACELET, about 1955
Navajo
Heavy double twisted wire;
2⅞ × ⅜ (7.3 × 1).
Provenance: Phoenix,
Arizona, 1960.

171 PAIR OF BRACELETS, about 1950
Hopi
Made by Lewis Lomay.
Heavy double twisted wire
overlaid with fine double twisted
wire; 2⅝ × ¼ (6.7 × .6).
Provenance: Santa Fe, New
Mexico.
Cf. Mera, p. 37, pl. 1.

172 BRACELET, about 1950
Navajo
Flattened double twisted wire;
stamped decoration; 2¹¹⁄₁₆ × ⅝
(6.8 × 1.6).
Provenance: unknown, 1953.
Cf. Mera, p. 42, pl. 12.

173 CHILD'S BRACELET, about 1940
Navajo
Two flattened double twisted
wires; set with small round
turquoise; 1½ × ⅝ (3.8 × 1.6).
Provenance: unknown.

Not shown:

174 BRACELET, 1940s
Navajo
Flattened double twisted wire;
set with three small elliptical
turquoises; stamped decoration;
$2^{7}/_{16} \times {}^{5}/_{16}$ (6.2 × 0.8).
Provenance: unknown, about
1953.

175 BRACELET, 1940s
Navajo
Two looped round wires enclosing
round wire; set with single round
turquoise; twisted wire and
teardrop decoration; $2^{7}/_{8} \times {}^{3}/_{4}$
(7.3 × 1.9).
Provenance: Hubbell's Trading
Post, Winslow, Arizona, 1956.
Bought as pawn.
Similar to no. 168.

176 BRACELET, 1940s
Navajo
Silver-plated copper; two round
wires enclosing four double wires;
$2^{1}/_{2} \times {}^{3}/_{4}$ (6.4 × 1.9).
Provenance: Turpen Trading Post,
Gallup, New Mexico, 1964.

177 BRACELET, 1940s–1950s
Navajo
Two looped round wires enclosing
round wire; set with single round
turquoise; twisted wire and bent
wire decoration; $2^{1}/_{2} \times {}^{15}/_{16}$
(6.4 × 2.4).
Provenance: unknown.
Similar to no. 168.

178 BRACELET, about 1950
Navajo
Double twisted flattened wire
in carinate form; stamped
decoration; $2^{7}/_{16} \times {}^{1}/_{4}$ (6.2 × 0.6).
Provenance: Hubbell's Trading
Post, Winslow, Arizona, 1953.
Bought as pawn.

179 BRACELET, about 1950
Navajo
Triple twisted wire band; $2^{5}/_{8} \times {}^{1}/_{4}$
(6.7 × 0.6).
Provenance: unknown.

180 BRACELET, 1950s
Navajo
Two flattened bands of round wire
twisted together with two fine
double twisted wires; $2^{7}/_{16} \times {}^{5}/_{8}$
(6.2 × 1.6).
Provenance: Crazy Horse,
Albuquerque, New Mexico, 1960.

181 BRACELET, 1950s
Navajo
Two half-round wires enclosing
flattened double twisted wire;
filed decoration; $2^{5}/_{16} \times {}^{1}/_{2}$
(5.9 × 1.3)
Provenance: unknown.

182 BRACELET, 1950s
Navajo
Two double twisted wires; set
with rectangular turquoise;
appliqué, teardrop, and stamped
decoration; $2^{1}/_{2} \times {}^{1}/_{2}$ (6.4 × 1.3).
Provenance: Quivira Shop,
Santa Fe, New Mexico, 1960.

183 BRACELET, about 1950
Navajo
Double twisted wire flattened
into carinated shape; stamped
decoration; $2^{3}/_{4} \times {}^{1}/_{4}$ (7 × 0.6).
Provenance: Tom Moore, Gallup,
New Mexico, 1953.

184 BRACELET, 1950s
Navajo
Double twisted wire overlaid with
fine double twisted wire; $2^{1}/_{2} \times {}^{1}/_{8}$
(6.4 × 0.3).
Provenance: unknown.

185 PAIR OF BRACELETS, 1950s
Navajo
Flattened double twisted wire
overlaid with fine double twisted
wire; $2^{1}/_{2} \times {}^{1}/_{8}$ (6.4 × 0.3).
Provenance: unknown.

186 CHILD'S BRACELET, 1950s
Navajo
Two round wires enclosing
flattened round wire twisted
together with two fine double
twisted wires; $2 \times {}^{1}/_{4}$
(5 × 0.6).
Provenance: unknown.

187 CHILD'S BRACELET, 1950s or later
Navajo
Two round wires enclosing
flattened double twisted wire;
$2^{1}/_{16} \times {}^{1}/_{4}$ (5.2 × 0.6)
Provenance: unknown.

188 CHILD'S BRACELET, 1965–1970
Santo Domingo Pueblo
Two round wires; set with single
round turquoise in serrated
bezel; twisted wire and teardrop
decoration; $1^{3}/_{4} \times {}^{1}/_{4}$ (4.4 × 0.6).
Provenance: Tony and Dorothy
Tortalita, Santa Fe, New Mexico,
1970.

189 190
191 192

189 BRACELET, 1950s or later
Navajo
Sheet band; set with two round
turquoises; appliqué and filed
decoration; 2¾ × 1⁵⁄₁₆ (7 × 3.3).
Provenance: Wright's Trading
Post, Albuquerque, New Mexico,
1972.

190 BRACELET, about 1950
Navajo
Sheet band; set with elliptical
Bisbee turquoise; repoussé and
stamped decoration; 2½ × 1⁷⁄₁₆
(6.4 × 3.7).
Provenance: Original Curio Store,
Santa Fe, New Mexico, 1954.

191 BRACELET, about 1950
Navajo
Carinated wire on sheet backing;
set with single flat elliptical
Blue Gem turquoise; stamped
decoration; 2½ × 1¹⁄₁₆ (6.4 × 2.9).
Provenance: Tom Moore, Gallup,
New Mexico, 1955.
Said to have belonged to Chee
Johnson's mother.

192 BRACELET, 1940s
Navajo
Sheet band; set with single
elliptical cabochon turquoise;
stamped decoration; 2½ × 1¼
(6.4 × 3.2).
Provenance: Hubbell's Trading
Post, Winslow, Arizona, 1954.
Bought as pawn.

Not shown:

193 CHILD'S BRACELET, about 1955
Santo Domingo Pueblo
Made by Joseph Tenorio.
Sheet band; set with one small
elliptical turquoise; filed
decoration; ½ × ⁵⁄₁₆ (1.3 × 0.8).
Provenance: Santa Fe Indian
School, Santa Fe, New Mexico,
1955.

194 BRACELET, about 1970
Euro-American
Made by Bill Holden, Taos, New
Mexico; maker's mark: BH
Sheet band; set with single flat
elliptical turquoise; filed,
stamped, and repoussé decora-
tion; 2½ × 2 (6.4 × 5).
Provenance: Carson House Shop,
Taos, 1975.

86

195 196 197
  198 199
    200

195 BRACELET, about 1940
Navajo
Two double twisted wires
enclosing sheet band; set with
seven elliptical turquoises;
teardrop and stamped decoration; 2¾ × 1 (7 × 2.5).
Provenance: George Rummage,
Gallup, New Mexico, 1956.

196 BRACELET, about 1940
Navajo
Two carinated bands enclosing
sheet band; set with eight
elliptical Nevada turquoises;
stamped decoration; 2¼ × 1
(5.7 × 2.5).
Provenance: George Rummage,
Gallup, New Mexico, 1954.
Cf. Mera, p. 32, pl. 5.

197 BRACELET, 1950s
Navajo
Six double twisted wires; set with
five elliptical Arizona turquoises;
2½ × ¹⁵⁄₁₆ (6.4 × 2.4).
Provenance: unknown.

198 BRACELET, about 1950
Hopi
Made by Lewis Lomay; maker's
mark: 〰
Hammered band; set with three
square Number 8 spiderweb
turquoises and four elliptical
cabochon corals; appliqué and
filed decoration; 2½ × ⁷⁄₁₆
(6.4 × 1.1).
Provenance: Santa Fe, New
Mexico.

199 BRACELET, 1930s
Navajo
Initials scratched inside: W D
Sheet band; one rectangular, two
round, and two square Burnham
turquoises; teardrop, twisted wire,
and spiral wire decoration;
2½ × ½ (6.4 × 1.3).
Provenance: Chief Joe Secakuku,
Winslow, Arizona, 1963.

200 BRACELET, late 1940s
Hopi
Made by Bert Puhuyestiwa;
maker's mark: 🦋
Hopi Silvercraft Guild mark.
Sheet band; set with seven
graduated elliptical turquoises
with twelve small round
turquoises interspersed; twisted
wire and stamped decoration;
2⅝ × 1 (6.7 × 2.5).
Provenance: Chief Joe Secakuku,
Winslow, Arizona, 1958.

Not shown:

201 BRACELET, 1940s
Navajo
Sheet band; set with five elliptical
cabochon Cerrillos turquoises;
2½ × ⁵⁄₁₆ (6.4 × 0.8).
Provenance: Fred Harvey Co.,
Albuquerque, New Mexico, 1950s.
Bought as pawn.

202 BRACELET, 1940s
Navajo
Three round wires; set with seven
elliptical turquoises on sheet
backing; teardrop and stamped
decoration; 2⅝ × ⅝ (6.7 × 1.6).
Provenance: Tom Moore, Gallup,
New Mexico, 1955.
Bought as pawn.

203 BRACELET, 1940s
Navajo
Ingot-cast band; set with five
triangular Burnham turquoises;
filed, teardrop, and stamped
decoration; 2⅝ × ½ (6.7 × 1.3).
Provenance: Tom Moore, Gallup,
New Mexico, 1953.

204 BRACELET, about 1945
Navajo
Two filed wires enclosing a band;
set with seven graduated elliptical
Lone Mountain turquoises;
appliqué and stamped decora-
tion; 2¾ × ¾ (7 × 1.9).
Provenance: Bright Angel Lodge,
Grand Canyon National Park,
Arizona, 1949.

205 PAIR OF BRACELETS, about 1950
Navajo
Two carinated bands enclosing
double twisted wire; set with five
elliptical Persian turquoises;
stamped decoration; 2⁷⁄₁₆ × ⅝
(6.2 × 1.6).
Provenance: Chief Joe Secakuku,
Winslow, Arizona, 1956.

206 BRACELET, about 1960
Navajo
Three twisted square wires
alternating with two square
wires; set with nine elliptical
and sixteen small round Nevada
turquoises; 3⅜ × ⅞ (8.6 × 2.2).
Provenance: Tom Bahti, Tucson,
Arizona, 1965.

207 BRACELET, 1960s or later
Santo Domingo Pueblo
Made by Tony Mirabal.
Sheet band; set with five
turquoises carved in the form
of owls; twelve bosses; 2⅞ × 1½
(7.3 × 3.8).
Provenance: Packard's Trading
Post, Santa Fe, New Mexico,
1975.

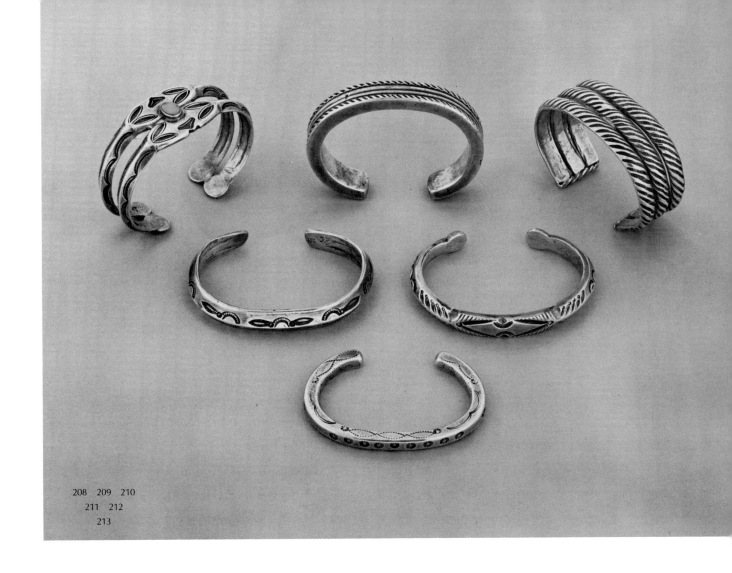

208 209 210
  211 212
    213

208 BRACELET, 1920s or later
Navajo
Two carinated bands joined at
center; set with single elliptical
Burnham turquoise; stamped
decoration; 2⅝ × 1¹/₁₆ (6.7 × 2.9).
Provenance: Santa Fe Indian
School, Santa Fe, New Mexico,
1955.

209 BRACELET, 1940s
Navajo
Heavy ingot-cast band; chased
and stamped decoration;
2¾ × ⁷/₁₆ (7 × 1.1).
Provenance: Tom Moore, Gallup,
New Mexico, 1953.

210 BRACELET, 1950s
Navajo
Three half-round wires; filed and
stamped decoration; 2⁹/₁₆ × ⁷/₁₆
(6.5 × 1.1).
Provenance: Quivira Shop,
Santa Fe, New Mexico, 1960.
Cf. Bedinger, p. 106, fig. 54a.

211 BRACELET, 1930s
Navajo
Hammered carinated band;
stamped decoration; 2¹³/₁₆ × ⅜
(7.1 × 1).
Provenance: Fred Harvey Co.,
Albuquerque, New Mexico, 1952.
Cf. Mera, p. 30, pl. 1.

212 BRACELET, about 1920–1930
Navajo
Cast carinated band; stamped
decoration; 2¹³/₁₆ × ⅜ (7.1 × 1).
Provenance: Maisel's, Albu-
querque, New Mexico, 1965.

213 SET OF FOUR BRACELETS,
about 1950
Navajo
Made by "Annie."
Heavy square wire band; stamped
decoration; each about 2½ × ¼
(6.4 × 0.6).
Provenance: Tom Moore, Gallup,
New Mexico, 1953.

Not shown:

214 BRACELET, 1930s
Navajo
Carinated band; stamped
decoration; 2⁹/₁₆ × ¼ (6.5 × 3.2).
Provenance: unknown.

215 BRACELET, about 1938
Navajo
Stamped: U.S. NAVAJO 1
Sheet band; stamped decoration;
2⁷/₁₆ × ⁷/₁₆ (6.2 × 1.1).
Provenance: unknown, 1956.

216 BRACELET, 1940s
Navajo
Hammered carinated band;
stamped decoration;
2¾ × ¼ (7 × 0.6).
Provenance: unknown.

217 BRACELET, 1940s
Navajo
Sheet band; stamped decoration;
2¼ × ½ (6.4 × 1.3).
Provenance: Turpen Trading Post,
Gallup, New Mexico, 1954.
Bought as pawn.

218 BRACELET, 1940s–1950s
Navajo
Square wire band; stamped
decoration; 2½ × ³/₁₆ (6.4 × 0.5).
Provenance: unknown, 1956.

219 BRACELET, about 1950
Navajo
Carinated band, probably cast;
2⁵/₈ × ⁵/₁₆ (6.7 × 0.8).
Provenance: Fred Harvey Co.,
Albuquerque, New Mexico, 1956.

220 BRACELET, about 1950
Navajo
Carinated wire band; stamped
decoration; 2½ × ¼ (6.4 × 0.6).
Provenance: unknown reservation
trading post, 1952.

221 BRACELET, about 1950
Navajo
Carinated wire band; stamped
decoration; 2½ × ¼ (6.4 × 0.6).
Provenance: Fred Harvey Co.,
Albuquerque, New Mexico, 1956.

222 BRACELET, about 1950
Navajo
Half-round band; chased and
stamped decoration; 2¼ × ¼
(6.4 × 0.6).
Provenance: unknown.

223 BRACELET, about 1950
Navajo
Sheet band; filed decoration;
2⁷/₁₆ × ¼ (6.2 × 0.6).
Provenance: Fred Harvey Co.,
Albuquerque, New Mexico, 1956.
Cf. Mera, p. 10, pl. 3.

224 BRACELET, about 1950
Navajo
Heavy sheet band; chased
decoration; 2¹¹/₁₆ × ⅜ (6.8 × 1).
Provenance: unknown.

225 BRACELET, about 1950
Navajo
Triple carinated band; twisted wire
decoration; 2½ × ½ (6.4 × 1.3).
Provenance: Fred Harvey Co.,
Albuquerque, New Mexico, 1956.

226 BRACELET, about 1950
Navajo
Two half-round wires enclosing
two bands and double twisted
wire; stamped decoration;
2½ × ⁵/₁₆ (6.4 × 0.8).
Provenance: Fred Harvey Co.,
Albuquerque, New Mexico, 1956.

227 BRACELET, about 1950
Navajo
Cast band; stamped decoration;
2¾ × ½ (7 × 1.3).
Provenance: George Rummage,
Gallup, New Mexico, 1950.

228 BRACELET, about 1950
Navajo
Half-round wire band; stamped
decoration; 2½ × ⁵/₁₆ (6.4 × 0.8).
Provenance: unknown.

229 BRACELET, 1950 or later
Navajo
Half-round band; stamped and
filed decoration; 2½ × ⅜
(6.4 × 1).
Provenance: unknown.

230 BRACELET, 1960s
Made by Joe Quintana; maker's
mark: JHQ
Heavy sheet band; chased and
stamped decoration; 2⁵/₈ × ⁹/₁₆
(6.7 × 1.4).
Provenance: Governor's Palace,
Santa Fe, New Mexico, 1970.

231 PAIR OF BRACELETS, about 1970
Navajo
Stamped: JOY
          IHM S/S
Heavy sheet band; chased deco-
ration; 2⅜ × ⅜ (6 × 1).
Provenance: Wooden Indian,
Washington, D.C., 1972.

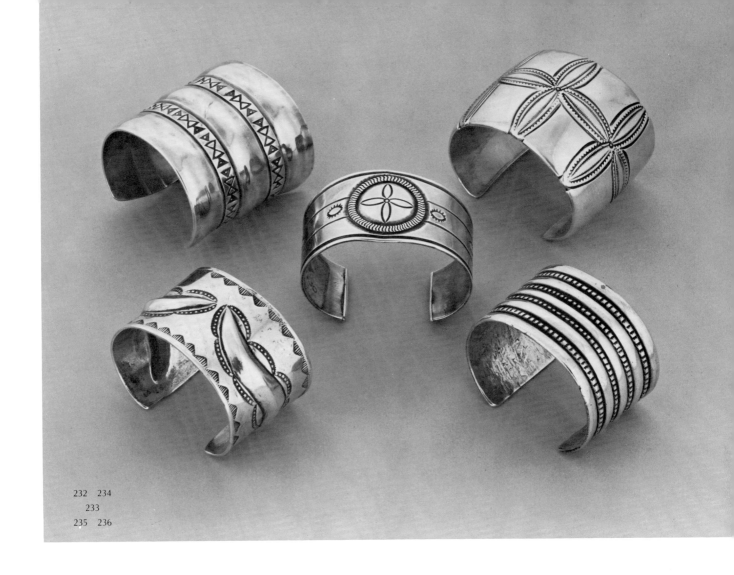

232 234
  233
235 236

232 PAIR OF BRACELETS, about 1950
Navajo
Sheet band; repoussé and
stamped decoration; 2¼ × 2½
(5.7 × 6.4).
Provenance: Turpen Trading Post,
Gallup, New Mexico, 1953.

233 BRACELET, 1960s
Navajo
Navajo Arts and Crafts Guild
label and stamp.
Sheet band; repoussé, stamped,
and chased decoration;
2⁹⁄₁₆ × 1½ (6.5 × 3.8).
Provenance: Wright's Trading
Post, Albuquerque, New Mexico,
1972.

234 BRACELET, 1960s
Navajo
Hollow sheet band; stamped
decoration; 2½ × 2⅛ (6.4 × 5.4).
Provenance: Sewell's, Scottsdale,
Arizona, 1975.

235 BRACELET, about 1940
Navajo
Sheet band; repoussé and
stamped decoration; 2⁷⁄₁₆ × 1⁹⁄₁₆
(6.2 × 4).
Provenance: C. G. Wallace,
Gallup, New Mexico, 1950s.
Wallace was said to have gotten
it from the silversmith, who had
worn it for ten to twelve years.

236 BRACELET, 1950s
Navajo
Sheet band; filed and chased
decoration; 2⅜ × 1⁹⁄₁₆ (6 × 4).
Provenance: Quivira Shop,
Santa Fe, New Mexico, 1960.

Not shown:

237 BRACELET, 1920s
Navajo
Hammered band; stamped and
chased decoration; 2⅜ × 1¼
(6 × 3.2).
Provenance: Taos, New Mexico,
1956.

238 BRACELET, about 1935
Navajo
Stamping at back in form of a
profile head.
Sheet band; repoussé and
stamped decoration; 2⁹⁄₁₆ × 1
(6.5 × 2.5).
Provenance: W. S. Dutton,
Santa Fe, New Mexico, 1957.

239 BRACELET, 1930s
Navajo
Sheet band; stamped and chased
decoration; 2½ × 1⅛ (6.4 × 2.9).
Provenance: Fred Harvey Co.,
Santa Fe, New Mexico, 1956.
Bought as pawn.

240 BRACELET, 1930s
Navajo
Sheet band; filed and stamped
decoration; 2⅝ × 1¼ (6.7 × 3.2).
Provenance: W. S. Dutton, Santa
Fe, New Mexico, 1957.

241 BRACELET, 1930s
Navajo
Sheet band; filed and stamped
decoration; 2⅜ × 1 (6 × 2.5).
Provenance: Irma Bailey,
Albuquerque, New Mexico, 1969.

242 BRACELET, about 1940
Navajo
Maker's mark: ⟨AD⟩
Stamped: HANDMADE
          STERLING
Sheet band; stamped and chased
decoration; 2⁹⁄₁₆ × 1⁵⁄₁₆ (6.5 × 3.3).
Provenance: Fred Harvey Co.,
Albuquerque, New Mexico, 1963.

243 BRACELET, 1940s
Navajo
Inscribed: YAZZ[—]
Sheet band; filed and stamped
decoration; 2⅝ × ⅞ (6.7 × 2.2).
Provenance: Price's All Indian
Shop, Albuquerque, New Mexico.

244 BRACELET, about 1950
Navajo
Heavy sheet band; chased and
stamped decoration; 2⅝ × 1¼
(6.7 × 3.2).
Provenance: House of Gifts,
Prescott, Arizona, 1953.

245 BRACELET, about 1950
Navajo
Sheet band; stamped decoration;
2½ × 1³⁄₁₆ (6.4 × 3).
Provenance: Armijo's Trading Post,
Gallup, New Mexico, 1956.

246 PAIR OF BRACELETS, 1950s
Navajo
Scallop-edged sheet band;
stamped decoration; 2¼ × 1³⁄₁₆
(5.7 × 3).
Provenance: Albuquerque,
New Mexico, 1960.

247 BRACELET, about 1960
Navajo
Made by Albert Benally; maker's
mark: AB and bear's paw ✋
Hollow sheet band; stamped
decoration; 2⅝ × 1 (6.7 × 2.5).
Provenance: Sewell's, Scottsdale,
Arizona, 1981.

248 BRACELET, about 1960
Navajo
Stamped: NAVAJO
Sheet band; filed and chased
decoration; 2¾ × 1½ (7 × 3.8).
Provenance: Crazy Horse,
Albuquerque, New Mexico, 1970.

249 BRACELET, 1960s
Navajo
Stamped: STERLING
Sheet band; filed and stamped
decoration; 2½ × 1½ (6.4 × 3.8).
Provenance: Wright's Trading Post,
Albuquerque, New Mexico, 1972.
Bought as pawn.

250 BRACELET, 1960s
Navajo
Stamped: STERLING
Sheet band; chased and stamped
decoration; 2½ × 1⁷⁄₁₆ (6.4 × 3.7).
Provenance: Crazy Horse,
Albuquerque, New Mexico, 1970.

251 BRACELET, 1960s
Navajo
Heavy sheet band; stamped and
filed decoration; 2⁵⁄₁₆ × ⅞
(5.9 × 2.2).
Provenance: Packard's Trading
Post, Santa Fe, New Mexico, 1975.

252 BRACELET, about 1965
Navajo
Made by David Taliman; maker's
mark: D. TALIMAN
Dapped sheet band; stamped and
chased decoration; 2⅜ × 1
(6 × 2.5).
Provenance: Kemp's, Santa Fe,
New Mexico.

253 BRACELET, 1968
Navajo
Made by Joe Suina.
Stamped: PACKARDS
          JSUINA
Sheet band; stamped and chased
decoration; 2⁷⁄₁₆ × 1¼ (6.2 × 3.8).
Provenance: Packard's Trading
Post, Santa Fe, New Mexico, 1968.
Made for the collector as a
reproduction of Mera, p. 11, pl. 6.

254 BRACELET, about 1970
Navajo
Made by Mark Chee; maker's
mark: bird in profile, CHEE
superimposed.
Sheet band; stamped and filed
decoration; 2⁷⁄₁₆ × 1⁵⁄₁₆ (6.2 × 3.3).
Provenance: Heard Museum
Shop, Phoenix, Arizona, 1977.

255 BRACELET, about 1973
Navajo
Made by Chief Joe Benally.
Sheet band; filed, chased, and
repoussé decoration; 2½ × 1¹¹⁄₁₆
(6.4 × 4.3).
Provenance: Packard's Trading
Post, Santa Fe, New Mexico, 1973.

256 BRACELET, 1970s
Navajo
Sheet band; repoussé and
stamped decoration; 2⅜ × 1⅜
(6 × 3.5).
Provenance: Sewell's, Scottsdale,
Arizona, 1979.

257
258 260
  259

257 BRACELET, about 1950
Navajo
Heavy sheet band; stamped and
filed decoration; 2½ × 1⅛
(6.4 × 2.9).
Provenance: unknown, 1956.

258 BRACELET, about 1940
Navajo
Scratched on inside: M M ADAMS
Sheet band; filed, chased, and
stamped decoration; 2⅝ × ¾
(6.7 × 1.9).
Provenance: Mrs. Richardson,
Gallup, New Mexico, 1953.

259 BRACELET, 1950s
Navajo
Made by John Silver, son of
Sam Silver.
Sheet band; filed decoration;
2⅜ × 1 (6 × 2.5).
Provenance: Turpen Trading Post,
Gallup, New Mexico, 1956.

260 BRACELET, about 1950
Navajo
Sheet band with carinated edges;
stamped and filed decoration;
2⁵⁄₁₆ × ¾ (5.9 × 1.9).
Provenance: Hilton Hotel Gift
Shop, Albuquerque, New Mexico,
1956.

Not shown:

261 BRACELET, 1920s
Navajo
Hammered band; stamped
decoration; $2^7/_{16} \times {}^7/_{16}$ (6.2 × 1.1).
Provenance: Asa Glascock,
Gallup, New Mexico, 1956.

262 BRACELET, 1930
Navajo
Hammered band; chased
decoration; $2^5/_8 \times {}^{15}/_{16}$ (6.7 × 2.4).
Provenance: Fred Harvey Co.,
Albuquerque, New Mexico, 1960.

263 CHILD'S BRACELET, about 1930
Navajo
Heavy sheet band; stamped
decoration; 2 × 1 (5 × 2.5).
Provenance: Hagberg's, Gallup,
New Mexico, 1965.
Bought as pawn.

264 BRACELET, about 1930
Navajo
Small carinated wire; stamped
decoration; $2^3/_8 \times 1^1/_4$ (6 × 3.2).
Provenance: unknown
Bought as pawn.

265 BRACELET, about 1935 or later
Navajo
Square wire hoop; stamped
decoration; $2^3/_4 \times {}^1/_8$ (7 × 0.3).
Provenance: unknown.

266 BRACELET, 1930s
Navajo
Sheet band with carved edges;
repoussé and stamped decoration;
$2^1/_2 \times {}^9/_{16}$ (6.4 × 1.4).
Provenance: Chester Copman,
Santa Fe Gift Shop, Santa Fe,
New Mexico, 1952.

267 BRACELET, about 1940
Navajo
Sheet band; repoussé and stamped
decoration; $2^1/_4 \times {}^3/_4$ (5.7 × 1.9).
Provenance: Chester Copman,
Santa Fe Gift Shop, Santa Fe,
New Mexico, 1952.

268 BRACELET, about 1940
Navajo
Sheet band; stamped decoration;
$2^1/_2 \times 1^1/_8$ (6.4 × 2.9).
Provenance: Hulderman,
Scottsdale, Arizona, 1965;
Dorothy Field Maxwell collection.

269 BRACELET, about 1940
Navajo
Hammered band; stamped
decoration; $2^5/_8 \times {}^{11}/_{16}$ (6.7 × 1.7).
Provenance: Taos Book Shop,
Taos, New Mexico, 1956.
Bought as pawn.

270 BRACELET, 1940s
Navajo
Scallop-edged sheet band;
stamped decoration; $2^3/_8 \times 1^{13}/_{16}$
(6 × 4.6).
Provenance: Fred Harvey Co.,
Albuquerque, New Mexico, 1940s.
Bought as pawn.

271 CHILD'S BRACELET, 1940s
Navajo
Half-round band; stamped
decoration; $2^1/_4 \times {}^1/_4$ (5.7 × 0.6).
Provenance: Hubbell's Trading
Post, Winslow, Arizona, 1953.
Bought as pawn.

272 PAIR OF BRACELETS, 1940s
Navajo
Cast half-round band; stamped
decoration; $2^1/_2 \times {}^7/_{16}$ (6.4 × 1.1).
Provenance: Tom Moore, Gallup,
New Mexico, 1953.

273 BRACELET, 1940s
Navajo
Three carinated wires; stamped
decoration; $2^1/_4 \times {}^5/_8$ (5.7 × 1.6).
Provenance: unknown.
Bought as pawn.

274 BRACELET, 1940s
Navajo
Sheet band; filed and stamped
decoration; $2^1/_2 \times {}^3/_8$ (6.4 × 1).
Provenance: unknown.

275 BRACELET, 1940s
Navajo
Scratched on inside: ELIZ
Heavy hammered band; stamped
decoration; $2^5/_8 \times {}^{13}/_{16}$ (6.7 × 2.1).
Provenance: Turpen Trading Post,
Gallup, New Mexico, 1957.
Same stamps as no. 276.

276 BRACELET, 1940s
Navajo
Scratched on inside: ELIZ
Heavy hammered band; stamped
decoration; $2^1/_2 \times {}^3/_4$ (6.4 × 1.9).
Provenance: Turpen Trading Post,
Gallup, New Mexico, 1954.
Bought as pawn.
Same stamps as no. 275.

277 BRACELET, 1940s
Navajo
Flattened teardrops soldered into
band; stamped decoration;
$2^1/_2 \times {}^1/_4$ (6.4 × 0.6).
Provenance: unknown.

278 BRACELET, 1940s
Navajo
Heavy hammered band; stamped
and filed decoration; $2^5/_8 \times {}^3/_4$
(6.7 × 1.9).
Provenance: Wright's Trading Post,
Albuquerque, New Mexico, 1953.

279 BRACELET, about 1950
Navajo
Sheet band; chased and stamped
decoration; $2^7/_{16} \times {}^5/_{16}$ (6.2 × 3.3).
Provenance: George Rummage,
Gallup, New Mexico, 1954.

280 BRACELET, about 1950
Navajo
Sheet band; appliqué and
stamped decoration; $2^1/_2 \times {}^1/_2$
(6.4 × 1.3).
Provenance: Fred Harvey Co.,
Albuquerque, New Mexico, 1956.

281 BRACELET, about 1950
Navajo
Sheet band; stamped decoration;
$2^1/_2 \times {}^7/_{16}$ (6.4 × 1.1).
Provenance: Hubbell's Trading
Post, Winslow, Arizona, 1954.

282 BRACELET, about 1950
Navajo
Scallop-edged sheet band;
stamped and teardrop decoration;
$2^1/_4 \times {}^1/_2$ (5.7 × 1.3).
Provenance: unknown.

283 BRACELET, about 1950
Navajo
Sheet band; stamped decoration;
$2^3/_4 \times {}^5/_{16}$ (7 × 0.8).
Provenance: Thieme Brothers,
Gallup, New Mexico, 1956.

284 BRACELET, about 1950
Navajo
Heavy sheet band; chased and
stamped decoration; $2^1/_2 \times {}^7/_{16}$
(6.4 × 1.1).
Provenance: Armijo's Trading
Post, Gallup, New Mexico, 1954.

285 BRACELET, about 1950
Navajo
Heavy sheet band; stamped and
filed decoration; 2¾ × 1 (7 × 2.5).
Provenance: unknown, 1960.

286 Pair of BRACELETS, about 1950
Navajo
Half-round band; filed
decoration; 2⁷/₁₆ × ³/₁₆ (6.2 × 0.5).
Provenance: Turpen Trading Post,
Gallup, New Mexico.

287 BRACELET, about 1950
Navajo
Heavy sheet band; chased and
stamped decoration; 2½ × ⁷/₁₆
(6.4 × 1.1).
Provenance: Fred Harvey Co.,
Albuquerque, New Mexico, 1956.

288 BRACELET, about 1950
Navajo
Sheet band enclosing carinated
wire; stamped decoration;
2½ × ⁷/₈ (7.4 × 2.2).
Provenance: Armijo's Trading
Post, Gallup, New Mexico, 1956.

289 BRACELET, about 1950
Navajo
Heavy sheet band; stamped
decoration; 2½ × ¹³/₁₆ (6.4 × 2.1).
Provenance: Armijo's Trading
Post, Gallup, New Mexico, 1956.

290 BRACELET, about 1950
Navajo
Sheet band; stamped decoration;
2½ × ⁹/₁₆ (6.4 × 1.4).
Provenance: Armijo's Trading
Post, Gallup, New Mexico, 1956.

291 BRACELET, about 1950
Navajo
Half-round wire band; stamped
and filed decoration; 2⁷/₈ × ³/₁₆
(7.3 × 0.5).
Provenance: Fred Harvey Co.,
Albuquerque, New Mexico, 1956.

292 BRACELET, about 1950
Navajo
Sheet band; stamped decoration;
2¼ × ⁹/₁₆ (5.7 × 1.4).
Provenance: Fred Harvey Co.,
Albuquerque, New Mexico, 1956.

293 BRACELET, about 1950
Navajo
Narrow sheet band overlaid with
bead wire; 2⁵/₁₆ × ⅛ (5.9 × 0.3).
Provenance: Fred Harvey Co.,
Albuquerque, New Mexico, 1956.

294 BRACELET, about 1950
Navajo
Heavy sheet band; chased and
stamped decoration; 2¹³/₁₆ × ¾
(7.1 × 1.9).
Provenance: George Rummage,
Gallup, New Mexico, 1954.

295 BRACELET, about 1950
Navajo
Scallop-edged sheet band;
stamped decoration; 2⅜ × ¾
(6 × 1.9).
Provenance: Hubbell's Trading
Post, Winslow, Arizona, 1954.
Same stamp as no. 296.

296 BRACELET, about 1950
Navajo
Scallop-edged sheet band;
stamped decoration; 2½ × ¾
(6.4 × 1.9).
Provenance: Hubbell's Trading
Post, Winslow, Arizona, 1954.
Same stamp as no. 295.

297 BRACELET, about 1950
Navajo
Sheet band; stamped decoration;
2⁵/₁₆ × ⁹/₁₆ (5.9 × 1.4).
Provenance: Jerry Chekerian,
Albuquerque, New Mexico, 1966.

298 BRACELET, about 1950
Navajo
Sheet band; stamped decoration;
2¼ × ⅝ (5.7 × 1.6).
Provenance: Jerry Chekerian,
Albuquerque, New Mexico, 1966.

299 BRACELET, 1950s
Navajo
Sheet band; stamped and chased
decoration; 2⁷/₁₆ × ¹¹/₁₆ (6.2 × 1.7).
Provenance: Chester Copman,
Santa Fe Gift Shop, Santa Fe,
New Mexico, 1959.

300 BRACELET, 1950s
Navajo
Sheet band; stamped and chased
decoration; 2½ × ⅝ (6.4 × 1.6).
Provenance: Chester Copman,
Santa Fe Gift Shop, Santa Fe,
New Mexico, 1959.

301 BRACELET, 1950s
Navajo
Sheet band; chased and stamped
decoration; 2½ × ⁷/₈ (6.4 × 2.2).
Provenance: Irma Bailey,
Albuquerque, New Mexico, 1969.

302 BRACELET, 1950s
Navajo
Sheet band; stamped and
appliqué decoration: 2½ × 1
(6.4 × 2.5).
Provenance: Sewell's, Scottsdale,
Arizona, 1972.

303 CHILD'S BRACELET, 1950s
Navajo
Sheet band; stamped decoration;
1¹³/₁₆ × ⁵/₁₆ (4.6 × 0.8).
Provenance: unknown.

304 PAIR OF BRACELETS, 1950s
Navajo
Heavy sheet band; chased
decoration; 2¾ × 1¹/₁₆ (7 × 2.7).
Provenance: unknown, 1960.

305 PAIR OF BRACELETS, 1950s
Navajo
Scallop-edged sheet band; chased
decoration; 2½ × 1½ (6.4 × 3.8).
Provenance: unknown, 1960.

306 PAIR OF BRACELETS, 1950s
Navajo
Scallop-edged band; chased and
stamped decoration; 2⅝ × 1⁹/₁₆
(6.7 × 4).
Provenance: unknown, 1960.

307 BRACELET, 1950s
Navajo
Sheet band; stamped and filed
decoration; 2⁹/₁₆ × 1 (6.5 × 2.5).
Provenance: unknown, 1960.

308 PAIR OF BRACELETS, 1950s
Navajo
Scallop-edged sheet band;
stamped and chased decoration;
2⁷/₁₆ × 1 (6.2 × 2.5).
Provenance: unknown, 1960.
Similar to no. 309.

309 PAIR OF BRACELETS, 1950s
Navajo
Scallop-edged band; chased and
stamped decoration; 2½ × 1¹/₁₆
(6.4 × 2.7).
Provenance: unknown, 1960.
Similar to no. 308.

310 BRACELET, 1950s
Navajo
Sheet band; filed and chased
decoration; 2⁷⁄₁₆ × 1 (6.2 × 2.5).
Provenance: unknown, 1960.
Similar to no. 311.

311 PAIR OF BRACELETS, 1950s
Navajo
Sheet band; filed and chased
decoration; 2³⁄₈ × ¹⁵⁄₁₆ (6 × 2.4).
Provenance: Albuquerque,
New Mexico, 1960.
Similar to no. 310.

312 BRACELET, 1950s
Navajo
Sheet band; chased and filed
decoration; 2¹⁵⁄₁₆ × 1 (7.5 × 2.5).
Provenance: Albuquerque,
New Mexico, 1960.

313 BRACELET, 1950s
Navajo
Sheet band; stamped, filed, and
appliqué decoration; 2½ × 1
(6.4 × 2.5).
Provenance: Sewell's, Scottsdale,
Arizona, 1972.

314 BRACELET, 1950s or later
Navajo
Sheet band; repoussé and
stamped decoration; 2¼ × ½
(5.7 × 1.3).
Provenance: Packard's Trading
Post, Santa Fe, New Mexico, 1973.
Same stamps as no. 315.

315 BRACELET, 1950s or later
Navajo
Sheet band; repoussé and
stamped decorations; 2⅛ × ¾
(5.4 × 1.9).
Provenance: Packard's Trading
Post, Santa Fe, New Mexico, 1973.
Same stamps as no. 314.

316 BRACELET, 1970
Navajo
Sheet band; chased and stamped
decoration; 2³⁄₈ × 1⅛ (6 × 2.9).
Provenance: unknown, 1970s.

317 319
318
320 321

317 BRACELET, 1950s
Navajo
Cast openwork band; stamped decoration; $2\frac{1}{2} \times 1\frac{3}{8}$ (6.4 × 3.5).
Provenance: Kemp's, Santa Fe, New Mexico, 1957.
Cast in two parts.

318 BRACELET, about 1950
Navajo
Maker's mark: JD
Cast band; set with four flat square turquoises and five squares of red material (two coral, two chalcedony, one plastic); $2\frac{5}{8} \times \frac{15}{16}$ (6.7 × 2.4).
Provenance: Nettie Wheeler, Muskogee, Oklahoma, 1952.
Cf. Mera, p. 28, pl. 12.

319 BRACELET, 1940s
Navajo
Stamped on inside: NAVAJO
Navajo Arts and Crafts Guild stamp.
Cast openwork band; stamped decoration; $2\frac{1}{2} \times 1\frac{1}{2}$ (6.4 × 3.8).
Provenance: Fred Harvey Co., Albuquerque, New Mexico, 1950(?).

320 BRACELET, about 1950
Navajo
Cast band in the form of a snake; $2\frac{1}{2} \times \frac{3}{4}$ (6.4 × 1.9).
Provenance: Tom Moore, Gallup, New Mexico, 1955.

321 BRACELET, about 1950
Navajo
Made by Tom Chee.
Cast band terminating in hands; set with single elliptical Burnham turquoise in serrated bezel; stamped decoration; $2\frac{3}{4} \times \frac{13}{16}$ (7 × 2.1).
Provenance: Tom Moore, Gallup, New Mexico, 1953.
Cf. King, p. 90, pl. 62.

Not shown:

322 BRACELET, 1930s or later
Navajo
Narrow cast band; stamped decoration; $2\frac{9}{16} \times \frac{3}{8}$ (6.5 × 1).
Provenance: Tom Moore, Gallup, New Mexico, 1953.

323 BRACELET, about 1950
Navajo
Cast band; filed and stamped decoration; $2\frac{3}{8} \times \frac{7}{16}$ (6 × 1.1).
Provenance: Fred Harvey Co., Albuquerque, New Mexico, 1956.

324 BRACELET, about 1950
Navajo
Cast band; filed and stamped decoration; $2\frac{3}{8} \times \frac{7}{16}$ (6 × 1.1).
Provenance: Fred Harvey Co., Albuquerque, New Mexico, 1956.

325 BRACELET, 1950s
Navajo
Made by Mike Thomas.
Cast band; stamped and filed decoration; $2\frac{3}{8} \times \frac{5}{8}$ (6 × 1.6).
Provenance: Turpen Trading Post, Gallup, New Mexico, 1956.

326 328
327
329 330

326 BRACELET, 1950s
Navajo
Cast openwork band; set with five
Morenci turquoises of irregular
shape; 2½ × 1⅝ (6.4 × 4.1).
Provenance: Turpen Trading Post,
Gallup, New Mexico, 1965.
Bought as pawn.

327 BRACELET, 1950s
Navajo
Cast openwork band; stamped
decoration; 2⁷⁄₁₆ × ⅝ (6.2 × 1.6).
Provenance: Quivira Shop,
Santa Fe, New Mexico, 1963.

328 BRACELET, about 1950
Cochiti Pueblo, in Navajo style
Made by Joe Quintana.
Cast openwork band; set with
triangular Cerrillos turquoise;
2½ × 1¾ (6.4 × 4.4).
Provenance: Joe and Teresita
Quintana, Sante Fe, New Mexico,
1956.

329 BRACELET, 1950s
Navajo
Cast openwork band; stamped
decoration; 2⅝ × 1⅜ (6.7 × 3.5).
Provenance: Fred Harvey Co.,
Albuquerque, New Mexico, 1960.
Bought as pawn.

330 BRACELET, about 1950
Navajo
Cast openwork band; 2¼ × 1¼
(5.7 × 3.2).
Provenance: Armijo's Trading
Post, Gallup, New Mexico, 1956.

Not shown:

331 BRACELET, about 1940
Navajo
Cast openwork band; set with
three Lone Mountain turquoises
in serrated bezels; stamped and
chased decoration; 2½ × 1¼
(6.4 × 3.2).
Provenance: Quivira Shop,
Santa Fe, New Mexico, 1963.

332 BRACELET, about 1955
Navajo
Cast openwork band; set with
single Royal Blue turquoise of
slightly irregular oval shape in
serrated bezel; 2½ × 1⅞
(6.4 × 4.8).
Provenance: Sewell's, Scottsdale,
Arizona, 1972.

333 BRACELET, about 1950
Navajo
Cast openwork band of brass-
colored metal; set with single
elliptical Number 8 spiderweb
turquoise; 2⁹⁄₁₆ × 2⁵⁄₁₆ (6.5 × 5.9).
Provenance: Turpen Trading Post,
Gallup, New Mexico, 1954.
Bought as pawn.

334 336
335
337 338

334 BRACELET, about 1965
Navajo
Cast openwork band with
contrasting unpolished areas in
center; 2¼ × 2⅝ (5.7 × 6.7).
Provenance: Sewell's, Scottsdale,
Arizona, 1977.

335 BRACELET, about 1950
Navajo
Cast band; set with two carved
turquoises in serrated bezels;
wire ring through hole in each
stone; teardrop and stamped
decoration; 2¼ × ⅞ (5.7 × 2.2).
Provenance: Fred Harvey Co.,
Albuquerque, New Mexico, 1963.
Leaves are Zuni style.

336 BRACELET, 1960s
Navajo
Cast openwork band; contrasting
unpolished areas at side; 2½ × 2
(6.4 × 5).
Provenance: Packard's Trading
Post, Santa Fe, New Mexico, 1973.

337 BRACELET, about 1950
Navajo, with Zuni influence
Cast band; flanked by two rows of
seven elliptical eastern Arizona
turquoises each (possibly Sleeping
Beauty); stamped decoration;
2½ × ¾ (6.4 × 1.9).
Provenance: Dick Marsh,
Santa Fe, New Mexico, 1954.

338 BRACELET, 1950s
Navajo
Cast openwork band; set with
rectangular turquoise; 2½ × 1¼
(6.4 × 3.2).
Provenance: Turpen Trading Post,
Gallup, New Mexico, 1963.
Bought as pawn.

Not shown:

339 BRACELET, about 1950
Navajo
Cast openwork band; large
turquoise of irregular shape
mounted on sheet with oxidized
contrasting background; teardrop
decoration; 2⁵⁄₁₆ × 1¹⁵⁄₁₆
(5.9 × 4.9).
Provenance: Turpen Trading Post,
Gallup, New Mexico, 1960.

340 BRACELET, about 1960
Navajo
Cast openwork band; 2½ × ½
(6.4 × 1.3).
Provenance: unknown.

341 342 343
344 345 346

341 BRACELET, 1940s
Zuni
Three bands; each set with
fourteen small square turquoises
in serrated bezels; teardrop and
stamped decoration; 2⁷⁄₁₆ × 1
(6.2 × 2.5).
Provenance: Dressman, Santa Fe,
New Mexico, 1954.
Bought as pawn.
Cf. King, p. 120, pl. 122.

342 BRACELET, about 1950
Zuni
Ten bands; each set with thirteen
small round and elliptical
turquoises in needlepoint style,
serrated bezels; teardrop and
stamped decoration; 2⁷⁄₁₆ × 1¹⁵⁄₁₆
(6.2 × 4.9).
Provenance: C. G. Wallace,
Gallup, New Mexico, 1950 or 1951.

343 BRACELET, 1960s
Zuni
Sheet band; set with one elliptical
and twenty small pear-shaped
turquoises in serrated bezels;
teardrop, appliqué, and stamped
decoration; 2½ × 1¹⁄₁₆ (6.4 × 2.7).
Provenance: Crazy Horse,
Albuquerque, New Mexico, 1970.

344 BRACELET, 1920s
Zuni style, possibly Navajo made
Split band; set with two heart-
shaped and forty-three round
Burnham turquoises forming
three clusters; bead wire and
stamped decoration; 2½ × 1¼
(6.4 × 3.2).
Provenance: unknown.

345 CHILD'S BRACELET, 1960s
Zuni
Round wire; set with cluster of
one round and nine pear-shaped
turquoises in serrated bezels;
1⅝ × ⅝ (4.1 × 1.6).
Provenance: unknown, about
1960.

346 BRACELET, 1940s
Zuni
Hammered band; channel-set
with ten triangular Morenci
turquoises in lozenge pattern and
two round turquoises; teardrop
and stamped decoration; 2⅝ × ½
(6.7 × 1.3).
Provenance: Dick Marsh, Santa Fe,
New Mexico, 1954.
Bought as pawn.

Not shown:

347 BRACELET, about 1930
Zuni
Five bands with teardrops and flattened double twisted wire interspersed at center; each set with fifteen small round turquoises; stamped decoration; 2½ × 1⅝ (6.4 × 4.1).
Provenance: unknown.

348 BRACELET, 1940s or later
Zuni
Sheet band; set with twenty small round turquoises; teardrop and stamped decoration; 2⁹⁄₁₆ × ¼ (6.5 × 0.6).
Provenance: unknown.

349 BRACELET, 1940s or later
Zuni
Sheet band; set with fifteen square turquoises in serrated bezels, enclosed by two rows of teardrops; stamped decoration; 2⁵⁄₁₆ × ⅝ (5.9 × 1.6).
Provenance: Hanns Hogan, Gallup, New Mexico.
Bought as pawn.

350 BRACELET, 1940s
Zuni
Sheet band; set with twenty small round turquoises; 2¹¹⁄₁₆ × ¹³⁄₁₆ (6.8 × 2.1).
Provenance: Quivira Shop, Santa Fe, New Mexico, 1952.

351 CHILD'S BRACELET, 1940s
Zuni
Three round wires; set with seventy-two very small round turquoises in three grid arrangements, serrated bezels; 2 × ¹¹⁄₁₆ (5 × 1.7).
Provenance: Fred Harvey Co., Albuquerque, New Mexico, 1956.
Bought as pawn.

352 BRACELET, about 1940
Zuni or Navajo
Sheet band; double twisted wire entwined in row of teardrops; stamped decoration; 2⅜ × ¼ (6 × 0.6).
Provenance: unknown.

353 BRACELET, about 1940
Zuni
Hammered band; set with eleven small round cabochon Arizona turquoises in serrated bezels, flanked by two rows of teardrops; stamped decoration; 2⅜ × ⁷⁄₁₆ (6 × 1.1).
Provenance: unknown.

354 BRACELET, 1940s
Zuni
Five sheet bands; each set with thirteen small round turquoises in serrated bezels; teardrop and stamped decoration; 2⅜ × 1⅜ 6 × 3.5).
Provenance: Hall's, Mesa Verde National Park, Colorado.
Bought as pawn.

355 CHILD'S BRACELET, about 1940
Zuni
Carinated wire; set with two rows of twelve small round turquoises each; teardrop decoration; 1⅞ × ¼ (4.8 × 0.6).
Provenance: Fred Harvey Co., Albuquerque, New Mexico, 1954.
Bought as pawn.

356 BRACELET, 1940s
Zuni
Sheet band; set with eleven rectangular and round turquoises in serrated bezels; stamped decoration; 2¾ × ³⁄₁₆ (7 × 0.5).
Provenance: Santa Fe, New Mexico, 1955.

357 BRACELET, about 1945
Zuni
Two sheet bands; each set with twenty elliptical needlepoint turquoises in serrated bezels; teardrop and stamped decoration; 2⅜ × ¹³⁄₁₆ (6 × 2.1).
Provenance: Hanns Hogan, Gallup, New Mexico, 1953.
Bought as pawn.

358 BRACELET, about 1950
Zuni
Four sheet bands; each set with fourteen small round turquoises in serrated bezels; teardrop and stamped decoration; 2⅜ × 1¹³⁄₁₆ (6 × 4.6).
Provenance: Chief Joe Secakuku, Winslow, Arizona, 1953.
Bought as pawn.

359 BRACELET, about 1950
Zuni
Sheet band; set with ten small round turquoises inlaid in large teardrops; teardrop and stamped decoration; 2½ × ¼ (6.4 × 0.6).
Provenance: Sante Fe Indian School, Santa Fe, New Mexico, 1955.

360 BRACELET, about 1950
Zuni
Sheet band; set with twelve small round turquoises inlaid in large stamped teardrops; teardrop and stamped decoration; 2½ × ¼ (6.4 × 0.6).
Provenance: Santa Fe Indian School, Santa Fe, New Mexico, 1955.

361 CHILD'S BRACELET, about 1950
Zuni
Sheet band; set with thirteen small round turquoises; teardrop and stamped decoration; 1¹³⁄₁₆ × ⅛ (4.6 × 0.3).
Provenance: unknown.

362 CHILD'S BRACELET, about 1950
Zuni
Sheet band; channel-set with ten small round turquoises; stamped decoration; 1¾ × ⅛ (4.4 × 0.3).
Provenance: unknown.

363 BRACELET, 1950s
Zuni
Three round wires; set with three clusters of small turquoises surrounding larger square turquoises; teardrop decoration; 2⁷⁄₁₆ × ⁹⁄₁₆ (6.2 × 1.4).
Provenance: Eric Kohlberg, Denver, Colorado, 1956.

364 BRACELET, 1960s
Zuni
Three sheet bands; set with abalone and Fox turquoise inlay on sheet mounting; appliqué and stamped decoration; 3 × 1⅞ (7.6 × 4.8).
Provenance: Nettie Wheeler, Muskogee, Oklahoma, 1968.

Necklaces

Necklaces of shell, stone, and turquoise, which go back to prehistoric times, and of coral beads brought by the Spanish have always been favorites of the southwestern Indians. The use of Spanish glass beads, however, declined until they all but disappeared in the late 1800s, to be temporarily replaced by glass artificial turquoise disk beads and ring sets imported during the early 1900s. Metal beads, crosses, and other kinds of pendants brought by the Spanish lost favor as the Indians began to work silver for themselves. Most of the necklaces in photographs from Bosque Redondo and from the early 1870s are of coral, shell, and stone, some with jaclas. Only a few silver necklaces made of buttons or spherical beads strung on a thong are to be seen, and a few silver beads do appear as slides on wire loop earrings. By the late 1870s, silver beads had become fairly common, probably as a result of the widespread mastery of soldering.

Most of the early necklaces were made of simple spherical beads only, but it was not long before various kinds of pendants were added. The most widespread and familiar was the naja, adopted from Spanish bridle ornaments. At first najas were hammered from annealed silver or cast ingots, and as early as 1870 some najas were cast. By the turn of the century many, if not most, were cast. This method permitted smiths to make double and triple najas quite easily, which they quickly did. So-called Pueblo crosses, with double bars and heart-shaped terminals, also were used as pendants, and plain crosses served as smaller necklace decorations, especially among the Pueblo peoples. Squash blossoms, copied from the pomegranate fruit buttons used by Spanish men along the slit sides of their pantaloons, appear slightly later on

Navajo necklaces, mounted on square shanks and interspersed with the spherical beads. Occasionally silver coins, usually dimes, were soldered to beads or shanks in place of the squash blossoms. As time passed, necklaces, like other jewelry, became more ornate and complex, with more turquoise sets.

In the teens and twenties the naja form became progressively more elaborate. The hammered or wire naja returned to favor, often echoing the pattern established in bracelets: two carinated wires enclosing a double twisted wire. By the early 1930s necklaces of two strands of smaller beads, held together with squash blossom beads on long shanks, had evolved. This more stable form prevented the squash blossom beads from flopping around or rotating inward, and it also provided a firmer base to support heavier squash blossom beads, particularly those set with turquoises. Eventually the strands of beads disappeared under the settings and served only as a supporting structure. In other types of necklace, the beads became more ornate and especially after the 1940s were stamped and fluted. The squash blossom form was also elaborated and varied, and in the same period beads terminating in "cornflowers," small cast najas, or "pumpkin seeds" appeared.

Zuni necklaces followed the trend toward elaboration. By the 1930s Zuni smiths were producing massive turquoise cluster necklaces with najas heavily studded with turquoise. Such necklaces continue to be typical of Zuni work.

For necklaces the length from clasp to pendant terminal is given, and for najas, the height.

J.B.W.
L.L.

365   366   367
365   367
368

365 BEAD NECKLACE, 1870–1880
Navajo or Pueblo
Single strand of spherical beads;
fourteen disks on shanks, some
with engraved sunburst design;
double naja of hammered wire
with hands as terminals; 14¾
(37.5).
Provenance: Taos Book Shop,
Taos, New Mexico, 1954.
Bought as pawn.

366 BEAD NECKLACE, 1900 or earlier
Probably Navajo
Single strand of graduated
flattened beads; 10¼ (26).
Provenance: W. S. Dutton,
Santa Fe, New Mexico, 1957.

367 CROSS NECKLACE, 1880–1900
Navajo or Pueblo
Single strand of spherical beads;
sixteen small cast crosses of two
types; large cast double-barred
cross as pendant; 17½ (44.5).
Provenance: Quivira Shop,
Santa Fe, New Mexico, 1952.

368 SQUASH BLOSSOM NECKLACE,
before 1900
Navajo
Single strand of flattened beads;
eleven squash blossom beads;
filed decoration on blossoms;
9¾ (24.8).
Provenance: Eleanor Beddell (?),
Santa Fe, New Mexico.

369 SQUASH BLOSSOM NECKLACE,
about 1910
Navajo
Single strand of spherical beads;
eight squash blossom beads; cast
double carinated naja with
stamped decoration at terminals
and upright squash blossom
surmounting shank, round flat
turquoise in serrated bezel at
center; 19⅛ (48.6).
Provenance: Raffaello Frilli,
Florence, Italy, 1965.

370 SQUASH BLOSSOM NECKLACE,
about 1900
Navajo
Single strand of spherical beads;
ten squash blossom beads, some
with filed decoration; cast
carinated naja set with three
round flat turquoises in serrated
bezels; 19 (48.3).
Provenance: Frances Quarles,
Taos, New Mexico, 1952.
Bought as pawn.

371 SQUASH BLOSSOM NECKLACE,
about 1910
Navajo
Single strand of irregular spherical
beads; eight squash blossom
beads; double naja of hammered
carinated wire with turquoise
pendant tied to center tab and
two oval turquoises set at
terminals (one with a silver
filling); 17¼ (43.8).
Provenance: Harold Street,
Taos, New Mexico, 1952; Woody
Crumbo, Taos.

372   373   374

372 SQUASH BLOSSOM NECKLACE,
     about 1900
     Navajo
     Single strand of spherical beads;
     twelve squash blossom beads;
     cast double carinated naja set
     with three round turquoises and
     square turquoise on shank; 14⅜
     (37.5).
     Provenance: W. S. Dutton,
     Santa Fe, New Mexico, 1957.

373 SQUASH BLOSSOM NECKLACE,
     about 1900, naja possibly later
     Navajo
     Single strand of spherical beads;
     eight small squash blossom
     beads; cast carinated naja with
     cross in center set with single
     elliptical turquoise; 14 (35.6).
     Provenance: Hubbell's Trading
     Post, Winslow, Arizona, 1955.
     Bought as pawn.

374 BEAD NECKLACE, 1910 or earlier
     Navajo
     Single strand of spherical beads;
     double carinated wire naja
     terminating in hands; 15⅜ (39).
     Provenance: Harold Street, Taos,
     New Mexico, 1959.

376
375 377

375 SQUASH BLOSSOM NECKLACE,
1900–1920
Navajo
Single strand of slightly elongated
beads; eighteen squash blossom
beads; triple naja of hammered
wire with repoussé decoration at
terminals and center, stamped
decoration on shank; 15 (38.1).
Provenance: Taos Book Shop,
Taos, New Mexico, 1954.
Bought as pawn.

376 SQUASH BLOSSOM NECKLACE,
naja probably about 1900, beads
probably later
Navajo
Single strand of slightly flattened
beads; eight squash blossom
beads; double naja with repoussé
leaves at apex and buttons at
terminals, stamped and filed
decoration; 18 (45.8).
Provenance: Price's All Indian
Shop, Albuquerque, New Mexico,
1964.
Said to be from Candelario
collection.

377 SQUASH BLOSSOM NECKLACE,
1920 or earlier
Navajo
Single strand of spherical beads;
eight squash blossom beads; cast
double naja with stamped and
filed decoration at terminals;
17¾ (45.1).
Provenance: Fred Harvey Co.,
Santa Fe, New Mexico, 1952.

Not shown:

378 SQUASH BLOSSOM NECKLACE,
about 1900–1920
Navajo
Single strand of slightly flattened
beads; eight squash blossom
beads; double carinated wire
naja with bosses at terminals;
18⅛ (46).
Provenance: Howard G. Dost,
Santa Fe, New Mexico, 1954.
Bought as pawn.

379 SQUASH BLOSSOM NECKLACE,
1910–1920
Navajo
Single strand of spherical beads;
ten squash blossom beads of
various types; double carinated
wire naja with repoussé
decoration at terminals and
center; 16¾ (42.1).
Provenance: Eric Kohlberg,
Denver, Colorado, 1955.
Bought as pawn.

380 CROSS NECKLACE, 1920 or earlier
Navajo
Single strand of flattened beads;
six crosses; double carinated naja
of hammered wire with bosses at
terminals; 12⅞ (32.7).
Provenance: Fred Harvey Co.,
Albuquerque, New Mexico,
before 1952.

382

381 383

381 CROSS NECKLACE, about 1930
     Cochiti Pueblo
     Four strands of tubular coral
     beads and round metal beads;
     fourteen small sheet crosses;
     large double-barred cross
     pendant with "bruised heart"
     terminal; single beads of jet and
     turquoise, small arrowhead;
     18¼ (46.3).
     Provenance: Teresita Quintana,
     Santa Fe, New Mexico, 1954.
     Said to be the wedding necklace
     of Cochiti smith Joe Quintana's
     mother-in-law.

382 CROSS NECKLACE, about 1900
     or earlier
     Pueblo
     Single strand of spherical brass
     trade beads; ten small brass
     crosses; large double-barred
     cross pendant with "bruised
     heart" terminal; filed decoration;
     18¼ (46.3).
     Provenance: Taos Book Shop,
     Taos, New Mexico, 1954.
     Said to have come from the
     shrine of a home chapel at
     Santa Clara Pueblo.

383 CROSS NECKLACE, about 1900
     or earlier
     Pueblo
     Single strand of spherical beads;
     sixteen small crosses and six coral
     beads; large double-barred cross
     pendant with "bruised heart"
     terminal; filed decoration; 17¼
     (43.8).
     Provenance: Eleanor Beddell,
     Santa Fe, New Mexico, 1952;
     Cornelia Thompson collection.

Not shown:

384 CROSS NECKLACE, stones possibly cut mid-nineteenth century, crosses modern
Probably Pueblo
Chunk and discoidal turquoise beads of various sizes; ten crosses of square wire; large double-barred cross pendant with "bruised heart" terminal; 18¾ (47.6).
Provenance: Brice and Judy Sewell, Taos, New Mexico, 1956; Frances Quarles collection.
Possibly a recombination of elements.

385 CROSS NECKLACE, 1930s or later
Pueblo
Single strand of large spherical beads; ten sheet crosses; large double-barred sheet cross pendant with "bruised heart" terminal; 21¼ (51.4).
Provenance: Harold Street, Taos, New Mexico, 1959.
Bought as Isleta, 1900–1925.

386 CROSS NECKLACE, 1940s
Navajo or Zuni
Single strand of silver beads; chunk turquoises, jet, variscite, unknown red beads, and eight silver crosses; large double-barred cross pendant with "bruised heart" terminal; 21½ (52.1).
Provenance: Frances Quarles, Taos, New Mexico, 1955.
Said to have been bought from a Navajo family by a trader named Daniels, this anomalous necklace more likely represents a Euro-American-made composite of several old Navajo and Zuni necklaces.

387 CROSS NECKLACE, about 1950
Navajo
Single strand of large flattened beads, smaller round beads at ends; twelve small square wire crosses; large beveled cross pendant; turquoise jacla; stamped decoration; 19⅝ (49.9).
Provenance: Tom Moore, Gallup, New Mexico, 1955.
Said to have been bought from a relative of the silversmith Tom Burnsides, Wide Ruins region. Jacla added by trader.

388 CROSS NECKLACE, 1950s
Pueblo
Single strand of round and tubular silver beads interspersed with tubular coral beads; twelve silver crosses of various types; one cross of white stone with turquoise inlay; 11⅞ (30.2).
Provenance: Fred Harvey Co., Albuquerque, New Mexico, 1960s. Strung by the collector.

390
389 391

389 SQUASH BLOSSOM NECKLACE, about 1930
Navajo
Single strand of spherical beads; twelve squash blossom beads; double carinated wire naja with single oval turquoise in center, stamped decoration at terminals, stamped plate at top of shank; 17¾ (45.1).
Provenance: Packard's Trading Post, Santa Fe, New Mexico, 1976.

390 SQUASH BLOSSOM NECKLACE, about 1930 or earlier
Navajo
Single strand of spherical beads; twenty squash blossom beads; hammered naja with cast cross as center pendant; stamped decoration; 14¾ (37.5).
Provenance: Eric Kohlberg, Denver, Colorado, 1953.

391 SQUASH BLOSSOM NECKLACE, 1920s
Navajo
Single strand of large slightly flattened beads; six squash blossom beads; triple naja surmounted by "oxbow," set with one elliptical and three square Cerrillos turquoises; filed decoration; 15 (38.1).
Provenance: Charlotte Goodrich, Albuquerque, New Mexico, 1961. Cf. Mera, p. 69, pl. 10.

393

392   394

392   SQUASH BLOSSOM NECKLACE,
      naja possibly about 1900, beads
      about 1930
      Navajo
      Single strand of spherical beads;
      fourteen squash blossom beads;
      hammered double carinated naja
      with stamped and repoussé
      decoration; 17½ (44.5).
      Provenance: Tom Bahti, Tucson,
      Arizona, 1965.

393   SQUASH BLOSSOM NECKLACE,
      about 1930
      Navajo
      Single strand of spherical beads;
      sixteen squash blossom beads;
      cast naja; 17¾ (45.1).
      Provenance: Tom Moore,
      Gallup, New Mexico, 1955.
      Naja of the type made by the
      Roanhorse family.

394   SQUASH BLOSSOM NECKLACE,
      1930s
      Navajo
      Single strand of spherical beads;
      fourteen squash blossom beads;
      cast naja with hands as terminals
      and large triangular turquoise at
      center; 15 (38.1).
      Provenance: Frances Quarles,
      Taos, New Mexico, 1954.

395 SQUASH BLOSSOM NECKLACE,
about 1950
Navajo
Double strand of small spherical
beads; sixteen squash blossoms
without beads; double carinated
wire naja with stamped and
repoussé decoration at terminals
and center; 15⅛ (38.4).
Provenance: Taos Book Shop,
Taos, New Mexico, 1954.
Bought as pawn.

396 SQUASH BLOSSOM NECKLACE,
1930s or later
Navajo
Double strand of slightly flattened
beads; sixteen squash blossom
beads; cast double naja with two
sets of hands as terminals; 14½
(36.8).
Provenance: Frances Quarles,
Taos, New Mexico, 1954.

397 SQUASH BLOSSOM NECKLACE, 1930s or later
Navajo
Double strand of small spherical beads; twenty-nine squash blossom beads; cast naja; 16 (40.7).
Provenance: Turpen Trading Post, Gallup, New Mexico, 1950.

398 SQUASH BLOSSOM NECKLACE, about 1930
Navajo
Single strand of small slightly flattened beads; thirty-eight squash blossom beads of graduated size; two flat triangular turquoises in bezel mounts attached at ends; cast naja set with two flat round turquoises at terminals; stamped decoration; 13⅛ (33.4).
Provenance: Eric Kohlberg, Denver, Colorado, 1955.

399 CHILD'S SQUASH BLOSSOM NECKLACE, about 1930
Navajo
Double strand of small spherical beads; twenty-four squash

blossom beads; cast triple naja with hands as terminals and cross in center; 12¼ (31.1).
Provenance: Bing Crosby Trading Post, Albuquerque, New Mexico, 1960.

Not shown:

400 SQUASH BLOSSOM NECKLACE, 1940s
Navajo
Double strand of spherical beads; fourteen small squash blossom beads; one larger squash blossom bead as pendant; 9⅞ (25.1).
Provenance: Turpen Trading Post, Gallup, New Mexico, 1953.
Bought as pawn.

401 CHILD'S SQUASH BLOSSOM NECKLACE, 1940s
Navajo
Double strand of small slightly flattened beads; twelve squash blossoms without beads; double carinated wire naja set with three small turquoises; 8¾ (21.6).
Provenance: Fred Harvey Co., Albuquerque, New Mexico, 1953.
Bought as pawn.

402 SQUASH BLOSSOM NECKLACE, about 1950
Navajo
Single strand of small spherical beads; nine squash blossom beads; no pendant; 8⅞ (22.5).
Provenance: Bright Angel Lodge, Grand Canyon National Park, Arizona, 1953.

403 CHILD'S SQUASH BLOSSOM NECKLACE, 1950s
Navajo
Single strand of small spherical beads; ten squash blossom beads; double carinated wire naja set with one small round turquoise at terminals (one stone missing); 8¾ (22.2).
Provenance: Aztec Shop, Scottsdale, Arizona, 1960.

404 405 406
407
408

404 BEAD NECKLACE, 1930s
Navajo
Single strand of spherical beads; double naja of half-round hammered wire, corona above shank set with three round cabochon turquoises; 12¾ (32.4).
Provenance: Frances Quarles, Taos, New Mexico, 1954.

405 BEAD NECKLACE, about 1930
Navajo
Single strand of small spherical beads; naja of carinated wire enclosing scalloped sheet crescent, set with one pear-shaped Blue Gem turquoise on center tab and two round Blue Gem turquoises at terminals, sheet ornament with stamped decoration above shank; 10 (25.4).
Provenance: Santa Fe, New Mexico, 1953.

406 BEAD NECKLACE, about 1930
Navajo
Single strand of spherical beads; naja of hammered half-round wire enclosed by double twisted flat wire, trapezoidal Cerrillos turquoise in serrated bezel at center, scallop-edged ornament with repoussé and stamped decoration above shank; 11¼ (28.6).
Provenance: Frances Quarles, Taos, New Mexico, 1952.

407 BEAD NECKLACE, 1970s
Navajo
Made by Sarah Debois, Cousins, New Mexico.
Single strand of slightly flattened beads; stamped decoration; 13 (33).
Provenance: Bernardine L. Garcia, Albuquerque, New Mexico, 1975.

408 BEAD NECKLACE, about 1950
Navajo
Single strand of slightly flattened beads; stamped decoration; 18½ (47).
Provenance: Frances Quarles, Taos, New Mexico, 1954.
Bought as pawn.

Not shown:

409 BEAD NECKLACE, 1930s
    Navajo
    Double strand of small spherical
    beads; triple naja of round and
    double twisted wire, set with six
    turquoises; 9⅜ (23.8).
    Provenance: Price's All Indian
    Shop, Albuquerque, New Mexico,
    1961.

410 BEAD NECKLACE, 1930s or later
    Navajo
    Single strand of ridged beads; cast
    double naja with "oxbow" at top,
    set with three Stennich turquoises;
    stamped decoration; 13½ (34.3).
    Provenance: Fred Harvey Co.,
    Albuquerque, New Mexico, 1955.

411 BEAD NECKLACE, 1930s or later
    Navajo
    Single strand of spherical beads;
    double naja of carinated wire with
    stamped decoration; 15⅜ (39.1).
    Provenance: unknown.

412 BEAD NECKLACE WITH NAJA,
    about 1950
    Navajo
    Single strand of spherical beads;
    hammered naja with small naja as
    pendant, stamped decoration;
    11¾ (29.9).
    Provenance: Tom Moore, Gallup,
    New Mexico, 1955.

413 NECKLACE, 1950s
    Navajo
    Single strand of spherical
    graduated beads; naja of two
    stamped carinated wires enclosing
    twisted wire; 12⅞ (32.7).
    Provenance: unknown.

414 BEAD NECKLACE WITH NAJA,
    about 1960
    Navajo
    Single strand of spherical beads;
    triple naja of carinated commercial
    wire, set with three turquoises;
    16¼ (41.3).
    Provenance: Price's All Indian
    Shop, Albuquerque, New Mexico,
    1968.
    Bought as pawn.

415
417
416 418

415 COIN NECKLACE, about 1950
Possibly Navajo
Single strand of spherical beads in
two sizes; five Mercury dimes on
shanks; nine elliptical turquoises
in bezels; 12⅜ (31.4).
Provenance: Petty's Curio,
Williams, Arizona, 1953.

416 COIN NECKLACE, about 1950
Pueblo
Single strand of spherical beads;
eighteen Mercury dimes on shanks;
cast double naja set with one
elliptical and two round turquoises;
14⅜ (36.5).
Provenance: George Rummage,
Gallup, New Mexico, 1955.

417 COIN NECKLACE, 1950s
Navajo
Single strand of slightly flattened
beads; thirty Mercury and Liberty
dimes on shanks; triple naja of
carinated wire, set with three
turquoises; stamped decoration;
17⅜ (44.2).
Provenance: Fred Harvey Co.,
Albuquerque, New Mexico, 1953.

418 COIN NECKLACE, about 1920
Pueblo
Single strand of irregular beads;
six squash blossom beads and eight
Liberty quarters on shanks; double
naja of carinated wire, set with
three round cabochon turquoises;
turquoise tied to neckband;
15½ (39.4).
Provenance: Teresita Quintana,
Santa Fe, New Mexico, 1956;
Cochita Quintana.

Not shown:

419 COIN NECKLACE, 1930–1950
Navajo
Double strand of small beads; ten
Mercury dimes, each set with a
small elliptical turquoise; double
carinated wire naja set with three
Burnham turquoises; 12 (30.5).
Provenance: Price's All Indian
Shop, Albuquerque, New Mexico,
1961.
Bought as pawn.

420 COIN NECKLACE, about 1950
Pueblo
Double strand of small beads;

thirty dimes on shanks; half-round
wire naja set with three elliptical
turquoises at center, triangular
turquoise pendant surrounded by
looped wire; 14½ (36.8).
Provenance: Turpen Trading Post,
Gallup, New Mexico, 1953.

421 COIN NECKLACE, about 1950
Navajo
Single strand of spherical beads;
fourteen Mercury dimes on
shanks; silver dollar attached as
pendant; 15¼ (39.3).
Provenance: Hanns Hogan,
Gallup, New Mexico, 1950.

422 COIN NECKLACE, about 1960
Navajo
Single strand of beads; twelve
Liberty dimes on shanks; cast naja
with hands as terminals, stamped
decoration; 15¾ (40).
Provenance: Charlotte Goodrich,
Albuquerque, New Mexico, 1963.

423 SQUASH BLOSSOM NECKLACE,
1940s–1950s
Navajo
Double strand of spherical beads;
fourteen squash blossoms overlaid
with "butterfly" plaques set with
red coral; naja of two square wires
enclosing double twisted wire, set
with elliptical red coral;
14½ (36.8).
Provenance: Quick Silver Shop,
Santa Fe, New Mexico, 1975.

424 SQUASH BLOSSOM NECKLACE,
1920s or later
Navajo
Double strand of spherical beads;
twenty-nine small squash blossoms
overlaid with "butterfly" plaques
set with small elliptical turquoises;
double naja of twisted square wire,
set with three round turquoises;
13⅞ (35.3).
Provenance: Fred Harvey Co.,
Santa Fe, New Mexico.

425 SQUASH BLOSSOM NECKLACE,
1940s–1950s
Navajo
Single strand of spherical beads;
ten squash blossom beads overlaid
with "butterfly" plaques set with
elliptical Blue Gem turquoises;
cast naja set with three turquoises;
stamped decoration; 14⅜ (36.5).
Provenance: Santa Fe, New
Mexico, 1954.

426 SQUASH BLOSSOM NECKLACE,
1930s
Navajo
Scratched inscription on back of
naja: [———] Flores
Double strand of spherical beads;
twenty squash blossoms overlaid
with hexagonal plaques set with
square Blue Gem turquoises; cast
double naja set with four
trapezoidal Blue Gem turquoises;
14⅛ (35.9)
Provenance: Kachina House,
Scottsdale, Arizona, 1959.

116

Not shown:

427 SQUASH BLOSSOM NECKLACE,
1930s
Navajo
Double strand of spherical beads;
sixteen squash blossoms overlaid
with "butterfly" plaques set with
round Burnham turquoises; naja
set with single row of round
Burnham turquoises; 11¾ (29.8).
Provenance: Turpen Trading Post,
Gallup, New Mexico, 1962.
Bought as pawn.

428 SQUASH BLOSSOM NECKLACE,
1930s
Navajo
Double strand of small spherical
beads; sixteen squash blossoms
overlaid with "butterfly" plaques
set with elliptical Cerrillos
turquoises; naja set with single
row of Cerrillos turquoises, large
oval Cerrillos turquoise as pendant;
11½ (29.2).
Provenance: Maisel's, Albuquerque, New Mexico, 1964.

429 SQUASH BLOSSOM NECKLACE,
1930s or 1940s
Navajo
Double strand of spherical beads;
twenty-eight squash blossoms
overlaid with "butterfly" plaques
set with elliptical Lone Mountain
turquoises; naja set with single
row of Lone Mountain turquoises,
"butterfly" pendant; 13½ (34.3).
Provenance: Tanner's, Scottsdale,
Arizona.

430 SQUASH BLOSSOM NECKLACE,
1940s
Navajo
Single strand of small spherical
beads; fourteen squash blossoms
overlaid with "butterfly" plaques
set with Battle Mountain
turquoises; naja set with single
row of small round turquoises of
various types; serrated bezels;
teardrop decoration; 11¾ (29.8).
Provenance: Frances Quarles,
Taos, New Mexico, 1955.

431 SQUASH BLOSSOM NECKLACE,
about 1940
Navajo
Double strand of spherical beads;
eighteen squash blossoms overlaid
with "butterfly" plaques set with
large elliptical cabochon turquoises
in scalloped bezels; naja of two
carinated wires enclosing double
twisted wire, set with three
elliptical cabochon turquoises;
stamped decoration; 14 (35.6).
Provenance: Turpen Trading Post,
Gallup, New Mexico, 1953.

432 BEAD NECKLACE, 1940s
Navajo
Double strand of slightly flattened
beads; thirty-two small Lone
Mountain turquoises on shanks;
naja set with single row of round
Lone Mountain turquoises;
stamped decoration; 15⅝ (39.7).
Provenance: Verkamp's, Grand
Canyon National Park, Arizona,
1949.

433 BEAD NECKLACE, 1950s
Navajo
Double strand of spherical beads;
fourteen Lone Mountain turquoises
on shanks; triple naja of carinated
and round wire, small center
pendant of Lone Mountain
turquoise; 12⅞ (32.8).
Provenance: George Rummage,
Gallup, New Mexico, 1960.

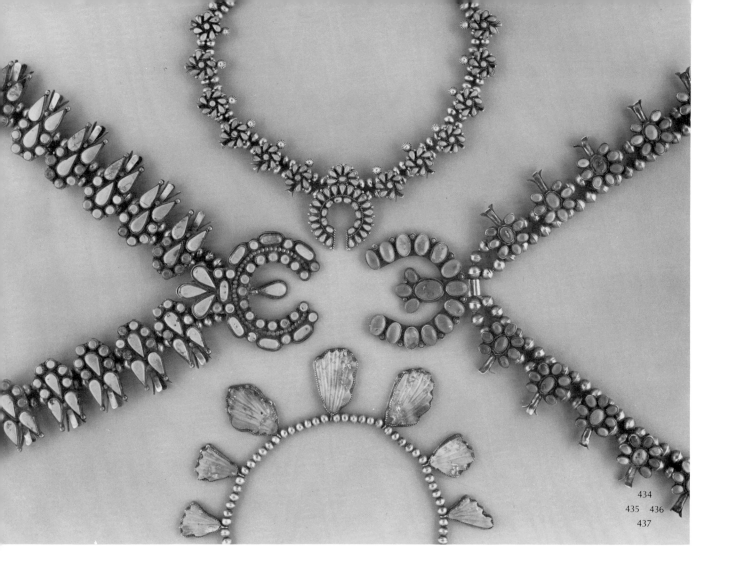

434 SQUASH BLOSSOM NECKLACE,
1940s
Zuni
Double strand of small spherical
beads; twelve squash blossoms set
with clusters of oval Villa Grove
turquoises; sheet naja set with
small oval and elliptical Villa Grove
turquoises; serrated bezels;
teardrop and twisted wire
decoration; 11⅛ (28.3).
Provenance: Hall's, Mesa Verde
National Park, Colorado, 1949.

435 SQUASH BLOSSOM NECKLACE,
1930s or later
Zuni
Double strand of spherical beads;
twelve squash blossoms overlaid
with large clusters of round and
pear-shaped Stennich turquoises;
sheet naja set with round, elliptical,
and pear-shaped Stennich
turquoises, center pendant;
serrated bezels; 16½ (41.9).
Provenance: Turpen Trading Post,
Gallup, New Mexico, 1953.

436 SQUASH BLOSSOM NECKLACE,
1930s–1940s
Probably Zuni
Double strand of spherical beads;
twelve squash blossoms overlaid
with clusters of small elliptical
Miami turquoises; sheet naja set
with elliptical Miami turquoises;
serrated bezels; 17 (43.2).
Provenance: Chief's Western Store,
Santa Fe, New Mexico, 1954.

437 SQUASH BLOSSOM NECKLACE,
about 1940
Zuni
Single strand of small spherical
beads; seven graduated Stennich
turquoise pendants carved in the
form of leaves, serrated bezels;
11¼ (28.6).
Provenance: Wright's Trading Post,
Albuquerque, New Mexico, 1952.

Not shown:

438 BEAD NECKLACE, 1940s
Zuni
Single strand of small beads;
eight clusters of round Morenci
turquoises; naja set with single
row of Morenci turquoises, one

large triangular Morenci turquoise
as center pendant; serrated bezels;
teardrop decoration; 13½ (34.3).
Provenance: Turpen Trading Post,
Gallup, New Mexico, 1955.
Bought as pawn.
Cf. Frank and Holbrook, p. 143.

439 SQUASH BLOSSOM NECKLACE,
1940s
Zuni
Double strand of spherical beads;
twelve squash blossoms overlaid
with clusters of oval and elliptical
Morenci turquoises; sheet naja set
with double row of round and oval
Morenci turquoises; serrated
bezels; twisted wire and teardrop
decoration; 14½ (35.9).
Provenance: Prescott, Arizona, 1953.

440 BEAD NECKLACE, about 1960
Navajo
Double strand of spherical beads;
ten flat cast squash blossoms of
variant type set with Blue Gem
turquoises of various shapes; cast
triple naja set with Blue Gem
turquoises; serrated bezels; 15⅛ (38.4).
Provenance: Harold Street, Taos,
New Mexico, 1963.

441 443

442

441 BEAD NECKLACE, 1930s
Navajo
Single strand of elongated beads
alternating with elliptical stamped
plaques; triangular turquoise
pendant in scallop-edged
mounting; stamped decoration;
11⅜ (28.9).
Provenance: Turpen Trading Post,
Gallup, New Mexico, 1952.

442 BEAD NECKLACE, about 1940
Probably Navajo
Scratched inscription on back of
pendant: I R J
Single strand of spherical beads;
four "butterfly" plaques set with
elliptical Miami turquoises;
"butterfly" pendant set with large
Miami turquoise of irregular shape;
stamped decoration; 13½ (34.3).
Provenance: Price's All Indian
Shop, Albuquerque, New Mexico,
1966.
Bought as pawn.

443 BEAD NECKLACE, about 1950
Navajo
Single strand of spherical beads
and chain links; double carinated
wire naja set with three round
cabochon turquoises; 17⅜ (44.2).
Provenance: Mary Bateman,
Hot Springs, Arkansas, 1951.

Not shown:

444 BEAD NECKLACE, 1930s
Navajo
Single strand of spherical beads;
square turquoise pendant
surrounded by bead wire and
twisted wire; 13 (33).
Provenance: unknown.

445 SQUASH BLOSSOM NECKLACE,
about 1940
Navajo
Single strand of spherical silver
and tubular coral beads; eight
squash blossom beads; carinated
wire naja set with three round
turquoises; 11¾ (29.9).
Provenance: Frances Quarles,
Taos, New Mexico, 1954.

446 BEAD NECKLACE, 1940s
Pueblo
Single strand of small beads; five
pendants in the form of feathers;
filed decoration; 10⅜ (26.4).
Provenance: Nettie Wheeler,
Muskogee, Oklahoma, 1952.

447 BEAD NECKLACE, 1940s
Zuni
Single strand of beads; turquoise
pendant carved in the form of a
leaf; 10¹³⁄₁₆ (27.5).
Provenance: Taos, New Mexico,
1956.

448 BEAD NECKLACE, about 1950
Pueblo
Single strand of tubular and round
beads with tubular coral beads
interspersed; turquoise pendant;
10¾ (27.3).
Provenance: Brice and Judy
Sewell, Taos, New Mexico, 1956;
Frances Quarles collection.

449 BEAD NECKLACE, 1950s
Navajo
Single strand of beads; seven cast
oval pendants with oxidized
centers; 10¼ (26.1).
Provenance: Turpen Trading Post,
Gallup, New Mexico, 1957.
Bought as pawn.

450 BEAD NECKLACE, about 1950
Navajo
Single strand of spherical beads;
sixteen repoussé leaf ornaments
set with round Morenci turquoises;
8⅜ (21.3).
Provenance: unknown.

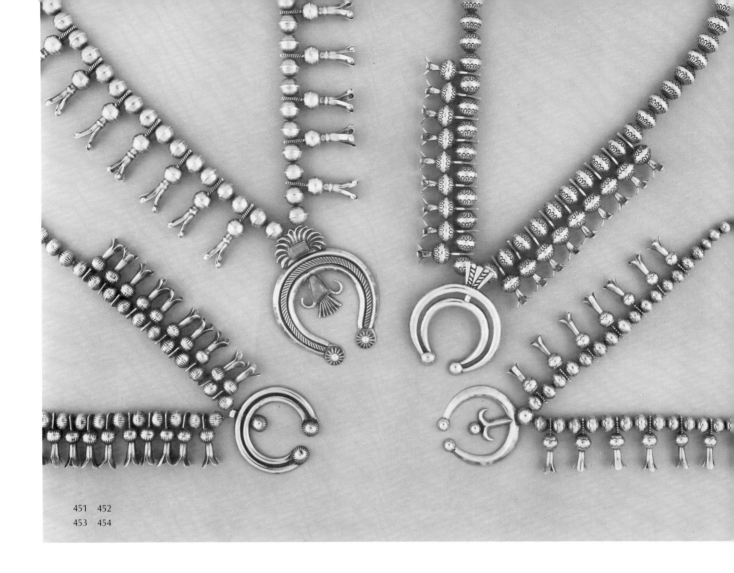

451 452
453 454

451 SQUASH BLOSSOM NECKLACE,
about 1960
Navajo
Single strand of ridged spherical
beads; sixteen squash blossom
beads; naja of two carinated wires
enclosing square wire, set with two
turquoises; 18 (45.7).
Provenance: Quivira Shop,
Santa Fe, New Mexico, 1962.
Bought as pawn.

452 SQUASH BLOSSOM NECKLACE,
1961
Navajo
Single strand of slightly flattened
beads; eighteen squash blossom
beads; cast double naja with
stamped decoration; 14¾ (37.5).
Provenance: Turpen Trading Post,
Gallup, New Mexico, 1961.
Made for the collector.

453 SQUASH BLOSSOM NECKLACE,
about 1960
Navajo
Single strand of spherical beads;
twenty squash blossom beads;
double naja of half-round wire
with bosses at center and
terminals; 14⅛ (35.8).
Provenance: Price's All Indian
Shop, Albuquerque, New Mexico,
1963.

454 SQUASH BLOSSOM NECKLACE,
1940s
Navajo
Single strand of spherical beads;
fourteen squash blossom beads;
cast naja with stamped decoration;
12⅝ (32.4).
Provenance: Hagberg's, Gallup,
New Mexico, 1956.
Bought as pawn.

Not shown:

455 SQUASH BLOSSOM NECKLACE,
1930s
Navajo
Single strand of flattened beads;
twelve squash blossom beads;
hammered naja with stamped
decoration; 16 (40.6).
Provenance: Packard's Trading
Post, Santa Fe, New Mexico,
1961.

456 SQUASH BLOSSOM NECKLACE,
1930s or later
Navajo
Single strand of graduated
spherical beads; fourteen squash
blossom beads; cast naja;
11⅛ (28.9).
Provenance: Fred Harvey Co.,
Grand Canyon National Park,
Arizona, 1953.

457 SQUASH BLOSSOM NECKLACE,
about 1935
Navajo
Single strand of large spherical
beads; twelve squash blossom
beads; cast naja; 17¾ (44.2).
Provenance: Turpen Trading Post,
Gallup, New Mexico, 1955.
Bought as pawn.

458 SQUASH BLOSSOM NECKLACE,
about 1935
Navajo
Single strand of spherical beads;
fourteen squash blossom beads;
cast carinated naja set with three
turquoises, stamped decoration;
16¼ (41.3).
Provenance: Turpen Trading Post,
Gallup, New Mexico, 1949.

459 SQUASH BLOSSOM NECKLACE,
about 1940
Navajo
Single strand of slightly flattened
beads; fourteen squash blossom
beads; double naja of carinated
wire with stamped decoration;
12⅜ (31.4).
Provenance: Fred Harvey Co.,
Albuquerque, New Mexico, 1959.

460 SQUASH BLOSSOM NECKLACE,
about 1940
Navajo
Single strand of graduated
spherical beads; twenty squash
blossom beads; double naja of
half-round wire; 14½ (36.8).
Provenance: Navajo Indian
Trading Post, Tucson, Arizona,
1965.
Bought as pawn.

461 SQUASH BLOSSOM NECKLACE,
1940s
Navajo
Single strand of spherical beads;
fourteen squash blossom beads;
double naja of carinated wire;
16¼ (41.3).
Provenance: Turpen Trading Post,
Gallup, New Mexico, 1959.

462 SQUASH BLOSSOM NECKLACE,
1940s
Navajo
Single strand of spherical beads;
twelve squash blossom beads;
twenty-two turquoise pendants
tied on; double carinated cast
naja set with three elliptical
turquoises; 15½ (39.4).
Provenance: Harold Street, Taos,
New Mexico, 1955.
Turquoise added by Harold Street.

463 SQUASH BLOSSOM NECKLACE,
about 1950
Navajo
Single strand of spherical beads;
ten squash blossom beads;
double naja of carinated wire
with turquoises on pendant and
terminals, twisted wire
decoration; 16⅛ (41).
Provenance: Fred Harvey Co.,
Albuquerque, New Mexico, 1961;
Palmer House, Chicago.

464 SQUASH BLOSSOM NECKLACE,
about 1950
Navajo
Single strand of fluted beads;
fourteen squash blossom beads;
triple naja of carinated and
double twisted wire; 13⅞ (35.3).
Provenance: Turpen Trading Post,
Gallup, New Mexico, 1952.

465 SQUASH BLOSSOM NECKLACE,
about 1950
Navajo
Single strand of graduated beads;
twenty squash blossom beads;
"oxbow" naja of carinated wire
enclosing double twisted wire,
Royal Blue turquoise as center
pendant, stamped decoration;
15 (38.1).
Provenance: Turpen Trading Post,
Gallup, New Mexico, 1956.

466 SQUASH BLOSSOM NECKLACE,
about 1950
Navajo
Single strand of spherical beads;
twelve squash blossom beads,
each soldered to second bead;
cast carinated double naja set
with three turquoises; 15¼ (38.8).
Provenance: Tom Moore, Gallup,
New Mexico, 1953.

467 SQUASH BLOSSOM NECKLACE,
1950s
Navajo
Single strand of spherical beads;
ten squash blossom beads; cast
naja with two pairs of inner
"arms" and small center pendant
of turquoise, stamped decoration;
13⅝ (34.6).
Provenance: George Rummage,
Gallup, New Mexico, 1960.

468 SQUASH BLOSSOM NECKLACE,
about 1960
Navajo
Stamped spherical beads; twelve
squash blossoms, stamped
decoration; carinated naja with
twisted wire; 14½ (36.8).
Provenance: Wright's Trading Post,
Albuquerque, New Mexico, 1975.

470
469 471

469 "CORNFLOWER" NECKLACE,
1950s
Navajo
Single strand of small beads; ten
cast "cornflowers" on shanks;
cast naja; 11¾ (28.8).
Provenance: Quivira Shop,
Santa Fe, New Mexico, 1959.

470 "CORNFLOWER" NECKLACE,
about 1935
Navajo
Single strand of spherical beads;
sixteen graduated hemispheres
terminating in cast "cornflowers";
carinated and square wire naja
with "cornflower" bead pendant;
stamped decoration; 13⅞ (35.5).
Provenance: Frank Patania,
Santa Fe, New Mexico, about
1939.

471 CHILD'S "CORNFLOWER"
NECKLACE, 1950s
Navajo
Double strand of small spherical
beads; twelve cast "cornflowers"
on shanks, set with elliptical
turquoises; cast naja set with
three elliptical Lone Mountain
turquoises at apex and terminals;
7⅜ (19.4).
Provenance: Packard's Trading
Post, Santa Fe, New Mexico,
1961.

Not shown:

472 "CORNFLOWER" NECKLACE,
1930s or later
Navajo
Single strand of spherical beads;
fourteen cast "cornflowers";
cast naja set with two small
round turquoises; 12½ (31.7).
Provenance: Fred Harvey Co.,
Albuquerque, New Mexico, 1955.
Bought as pawn.

474

473 475

473 SQUASH BLOSSOM NECKLACE,
about 1950
Navajo
Double strand of spherical
beads; fourteen small beads
terminating in najas of carinated
wire; cast double naja set with
one triangular and two round
turquoises; 14¼ (36.2).
Provenance: George Rummage,
Gallup, New Mexico, 1954.
Cf. Frank and Holbrook, p. 174.

474 SQUASH BLOSSOM NECKLACE,
1930s or later
Navajo
Single strand of small spherical
beads; fourteen small beads
terminating in small najas
of triangular wire; carinated
wire naja with twisted wire
decoration; 12³⁄₁₆ (31).
Provenance: Frances Quarles,
Taos, New Mexico, 1955.
Bought as pawn.

475 SQUASH BLOSSOM NECKLACE,
about 1940
Navajo
Single strand of slightly flattened
beads; six squash blossom
beads; eight beads terminating
in cast najalike ornaments; cast
carinated double naja; 13¾
(34.9).
Provenance: Eric Kohlberg,
Denver, Colorado, 1947.

Not shown:

476 NECKLACE, about 1956
Navajo
Made by Sam Silver.
Single strand of small spherical
beads; sixteen cast crosses
terminating in najas; cast
double naja with pendant cross
in center; 13¾ (34.9).
Provenance: Turpen Trading
Post, Gallup, New Mexico 1956.
Made for Tobe Turpen as a copy
of an old necklace in the smith's
possession.

477 NECKLACE, 1970s
Navajo
Single strand of cast eight-sided
beads; twelve cast najas on
shanks; cast naja terminating in
hands; 11¹³⁄₁₆ (30).
Provenance: Wright's Trading
Post, Albuquerque, New Mexico,
1976.

479

478   480

478 "CORNFLOWER" NECKLACE,
     about 1950
     Navajo
     Single strand of flattened beads;
     fourteen cast "cornflower"
     beads; naja of half-round wire
     with "cornflower" bead as
     shank; 15 3/16 (38.6).
     Provenance: Turpen Trading
     Post, Gallup, New Mexico, 1956.
     Bought as pawn.

479 CROSS NECKLACE, about 1935
     Navajo
     Single strand of spherical beads;
     seven sheet crosses (one
     missing); cast naja; filed
     decoration; 13 3/4 (34.9).
     Provenance: Packard's Trading
     Post, Santa Fe, New Mexico,
     1961.

480 "PUMPKIN SEED" NECKLACE,
     1933 or later
     Navajo
     Made by Annie Mudwater.
     Single strand of spherical beads;
     ten cast pear-shaped "pumpkin
     seeds," each set with an elliptical
     turquoise; cast naja set with
     elliptical turquoise; 15 1/8 (38.9).
     Provenance: Ann Clark, Phoenix,
     Arizona, 1973; Tom Moore,
     Gallup, New Mexico.
     Cf. King, p. 156, pl. 208.

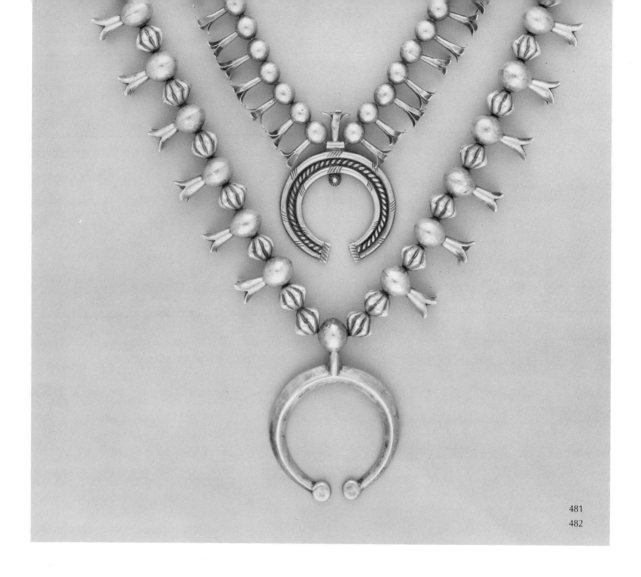

481
482

481 SQUASH BLOSSOM NECKLACE, about 1940
Navajo
Single strand of spherical beads; eighteen squash blossom beads strung directly on necklace; triple naja of two round wires enclosing double twisted wire, upright squash blossom surmounting shank; 15⅛ (38.4).
Provenance: Fred Harvey Co., Albuquerque, New Mexico, before 1952.

482 SQUASH BLOSSOM NECKLACE, about 1970
Euro-American
Made by Wolf Reed.
Single strand of gadrooned beads; fourteen squash blossom beads strung directly on necklace; cast carinated naja with bead as shank; 15⅛ (38.4).
Provenance: Packard's Trading Post, Santa Fe, New Mexico, 1976.

Not shown:

483 SQUASH BLOSSOM NECKLACE, about 1935
Navajo
Single strand of large spherical beads; sixteen squash blossom beads strung directly on necklace; double naja of carinated wire and twisted square wire, set with single turquoise; 16¾ (42.5).
Provenance: Turpen Trading Post, Gallup, New Mexico, 1953. Bought as pawn.

484 SQUASH BLOSSOM NECKLACE, about 1935
Navajo
Made by the Roanhorse family.
Single strand of spherical beads; thirty squash blossom beads strung directly on necklace; cast naja; 16³⁄₁₆ (41.1).
Provenance: Tom Moore, Gallup, New Mexico, 1953.

485 SQUASH BLOSSOM NECKLACE, about 1940
Navajo
Single strand of thirty squash

blossom beads strung directly on necklace; double naja of carinated wire, set with ten round turquoises; 13¾ (34.9).
Provenance: Turpen Trading Post, Gallup, New Mexico, 1952.

486 SQUASH BLOSSOM NECKLACE, 1940s–1950s
Navajo
Single strand of small spherical beads; ten squash blossom beads strung directly on necklace; naja of carinated wire with lozenge-shaped turquoise as center pendant, stamped decoration; 11⁹⁄₁₆ (29.5).
Provenance: Frances Quarles, Taos, New Mexico, 1954. Bought as pawn.

487 CHILD'S SQUASH BLOSSOM NECKLACE, about 1960
Navajo
Single strand of small ridged beads; fourteen squash blossom beads strung directly on necklace; triple naja of carinated wires enclosing double twisted wire; 10¹⁄₁₆ (25.5).
Provenance: unknown.

488   489
490   491

488 SQUASH BLOSSOM NECKLACE,
     about 1960
     Navajo
     Squash blossoms and naja made
     by Alice Watson.
     Double strand of fluted beads;
     fourteen squash blossoms, each
     overlaid with a Fox turquoise of
     irregular shape; double naja
     of carinated wire with Fox
     turquoises at terminals and
     fluted bead pendant, stamped
     decoration; 16⅜ (41.1).
     Provenance: Turpen Trading
     Post, Gallup, New Mexico, 1963.

489 SQUASH BLOSSOM NECKLACE,
     1960s
     Navajo
     Double strand of slightly
     flattened beads; twenty-two
     squash blossom beads, each
     overlaid with a Burnham
     turquoise of irregular shape;
     cast naja set with four Burnham
     turquoises; 16¼ (41.3).
     Provenance: Florence Strange,
     Santa Fe, New Mexico, 1970;
     Mrs. Ramon Calabaza.

490 SQUASH BLOSSOM NECKLACE,
     1940s
     Navajo
     Double strands of spherical
     beads; eighteen squash
     blossoms, each overlaid with
     two irregularly shaped Blue
     Gem turquoises; triple naja of
     two carinated wires enclosing
     filed half-round wire, set with
     eight Blue Gem turquoises
     of various shapes; teardrop
     decoration; 15½ (39.5).
     Provenance: Turpen Trading
     Post, Gallup, New Mexico, 1955.

491 "CORNFLOWER" NECKLACE,
     1950s
     Zuni
     Double strand of spherical
     beads; twelve "cornflowers,"
     each set with large Morenci
     turquoise of irregular shape;
     sheet naja set with twelve
     Morenci turquoises of irregular
     shape, stamped and repoussé
     decoration; 16¾ (41.5).
     Provenance: Fred Harvey Co.,
     Albuquerque, New Mexico, 1957.
     Bought as pawn.

Not shown:

492 SQUASH BLOSSOM NECKLACE,
     1940s
     Navajo
     Double strand of spherical
     beads; twelve squash blossoms,
     each overlaid with two
     turquoises of irregular shape;
     naja set with eight turquoises
     of irregular shape, twisted
     wire decoration; 14⁹⁄₁₆ (37).
     Provenance: Hagberg's, Gallup,
     New Mexico, 1956.

493 SQUASH BLOSSOM NECKLACE,
     about 1950
     Navajo
     Double strand of spherical
     beads; twelve squash blossoms
     overlaid with "butterfly"
     plaques, each set with Lone
     Mountain turquoise; triple naja
     of carinated wire enclosing filed
     round wire, set with eight
     turquoises of various shapes;
     16³⁄₁₆ (41.1).
     Provenance: Price's All Indian
     Shop, Albuquerque, New
     Mexico, 1968.
     Bought as pawn.

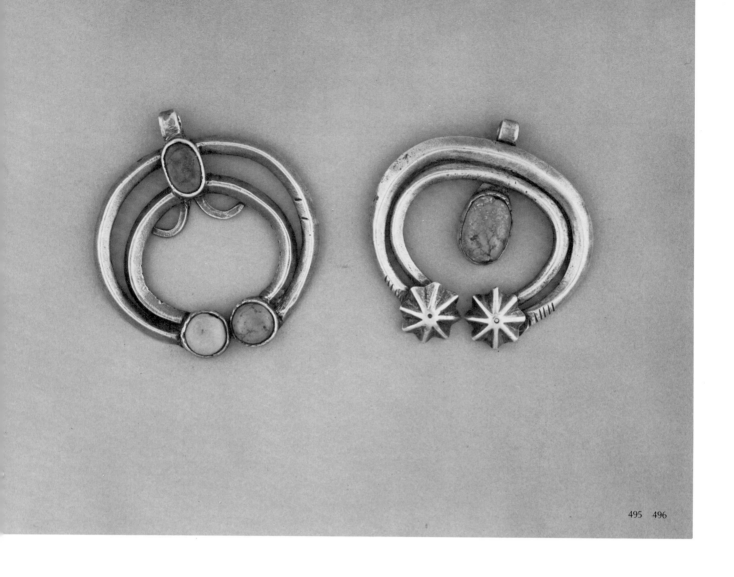

495 NAJA, about 1910
Navajo
Double naja of carinated wire;
set with one elliptical turquoise
at apex and two round cabochon
turquoises at terminals; 2⅝ (6.7).
Provenance: W. S. Dutton,
Santa Fe, New Mexico, 1957.

496 NAJA, about 1910
Navajo
Double naja of carinated wire;
set with elliptical cabochon
turquoise at center; repoussé
ornaments at terminals; filed
decoration; 2½ (6.4).
Provenance: W. S. Dutton,
Sante Fe, New Mexico, 1957.

494 "CORNFLOWER" NECKLACE,
1960s
Zuni
Double strand of spherical
beads; twelve "cornflowers,"
each set with elliptical
turquoises of various shapes;
15⁹⁄₁₆ (39.5).
Provenance: Ann Clark, Phoenix,
Arizona, 1973.

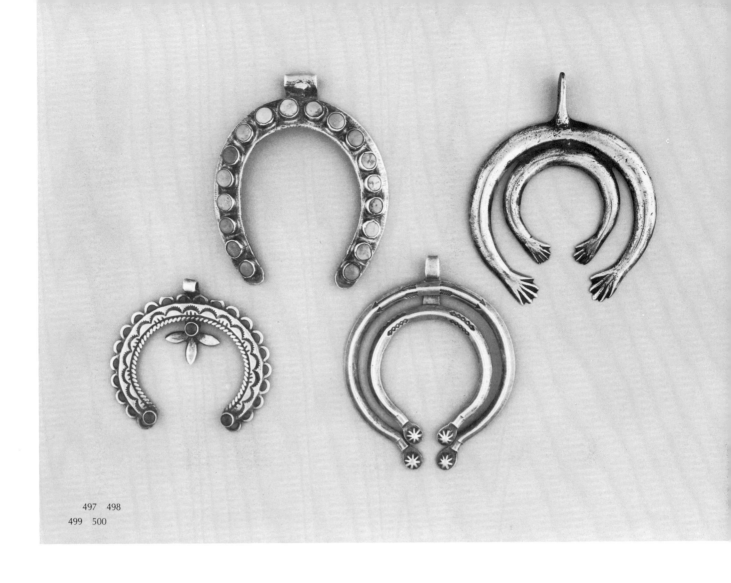

497 498
499 500

497 NAJA, about 1930
Navajo
Sheet naja; set with eighteen
small round turquoises; 2½ (6.4).
Provenance: Hubbell's Trading
Post, Winslow, Arizona, 1950.
Bought as pawn.

498 NAJA, 1930s or later
Navajo
Double cast naja with hands as
terminals; 2⅝ (6.7).
Provenance: Turpen Trading
Post, Gallup, New Mexico, 1954.
Bought as pawn.

499 NAJA, about 1930
Navajo
Sheet naja; set with three small
round turquoises; twisted wire,
bent wire, and stamped
decoration; 1¾ (4.4).
Provenance: Tom Bahti, Tucson,
Arizona, 1959.

500 NAJA, about 1930
Navajo
Double naja of carinated wire;
repoussé and stamped
decoration; 2½ (6.4).
Provenance: Fred Harvey Co.,
Albuquerque, New Mexico, 1957.

Not shown:

501 NAJA, 1930s
Navajo
Triple naja of twisted square
wires enclosing half-round wire;
set with three Lone Mountain
turquoises at center and
terminals; 2¼ (5.7).
Provenance: Hanns Hogan,
Gallup, New Mexico, 1950.

502 NAJA, 1930s or later
Navajo
Triple naja of half-round wires
enclosing double twisted wire;
set with three turquoises on
plaque at center; repoussé
decoration; 1⅝ (4).
Provenance: Hubbell's Trading
Post, Winslow, Arizona, 1953.

503 NAJA, about 1940
Navajo
Triple naja of half-round wire;
set with square Cerrillos
turquoise at apex; repoussé and
stamped decoration; 2¼ (5.7).
Provenance: Tom Bahti, Tucson,
Arizona, 1959.
Bought as pawn.

504 NAJA, about 1940
Navajo
Triple naja of carinated wires
enclosing round wire; set with
four Fox turquoises at apex,
center, and terminals; 2½ (6.4).
Provenance: C. G. Wallace,
Gallup, New Mexico, 1963.

505 507
506
508 509

505 NAJA, about 1950
Navajo
Cast naja; stamped decoration;
2¼ (5.7).
Provenance: Santa Rita Hotel,
Tucson, Arizona, 1959.

506 NAJA, 1950s or later
Navajo
Cast naja; set with two elliptical
turquoises in serrated bezels;
filed decoration; 2¾ (7).
Provenance: Irma Bailey,
Albuquerque, New Mexico,
1975.

507 NAJA, 1950
Navajo
Cast carinated naja; 3 (7.6).
Provenance: Packard's Trading
Post, Santa Fe, New Mexico,
1973.

508 NAJA, 1950s or later
Navajo
Cast carinated naja; set with
oval Lone Mountain turquoise
at apex; 3 (7.6).
Provenance: Quivira Shop,
Santa Fe, New Mexico, 1973.

509 NAJA, about 1960
Navajo
Made by Chee Yazzie.
Naja of two carinated wires
enclosing double twisted wire;
set with two Tiffany Cerrillos
turquoises of irregular shape at
terminals and three similar
stones on "oxbow" appliqué;
filed decoration; 2¾ (7).
Provenance: Turpen Trading
Post, Gallup, New Mexico, 1960.
Made for the collector as copy
of a naja on a necklace in stock.

Not shown:

510 NAJA, about 1935
Navajo
Double naja of carinated wire
and double twisted wire; set
with five small round turquoises;
1⅝ (4.1).
Provenance: Original Curio
Store, Santa Fe, New Mexico,
1956.

511 NAJA, about 1940
Santo Domingo Pueblo
Made by Vidal Aragon; maker's
mark: VA ➤
Cast naja; Morenci turquoise
of irregular shape as center
pendant; filed decoration;
2 (5.1).
Provenance: Packard's Trading
Post, Santa Fe, New Mexico,
1965.
Bought as pawn.

512 NAJA, 1940–1950
Navajo
Cast naja with hands as
terminals; set with two elliptical
Number 8 turquoises at "wrists";
1¾ (4.4).
Provenance: Fred Harvey Co.,
Albuquerque, New Mexico 1957.

513 NAJA, 1940–1950
Navajo
Triple naja of carinated wires
enclosing double twisted wire;
set with single elliptical
turquoise at center; stamped
decoration; 3¼ (8.3).
Provenance: Irma Bailey,
Albuquerque, New Mexico, 1956.

514 NAJA, about 1950
Santo Domingo Pueblo
Made by Vidal Aragon; maker's
mark: VA ➤
Cast carinated naja; stamped
decoration; 1⅝ (4.1).
Provenance: Chester Copman,
Santa Fe Gift Shop, Santa Fe,
New Mexico, 1959.

515 NAJA, about 1950
Navajo
Cast half-round naja; small naja
of square wire as center
pendant; stamped and
filed decoration; 3¾ (9.5).
Provenance: Tom Moore,
Gallup, New Mexico, 1955.

516 NAJA, about 1950
Navajo
Naja of carinated wire; set with
three small round turquoises;
1½ (3.8).
Provenance: Old Wooden
Indian, near Taos, New Mexico,
1965.

517 NAJA, about 1950
Navajo
Triple naja of square wires
enclosing filed wire; stamped
decoration; 3½ (8.9).
Provenance: Tom Moore,
Gallup, New Mexico, 1955.

518 NAJA, about 1950
Navajo
Sheet naja; set with three
Stennich turquoises at center
and terminals; stamped
decoration; 2 (5.1).
Provenance: unknown, 1954.

519 NAJA, about 1950
Navajo
Double naja of half-round wire;
set with round cabochon
Morenci turquoise at center;
filed decoration; 1¼ (3.2).
Provenance: Mr. Daniel, Tucson,
Arizona, 1959.

520 NAJA, 1950
Navajo
Double naja of carinated wires;
set with Miami turquoise at
center; stamped decoration;
1½ (3.8).
Provenance: Chester Copman,
Santa Fe Gift Shop, Santa Fe,
New Mexico, 1957.

521 NAJA, 1950s
Navajo
Cast openwork naja; 2¾ (7).
Provenance: Turpen Trading
Post, Gallup, New Mexico, 1965.

522 NAJA, 1950s or later
Navajo
Cast naja with hands as
terminals; 1¼ (3.2).
Provenance: Half Red Man,
Tucson, Arizona, 1973.

523 NAJA, 1950s
Navajo
Triple naja of carinated wire
enclosing half-round wire;
elliptical Blue Gem turquoise as

pendant; stamped and filed
decoration; 1¾ (4.4).
Provenance: Packard's Trading
Post, Santa Fe, New Mexico,
1965.
Bought as pawn.

524 NAJA ON CHAIN, about 1955
Navajo
Double naja of round wire;
set with three small round
turquoises in serrated bezels;
2 (5.1).
Provenance: Chester Copman,
Santa Fe Gift Shop, Santa Fe,
New Mexico, 1957.

525 NAJA, about 1960
Navajo
Cast openwork naja; stamped
decoration; 2¾ (7).
Provenance: C. G. Wallace,
Gallup, New Mexico, 1963.

526 NAJA, about 1960
Navajo
Cast naja with hands as
terminals; stamped decoration;
2½ (6.4).
Provenance: C. G. Wallace,
Gallup, New Mexico, 1963.

527 NAJA, about 1960
Navajo
Naja of half-round wire; reverse
curve center device; filed
decoration; 2⅝ (6.7).
Provenance: Reese Vaughn,
Scottsdale, Arizona, 1960.
Made as copy of a naja on a
necklace in stock.

528 NAJA, 1960s
Navajo
Cast carinated naja with
"cornflowers" as terminals; filed
decoration; 2½ (6.4).
Provenance: Packard's Trading
Post, Sante Fe, New Mexico,
1973.
Similar to no. 529.

529 NAJA, 1960s
Navajo
Cast carinated naja with
"cornflowers" as terminals;
2½ (6.4).
Provenance: Packard's Trading
Post, Santa Fe, New Mexico,
1969.
Bought as pawn.
Similar to no. 528.

530 NAJA, 1960s
Navajo
Cast carinated naja; 2¾ (7).
Provenance: Packard's Trading
Post, Santa Fe, New Mexico, 1969.
Bought as pawn.

531 NAJA, 1960s
Navajo
Triple naja of half-round wire
enclosing double twisted wire;
elliptical turquoise at center;
filed decoration; 1⅛ (2.9).
Provenance: Packard's Trading
Post, Santa Fe, New Mexico,
1969.

532 NAJA, about 1963
Navajo
Cast carinated naja with hands
as terminals; 1⅜ (3.5).
Provenance: Vada Glennon,
Gallup, New Mexico, 1963.

533 NAJA, about 1963
Navajo
Cast carinated naja with hands
as terminals; 1 (2.5).
Provenance: Vada Glennon,
Gallup, New Mexico, 1963.

534 NAJA, about 1963
Navajo
Cast carinated naja with
hands as terminals; stamped
decoration; 2¼ (5.7).
Provenance: Vada Glennon,
Gallup, New Mexico, 1963.
Similar to no. 535.

535 NAJA, about 1963
Navajo
Cast carinated naja with
hands as terminals; stamped
decoration; 2¼ (5.7).
Provenance: Vada Glennon,
Gallup, New Mexico, 1963.
Similar to no. 534.

536 NAJA, about 1963
Navajo
Cast carinated naja with bosses
at terminals; 2 (5.1).
Provenance: Vada Glennon,
Gallup, New Mexico, 1963.

537 NAJA, about 1964
Navajo
Triple naja of square wire; set
with two elliptical Lone
Mountain turquoises in
scalloped bezels at apex
and center; 3 (7.6).
Provenance: Tobe Turpen, Sr.,
Albuquerque, New Mexico,
1964.

538 NAJA, about 1965
Navajo
Triple naja of carinated wires
enclosing double twisted wire;
set with four elliptical Blue Gem
turquoises at center, apex, and
terminals; "oxbow" at top; filed
decoration; 2¾ (7).
Provenance: Turpen Trading
Post, Gallup, New Mexico, 1965.

539 NAJA, 1968
Navajo
Cast carinated naja with two
pairs of inner "arms" soldered
on; Blue Gem turquoise at
center; twisted wire and
stamped decoration; 3 (7.6).
Provenance: Jerry Chekerian,
Albuquerque, New Mexico,
1968.

540 NAJA, 1969
Navajo
Cast naja; stamped decoration;
1⅜ (3.5).
Provenance: Packard's Trading
Post, Santa Fe, New Mexico,
1969.

541 NAJA, about 1969
Navajo
Cast carinated openwork naja;
2½ (6.4).
Provenance: Packard's Trading
Post, Santa Fe, New Mexico,
1969.

542 NAJA, about 1970
Zuni
Sheet naja; channel-set with
seven round Morenci turquoises;
teardrop decoration; ¾ (0.9).
Provenance: Irma Bailey,
Albuquerque, New Mexico,
1970.

543 NAJA, about 1973
Navajo
Cast openwork naja; set with
elliptical spiny oyster shell on
oxidized background; 3 (7.6).
Provenance: Quivira Shop, Santa
Fe, New Mexico, 1973.

544 NAJA, about 1973
Navajo
Cast double naja; set with
elliptical cabochon turquoises
at apex, center, and terminals;
3⅛ (7.9).
Provenance: Packard's Trading
Post, Santa Fe, New Mexico,
1973.

545 NAJA, about 1976
Navajo
Cast openwork naja; 2½ (6.4).
Provenance: Old Territorial
Shop, Scottsdale, Arizona, 1976.

Belts

The silver concha belt is one of the oldest and most characteristic Navajo ornaments. The earliest conchas appear to have been copied from Spanish prototypes used as buckles and to garnish saddles, bridles, and perhaps belts. Early Navajo-made conchas were oval or round, slightly convex, and decorated with a scalloped edge of "petals" pierced by small holes, which surrounded a raised, tooled band. In the center, two triangular or sometimes semicircular holes were cut, with a vertical bar left between. A narrow leather strap passing through the holes and over the bar strung several conchas into a belt. Early buckles tended to be silver copies of harness buckles. Although open-centered conchas remained popular until about 1900, conchas with decorative closed centers, attached to the belt by a metal sleeve in the back, were being made by the 1880s, when the technique of soldering had been mastered.

As belts became more complex and ornate, buckles followed suit, and by the turn of the century both wrought and cast buckles were being made independently of the silver belts. Even though stamping, repoussé, and turquoise mounting had become common in the late 1800s, the scalloped and perforated edge of the concha continued to be a standard feature. Many belts made after 1900 have vertical "butterfly" plaques mounted between the oval conchas. In the 1920s and 1930s conchas of various sizes were produced—some of them very large—and many belts of small conchas were made for the tourist market. At about the same time, smiths began setting a few concha belts with stones. Although some smiths have experimented with novel concha shapes, particularly round and square, the oval form has remained the standard. The conchas on some modern belts are cast.

The first measurement given is the length of the belt, and the second is the width of the concha. In dimensions of buckles, width precedes height.

J.B.W.
L.L.

547
548

546 CONCHA BELT, 1870–1890
Navajo
Leather belt, buckle missing; six
elliptical conchas with
lozenge-shaped center openings;
punched, chased, and stamped
decoration; 37, 3¾ (94, 9.5).
Provenance: Eleanor Beddell,
Santa Fe, New Mexico, 1956;
James McMillan, Spanish and
Indian Trading Co., Santa Fe;
Munich antique shop; unknown
German artist who lived near
Flagstaff, Arizona, about 1900.

547 CONCHA BELT, 1880–1900
Navajo
Leather belt with rectangular
buckle; seven elliptical conchas
with repoussé centers; stamped,
chased, and punched decoration;
39, 4¾ (99, 12).
Provenance: Howard G. Dost,
Santa Fe, New Mexico, 1954.
Cf. Frank and Holbrook, p. 195.

548 CONCHA BELT, 1880–1900
Navajo
Leather belt with rectangular
buckle; seven elliptical conchas
with closed centers; punched,
chased, stamped, and repoussé
decoration; 41, 4 (104.1, 10.1).
Provenance: Fred Harvey Co.,
Albuquerque, New Mexico, 1953.

549
550
551

549 CONCHA BELT, about 1930
Navajo
Leather belt with rectangular
buckle set with two irregularly
shaped Cerrillos turquoises;
seven elliptical conchas; chased
and stamped decoration; 45, 3¾
(114.3, 9.5).
Provenance: Charlotte Goodrich,
Albuquerque, New Mexico, 1963.

550 CONCHA BELT, about 1930
Navajo
Leather belt with rectangular
buckle; five large elliptical
conchas with rectangular open
centers; chased, stamped, and
repoussé decoration; 41, 5¾
(104.1, 14.6).
Provenance: George Rummage,
Gallup, New Mexico, 1957; Rose
Mary Charley, who said her
father made it.
Bought as pawn.

551 CONCHA BELT, about 1940
Navajo
Leather belt with elliptical
buckle; thirteen small conchas,
each set with single small

round Sleeping Beauty turquoise;
stamped decoration; 32½,
2 (82.6, 5).
Provenance: Fred Harvey Co.,
Albuquerque, New Mexico, late
1940s.

Not shown:

552 CONCHA BELT, 1930s
Navajo
Leather belt with rectangular
buckle set with four elliptical
Blue Gem turquoises; six
elliptical conchas and seven
"butterfly" plaques, each set
with single Blue Gem turquoise;
stamped and repoussé
decoration; 39¾, 3½ (101, 8.9).
Provenance: Fred Harvey Co.,
Albuquerque, New Mexico,
1952.

553 CONCHA BELT, about 1930
Navajo
Buckle made by Tom Chee.
Leather belt with cast openwork
buckle; nine elliptical conchas
with lozenge-shaped center

openings; stamped decoration;
32, 3⅛ (81.3, 8).
Provenance: Nettie Wheeler,
Muskogee, Oklahoma, 1940s.
Bought as pawn.

554 CONCHA BELT, 1930s
Navajo
Leather belt with elliptical
buckle; seven elliptical conchas
and eight "butterfly" plaques;
repoussé and stamped
decoration; 34½, 2¾ (87.6, 7).
Provenance: Turpen Trading
Post, Gallup, New Mexico, 1940s.

555 CONCHA BELT, about 1940
Navajo
Leather belt with rectangular
buckle set with four elliptical
Blue Gem turquoises; five
conchas and four "butterfly"
plaques, each set with single
Blue Gem turquoise; stamped,
chased, and repoussé decoration;
38½, 4¼ (97.8, 10.8).
Provenance: Fred Harvey Co.,
Albuquerque, New Mexico, 1955.

556 CONCHA BELT, about 1930
Navajo
Silk band; fifteen small elliptical
conchas; stamped and repoussé
decoration; 27½, 1¼ (69.9, 3.2).
Provenance: unknown.

557 CONCHA BELT, 1930s
Navajo
Leather belt with buckle in
modified "butterfly" shape; nine
conchas and eight conventional
"butterfly" plaques, each set with
small elliptical turquoise; chased
and repoussé decoration; 40, 2½
(101.6, 6.4).
Provenance: Turpen Trading Post,
Gallup, New Mexico, 1960.

558 CONCHA BELT, about 1940
Navajo
Leather belt with lozenge-shaped
buckle; nine lozenge-shaped
conchas, each set with single
elliptical Stennich turquoise;
stamped, chased, and repoussé
decoration; 36¾, 2¾ (93.3, 7).
Provenance: Fred Harvey Co.,
Albuquerque, New Mexico, late
1960s.

Not shown:

559 CONCHA BELT, about 1930
Navajo
Leather belt with rectangular
buckle; twelve elliptical conchas
and eleven "butterfly" plaques;
stamped and repoussé decora-
tion; 31¾, 1⅜ (80.6, 3.5).
Provenance: Taos Book Shop,
Taos, New Mexico, 1956.
Bought as pawn.

560 CONCHA BELT, 1930s
Navajo
Leather belt with conventional
horseshoe buckle; stamped
decoration; thirty-one repoussé
quarters; 42¾, ¾ (108.6, 2).
Provenance: Taos Book Shop,
Taos, New Mexico, 1959.
Quarters added later, probably
in the 1950s.

561 CONCHA BELT, about 1945
Navajo
Leather belt with older
rectangular buckle set with
six elliptical Battle Mountain
turquoises; ten elliptical
conchas and nine "butterfly"
plaques of aluminum;
38¼, 2 (97.1, 5).
Provenance: Turpen Trading
Post, Gallup, New Mexico, 1959.

562
563
564

562 CONCHA BELT, about 1950
Navajo
Leather belt with rectangular
buckle; seven elliptical conchas
with elliptical center openings;
stamped, chased, and repoussé
decoration; 36, 3⅝ (91.4, 9.2).
Provenance: George Rummage,
Gallup, New Mexico, 1954.

563 CONCHA BELT, about 1950
Navajo
Leather belt with rectangular
buckle; ten elliptical conchas;
stamped and repoussé decoration;
49½, 2¾ (125.7, 7).
Provenance: Turpen Trading Post,
Gallup, New Mexico, 1954.
Made to order for the trader as
copy of an old belt in pawn.

564 CONCHA BELT, about 1970
Navajo
Made by Charlie Lee.
Leather belt with rectangular
buckle; ten elliptical conchas;
stamped, chased, and repoussé
decoration; 49, 3 (124.5, 7.6).
Provenance: Sewell's, Scottsdale,
Arizona, 1976.

Not shown:

565 CONCHA BELT, about 1950
Navajo
Leather belt with rectangular
buckle; ten elliptical conchas,
eleven "butterfly" plaques;
repoussé and stamped decoration;
34, 1½ (86.4, 3.8).
Provenance: Dressman, Santa Fe,
New Mexico, 1955.

566 CONCHA BELT, 1950s
Navajo
Leather belt with rectangular
buckle; eight elliptical conchas
cast from older piece; stamped
decoration; 32½, 3 (82.6, 7.6).
Provenance: Turpen Trading Post,
Gallup, New Mexico, 1957.

567 CONCHA BELT, 1960s
Navajo
Leather belt with rectangular
buckle; eight elliptical conchas,
each set with elliptical Persian
turquoise; stamped and repoussé
decoration: 46, 3¾ (116.8, 9.5).
Provenance: Packard's Trading
Post, Santa Fe, New Mexico, 1973.

568 CONCHA BELT, about 1970
Navajo
Made by Ben Lee.
Leather belt with "butterfly"
buckle; nine elliptical conchas;
stamped, chased, and repoussé
decoration; 50½, 3⅞ (128.3, 9.8).
Provenance: Scottsdale, Arizona,
1978.

569 CONCHA BELT, 1970s
Navajo
Made by Ben Lee.
Leather belt without buckle;
eight elliptical conchas; stamped
decoration; 43, 4⅛ (109.2, 10.5).
Provenance: Sewell's, Scottsdale,
Arizona, 1981.

570 CONCHA BELT, 1960s
Navajo
Leather belt with rectangular
buckle; six round conchas and
six modified "butterfly" plaques,
each set with a round turquoise;
chased and appliqué decoration;
32½, 3 (82.6, 7.6).
Provenance: unknown.

571 CONCHA BELT, about 1970
Navajo
Leather belt with cast openwork
buckle; ten cast openwork
conchas, each set with elliptical
Morenci turquoise; twisted wire
decoration; 48, 7¼ (121.9, 5.7).
Provenance: Quivira Shop,
Santa Fe, New Mexico, 1973.

Not shown:

572 CONCHA BELT, 1950
Navajo
Twelve round conchas linked by
elliptical plaques; stamped
decoration; 22¾, 1½ (57.8, 3.8).
Provenance: Fred Harvey Co.,
Albuquerque, New Mexico, 1950s.

573 CONCHA BELT, about 1950
Navajo
Leather belt with cast openwork
buckle; nine cast conchas and
eight cast "butterfly" plaques;
stamped decoration; 35¼, 1¾
(89.5, 4.4).
Provenance: Turpen Trading Post,
Gallup, New Mexico, 1956.

574 CONCHA BELT, about 1960
Navajo
Leather belt with cast openwork
buckle; thirteen cast openwork
conchas; 34, 1⅞ (86.4, 4.8).
Provenance: Turpen Trading Post,
Gallup, New Mexico, 1960.

575 576
577 578

575 CONCHA, 1870–1880
   Navajo
   Single round concha; lozenge-
   shaped center opening; chased
   and stamped decoration; 3½ (8.9).
   Provenance: Turpen Trading Post,
   Gallup, New Mexico, 1961.

576 BELT BUCKLE, about 1930
   Navajo
   Rectangular sheet buckle; set
   with two elliptical turquoises in
   serrated bezels; stamped and
   chased decoration; 3 × 2½
   (7.6 × 6.4).
   Provenance: Quivira Shop,
   Santa Fe, New Mexico, 1973.

577 BELT BUCKLE, 1930s
   Navajo
   Maker's mark: G . N . M . and
   curved arrow.
   Rectangular sheet buckle; set
   with large lozenge-shaped
   Cerrillos turquoise; repoussé and
   stamped decoration; 3⅝ × 2¼
   (9.2 × 5.7).
   Provenance: Price's All Indian
   Shop, Albuquerque, New Mexico,
   1969.
   Bought as pawn.

578 BELT BUCKLE, about 1960
   Navajo
   Cast openwork buckle; set with
   two Lone Mountain turquoises;
   3 × 2⅜ (7.6 × 6).
   Provenance: Tom Bahti, Tucson,
   Arizona, 1965.

Not shown:

579 BELT BUCKLE, about 1930
Navajo
Rectangular buckle; set with two elliptical turquoises in serrated bezels; repoussé and stamped decoration; 3¾ × 3¼ (9.5 × 8.3).
Provenance: Clay Lockett, Gallup, New Mexico, 1953.
Stones are replacements.

580 BELT BUCKLE, about 1930
Navajo
Rectangular buckle; set with four elliptical Battle Mountain turquoises; stamped and repoussé decoration; 3¼ × 2½ (8.3 × 6.4).
Provenance: Fred Harvey Co., Albuquerque, New Mexico, 1965.
Bought as pawn.

581 BELT BUCKLE, about 1930
Navajo
Rectangular buckle; set with sixteen Lone Mountain turquoises; repoussé and stamped decoration; 3⅝ × 2¾ (9.2 × 7).
Provenance: Price's All Indian Shop, Albuquerque, New Mexico, 1966.

582 BELT BUCKLE, 1930s
Navajo
Rectangular buckle; set with six elliptical turquoises; stamped decoration; 2¾ × 2⅛ (7 × 5.4).
Provenance: Asa Glascock, Gallup, New Mexico, 1956.

583 BELT BUCKLE, about 1940
Navajo
Cast openwork buckle; 2¼ × 3 (5.7 × 7.6).
Provenance: George Rummage, Gallup, New Mexico, 1954.

584 BELT BUCKLE, 1940s
Navajo
Rectangular buckle; stamped decoration; 2¾ × 2¼ (7 × 5.7).
Provenance: Tom Bahti, Tucson, Arizona, 1965.

585 BELT BUCKLE, 1940s or later
Navajo
Cast openwork buckle; set with four round turquoise beads, filled with silver; 3¼ × 2¼ (8.3 × 5.7).
Provenance: George Rummage, Gallup, New Mexico, 1954.

586 BELT BUCKLE, about 1950
Navajo
Stamped: STERLING and thunderbird mark.
Elliptical "concha" buckle with square open center; hammered, punched, chased, and stamped decoration; 3 × 2½ (7.6 × 6.4).
Provenance: Fred Harvey Co., Albuquerque, New Mexico, 1954.

587 BELT BUCKLE, about 1950
Navajo
Elliptical buckle; set with elliptical turquoise; repoussé and stamped decoration; 3½ × 2½ (8.9 × 6.4).
Provenance: Tom Moore, Gallup, New Mexico, 1954.
Bought as pawn.

588 BELT BUCKLE, about 1950
Navajo
Maker's mark: M
Cast buckle in horseshoe shape; stamped decoration; 2 × 1¾ (5 × 4.4).
Provenance: Tom Moore, Gallup, New Mexico, 1953.

589 BELT BUCKLE, 1950s
Navajo
Cast openwork buckle; 3⅜ × 2½ (8.6 × 6.4).
Provenance: Turpen Trading Post, Gallup, New Mexico, 1960.
Bought as pawn.

590 BELT BUCKLE, 1950s
Navajo
Cast openwork buckle; 3½ × 2¾ (8.9 × 7).
Provenance: George Rummage, Gallup, New Mexico, 1957.

591 BELT BUCKLE, about 1950
Navajo
Rectangular buckle; stamped decoration; 1½ × 1⅛ (3.8 × 2.9).
Provenance: Fred Harvey Co., Albuquerque, New Mexico, 1950s.
Bought as pawn.

592 BELT BUCKLE, about 1950
Navajo
Cast buckle in horseshoe shape; stamped decoration; 2½ × 2½ (6.4 × 6.4).
Provenance: Tom Moore, Gallup, New Mexico, 1953.

593 BELT BUCKLE, 1950s
Navajo
Cast openwork buckle; 3¾ × 2¾ (9.5 × 7).
Provenance: unknown, 1956.

594 BELT BUCKLE, about 1960
Navajo
Cast openwork buckle; stamped decoration; 3¾ × 2¼ (9.5 × 5.7).
Provenance: Hagberg's, Gallup, New Mexico, 1965.
Bought as pawn.

595 BELT BUCKLE, 1960s
Navajo
Cast openwork buckle; "stamped" decoration in mold; 3 × 2 (7.6 × 5).
Provenance: Irma Bailey, Albuquerque, New Mexico, 1969.

Ketohs

Throughout the time the Navajo used the bow and arrow as a weapon, archers wore a leather band called a ketoh to protect their wrists from the sting of the bowstring. When metals became available—brass, copper, sheet tin, and finally silver—they began to attach decorative metal plaques to the leather. The earliest ketohs appear in photographs taken at Bosque Redondo in the 1860s. By the 1870s silver-mounted ketohs were common, and long after their use as wrist guards ceased, they continued to be made and worn as ornaments.

Both cast and wrought ketohs followed the general development in decorative techniques, becoming more ornate as time went on; however, the rectangular form of the silver mounting has remained unchanged since earliest days. Almost always the designs of these pieces focus on the center, where stones are frequently set and decorative lines converge. The surface is usually divided by diagonal or perpendicular lines into symmetrical quadrants, although a few interesting exceptions can be seen in the Doneghy collection. Ketohs are generally more massive in scale and decoration than other forms of silverwork and thus afford a good example of the sculptural quality of Navajo silver. They are made today primarily for the curio trade, but the old ones are still worn during various dances and ceremonies.

The measurement given is the height of the silver mounting.

J.B.W.
L.L.

596 597 598
599 600

596 KETOH, about 1910
Navajo
Sheet mounting on leather band;
set with single elliptical turquoise;
repoussé and stamped decoration;
3¾ (9.5).
Provenance: Chester Copman,
Santa Fe Gift Shop, Santa Fe,
New Mexico, 1961.

597 KETOH, 1890s
Navajo
Sheet mounting on leather band;
chased and stamped decoration;
four repoussé buttons on one
side; 3⅜ (8.6).
Provenance: Clay Lockett,
Tucson, Arizona, 1959.
Cf. Frank and Holbrook, p. 135.

598 KETOH, about 1900
Navajo
Sheet mounting on leather band;
set with single elliptical
turquoise; stamped decoration;
3⅝ (9.2).
Provenance: Tanner's, Scottsdale,
Arizona, 1976.
Turquoise is a later addition.

599 CHILD'S KETOH, 1890s
Navajo
Sheet mounting on leather band;
set with single elliptical turquoise;
repoussé and stamped decoration;
3⅛ (7.9).
Provenance: Taos Book Shop,
Taos, New Mexico, 1961.

600 KETOH, about 1900
Navajo
Sheet mounting on leather band;
set with one triangular and two
elliptical Battle Mountain
turquoises; repoussé and stamped
decoration; 4 (10.1).
Provenance: Packard's Trading
Post, Santa Fe, New Mexico,
1961.
Turquoises are a later addition.

601 602
603 604

601 KETOH, 1920s
Navajo
Cut into leather: HERBEI
Cast mounting on leather band;
set with one rectangular and four
oval Stennich turquoises; stamped
decoration; silver button as
fastener; 4¼ (10.8).
Provenance: Sewell's, Scottsdale,
Arizona, 1978.

602 KETOH, about 1930
Navajo
Cast mounting on leather band;
set with single cabochon Nevada
turquoise; 3½ (8.9).
Provenance: Eric Kohlberg,
Denver, Colorado, 1949; Margery
Bedinger collection.
Illustrated in Bedinger, p. 54,
fig. 21b.

603 KETOH, about 1920
Navajo
Cast openwork mounting on
leather band; set with five
elliptical cabochon turquoises
in serrated bezels; stamped
decoration; 3½ (8.9).

Provenance: Hubbell's Trading
Post, Ganado, Arizona, 1953.
Bought as pawn.

604 KETOH, about 1930
Navajo
Cast mounting on leather band
(perhaps an old wallet?); set with
single elliptical cabochon
turquoise; 3³⁄₁₆ (8).
Provenance: Crucita Cate (Santo
Domingo Pueblo), Santa Fe,
New Mexico, 1951.

Not shown:

605 KETOH, 1920s
Navajo
Cast openwork mounting on
leather band; set with one large
rectangular and two small round
Cerrillos turquoises; stamped
decoration; 4⅜ (11.1).
Provenance: Maisel's, Albuquerque, New Mexico, 1955.

606 KETOH, 1920s
Hopi
Cast openwork mounting on
leather band; set with single

round cabochon turquoise;
3⅝ (9.2).
Provenance: Chief Joe Secakuku,
Winslow, Arizona, 1953.

607 KETOH, 1930s
Navajo
Cast openwork mounting on
leather band; set with five
elliptical cabochon turquoises;
3½ (8.9).
Provenance: Turpen Trading Post,
Gallup, New Mexico, 1952.

608 KETOH, 1930s
Navajo
Cast mounting on leather band;
set with one round and two
elliptical turquoises; 4 (10.1).
Provenance: Turpen Trading Post,
Gallup, New Mexico, 1962.
Bought as pawn.

610
609 611
612

609 KETOH, about 1920
Navajo
Sheet mounting on leather band;
set with nine turquoises of various
shapes; repoussé and stamped
decoration; 3⅜ (8.6).
Provenance: W. S. Dutton,
Santa Fe, New Mexico, 1957.

610 KETOH, about 1940
Navajo
Sheet mounting on leather band;
set with single elliptical Nevada
turquoise; 3⅞ (9.8).
Provenance: Eric Kohlberg,
Denver, Colorado, 1956.

611 KETOH, about 1940
Navajo
Sheet mounting on leather band;
set with single elliptical
Cerrillos turquoise; repoussé and
stamped decoration; five dimes
on each side; 3⅜ (8.6).
Provenance: Eric Kolhberg,
Denver, Colorado, 1949.
Cf. Heard Museum, p. 42.

612 CHILD'S KETOH, 1930s or later
Navajo
Sheet mounting on leather band;
set with five elliptical Miami
turquoises; chased and stamped
decoration; 2½ (6.4).
Provenance: Albuquerque,
New Mexico, 1952.

Not shown:

613 CHILD'S KETOH, about 1930
Navajo
Sheet mounting; set with single
elliptical Blue Gem turquoise in
serrated bezel; repoussé and
stamped decoration; 2⅝ (6.7).
Provenance: Hubbell's Trading
Post, Winslow, Arizona, 1953.
Said to have been pawned.

614 KETOH, about 1940
Navajo
Sheet mounting on bracelet band;
set with single turquoise of
irregular shape; repoussé, chased,
and stamped decoration; 3¼ (8.3).
Provenance: Eric Kohlberg,
Denver, Colorado, 1948.

615 KETOH, about 1940
Navajo
Sheet mounting; set with single
elliptical Battle Mountain
turquoise; repoussé and stamped
decoration: 3¾ (9.5).
Provenance: Hubbell's Trading
Post, Winslow, Arizona, 1954.

616 617 618

616 KETOH, about 1950
     Hopi
     Made by Valjean Lomaheftewa;
     maker's mark: crescent moon.
     Hopi Silvercraft Guild mark.
     Sheet mounting on leather band;
     set with single elliptical Miami
     turquoise; bead wire, repoussé,
     and stamped decoration;
     3⁷/₁₆ (8.7).
     Provenance: Chief Joe Secakuku,
     Winslow, Arizona, 1953.

617 KETOH, about 1950
     Navajo
     Sheet mounting; repoussé and
     stamped decoration; 4 (10.1).
     Provenance: Clay Lockett, Gallup,
     New Mexico, 1953.

618 KETOH, 1930s–1940s
     Navajo
     Sheet mounting on leather band;
     set with five Miami turquoises;
     stamped and repoussé decoration;
     3½ (8.9).
     Provenance: Eric Kohlberg,
     Denver, Colorado, 1956.

Not shown:

619 KETOH, 1940s
     Navajo
     Sheet mounting on leather band;
     stamped decoration; 3⅝ (9.2).
     Provenance: Tesuque Trading
     Post, Santa Fe, New Mexico, 1954.

620 KETOH, 1940s
     Navajo
     Sheet mounting on leather band;
     set with single elliptical Miami
     turquoise; repoussé and stamped
     decoration; 4 (10.1).
     Provenance: Hubbell's Trading
     Post, Winslow, Arizona, 1952.

621 KETOH, about 1950
     Navajo
     Sheet mounting; set with fifteen
     elliptical Battle Mountain
     turquoises of graduated size;
     stamped decoration; 3⅝ (9.2).
     Provenance: Hubbell's Trading
     Post, Winslow, Arizona, 1953.

623

622   624

625

622 KETOH, about 1950
Navajo
Cast openwork mounting on
leather band; set with single
square turquoise drilled as a
bead; filed decoration; 3⅜ (8.6).
Provenance: Clay Lockett,
Tucson, Arizona, 1959.

623 KETOH, 1940s
Navajo
Cast openwork mounting on
leather band; set with single
triangular Cerrillos turquoise;
3⅝ (9.2).
Provenance: Fred Harvey Co.,
Albuquerque, New Mexico, 1953.
Similar to nos. 627 and 628.

624 KETOH, about 1960
Navajo
Navajo Arts and Crafts Guild tag.
Cast openwork mounting on
leather band; set with three
Morenci turquoises of irregular
shape; teardrop decoration;
3¹⁵⁄₁₆ (10).
Provenance: Rainbow Man,
Santa Fe, New Mexico, 1962.

625 CHILD'S KETOH, about 1970
Navajo
Cast openwork mounting;
stamped decoration; 2¼ (5.7).
Provenance: Packard's Trading
Post, Santa Fe, New Mexico, 1973.
Bought as pawn.
Cf. Mera, p. 60, pl. 6.

Not shown:

626 KETOH, 1940s
Navajo
Cast openwork mounting; set
with single elliptical cabochon
Royal Blue turquoise; 4 (10.1).
Provenance: Hubbell's Trading
Post, Winslow, Arizona, 1953.
Bought as pawn.

627 KETOH, 1940s
Navajo
Cast openwork mounting on
leather band; set with single
rectangular turquoise; six dimes
on each side; 3¼ (8.3).
Provenance: Fred Harvey Co.,
Albuquerque, New Mexico, 1952.
Similar to nos. 623 and 628.

628 KETOH, 1940s
Navajo
Cast openwork mounting; set
with single square Burnham
turquoise; 3³⁄₁₆ (8).
Provenance: Hanns Hogan,
Gallup, New Mexico, 1950(?).
Similar to nos. 623 and 627.

629 KETOH, about 1950
Navajo
Cast openwork mounting; set
with single elliptical Villa Grove
turquoise; 4 (10.1).
Provenance: Frances Quarles,
Taos, New Mexico, 1954.

630 KETOH, 1950s
Navajo
Cast openwork mounting on
leather band; set with triangular
Nevada turquoise; 3¾ (9.5).
Provenance: Price's All Indian
Shop, Albuquerque, New Mexico,
1962.

631 KETOH, 1950s
Navajo
Cast openwork mounting on
leather band; inlaid with ten
channel-set turquoises; 3⅝ (9.2).
Provenance: Turpen Trading Post,
Gallup, New Mexico, 1965.
Bought as pawn.

632 KETOH, about 1960
Navajo
Navajo Arts and Crafts Guild
stamp.
Cast openwork mounting on
leather band; stamped
decoration; 2⅞ (7.3).
Provenance: Rainbow Man,
Santa Fe, New Mexico, 1962.
Red ribbon at the New Mexico
State Fair, 1960.

633 CHILD'S KETOH, about 1960
Navajo
Cast openwork mounting on
leather band; 3 (7.6).
Provenance: Turpen Trading Post,
Gallup, New Mexico, 1965.
Bought as pawn.

634 KETOH, about 1960
Navajo
Cast openwork mounting; 3 (7.6).
Provenance: Packard's Trading
Post, Santa Fe, New Mexico, 1970.
Bought as pawn.

635 KETOH, about 1960
Navajo
Cast openwork mounting on
leather band; set with three
round turquoises; 3¼ (8.3).
Provenance: Turpen Trading Post,
Gallup, New Mexico, 1961.

636 KETOH, about 1970
Navajo
Cast openwork mounting on
leather band; set with single
Sleeping Beauty turquoise of
irregular shape; 3³⁄₁₆ (8).
Provenance: Treasure Chest,
Santa Fe, New Mexico, 1976.

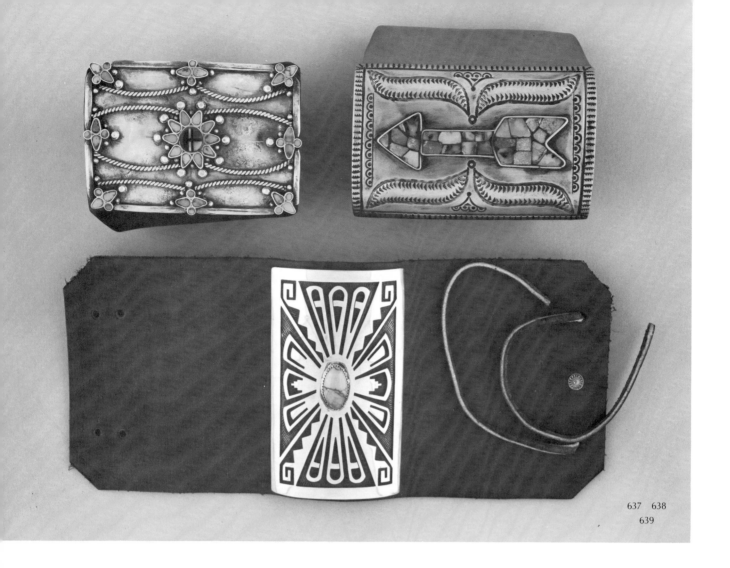

637 637
639

637 KETOH, about 1950
Zuni
Sheet mounting on leather band;
set with channel and inlay designs
of Morenci turquoises and red,
black, and white stones; twisted
wire and teardrop decoration;
3¾ (9.5).
Provenance: Hotevilla, Arizona,
1952.

638 KETOH, 1940s
Santo Domingo Pueblo
Sheet mounting on leather band;
set with large turquoise mosaic
inlay in the form of an arrow;
repoussé, chased, and stamped
decoration; 4¹⁄₁₆ (10.3).
Provenance: Original Curio Store,
Santa Fe, New Mexico, 1955.

639 KETOH, 1970s
Hopi
Made by Bobby Secakuku.
Hopi Silvercraft Guild mark on
separate silver disk.
Overlay mounting on leather
band; set with single elliptical
Fox turquoise in serrated bezel;
4 (10.1).
Provenance: Tewa Weavers,
Albuquerque, New Mexico, 1978.

Bags

Because their pants lacked pockets, Navajo men used to carry "pocket" items in a leather pouch hung from a strap over the shoulder. Such bags are frequently called medicine pouches, since medicine was sometimes carried in them. Photographs of the 1860s and 1870s show small, short-flap pouches with wide straps. They are decorated with silver buttons and many have beadwork designs at the edges and center. By 1880, beadwork had all but disappeared as silver buttons and cast ornaments appeared in greater and greater quantity. As silver decoration increased, the flaps were made longer than the pouches. Medicine pouches are rarely made today, and even the old ones are seen only on special occasions.

The height of the bag alone is given first, followed by the length from the bottom of the bag to the middle of the strap.

J.B.W.

640 641

640 BAG, about 1900
Navajo
Leather bag with cast ornament
and repoussé buttons on flap;
shell on thong closure; fluted and
hemispheric buttons on strap;
6¾ × 26¼ (17.2 × 66.3).
Provenance: W. S. Dutton,
Santa Fe, New Mexico, 1957.
Cf. Heard Museum, p. 39.

641 BAG, about 1935
Navajo
Leather flap without pouch; two
contemporary conchas and two
older "butterfly" ornaments;
leather strap with two "butterfly"
ornaments and sixty-five Mercury
dimes; 6¾ × 26 (17.2 × 66).
Provenance: On West, Gallup,
New Mexico, 1955.

150

642 643

642 BAG, 1925 or earlier
Navajo or Hopi
Stamped inside: C. S. Garcia,
Elko, Nevada
Leather bag with tooled floral
design; stamped and fluted button
ornaments; center ornament set
with single flat rectangular
turquoise; 6½ × 27 (16.5 × 68.5).
Provenance: Reese Vaughn,
Scottsdale, Arizona, 1960, who
bought it from Hopi chief
Tewequaptewa, Old Oraibi,
Arizona, in the 1930s.

643 BAG, 1900–1925
Navajo
Leather bag with stamped deco-
ration; hemispheric and fluted
buttons; 5½ × 23½ (14 × 58.2).
Provenance: Taos Book Shop,
Taos, New Mexico, 1956; Ralph
Meyer collection.

Not shown:

644 BAG, 1940s
Navajo
Leather bag with stamped and
fluted buttons; 6½ × 23½
(16.5 × 58.2).
Provenance: Taos Book Shop,
Taos, New Mexico, 1956.
Bought as pawn.

Dress Ornaments, Buttons, and Pins

The objects in this category all serve to decorate clothing. Buttons were not commonly used as fasteners in the early period of silverwork, but photographs from the end of the nineteenth century show some buttons being put to this use. Small decorative buttons, made by pounding a dime or a small silver disk into a die and thus producing a hollow hemisphere, were and are ubiquitous. They were attached to pants, blouses, pouches, bridles, and other items by means of a loop soldered onto the back. Rows of buttons outlined pouch straps as well as the collar edges, cuffs, and seams of blouses and shirts and even the sides of ketohs. By the end of the nineteenth century small buttons were often fluted with a file or a fluted die. Larger, conchalike buttons, often chased or stamped and sometimes set with turquoise, adorned moccasins and other articles. Later, many buttons were made by soldering loops to the backs of dimes, quarters, or (rarely) other coins. When the technique of casting silver was mastered in the 1870s, smiths added openwork buttons to their repertory.

After the turn of the century, the rows of small buttons evolved into larger dress ornaments. Some of these, such as "butterfly" plaques, were made in multiples and attached in rows to women's blouses. Others were made in pairs designed to be attached to collars or worn at the shoulders, replacing the earlier arrangement of small buttons.

Nineteenth-century Navajo women fastened their hand-woven garments together at the shoulder with manta pins. This early form, which is not represented in the Doneghy collection, disappeared as styles of dress changed. It was replaced in the early tourist period by silver and turquoise plaques with conventional pin clasps, which have never been widely used by the Navajo.

Where a single measurement is given it is the maximum dimension of the piece. For round buttons the diameter is given.

J.B.W.
L.L.

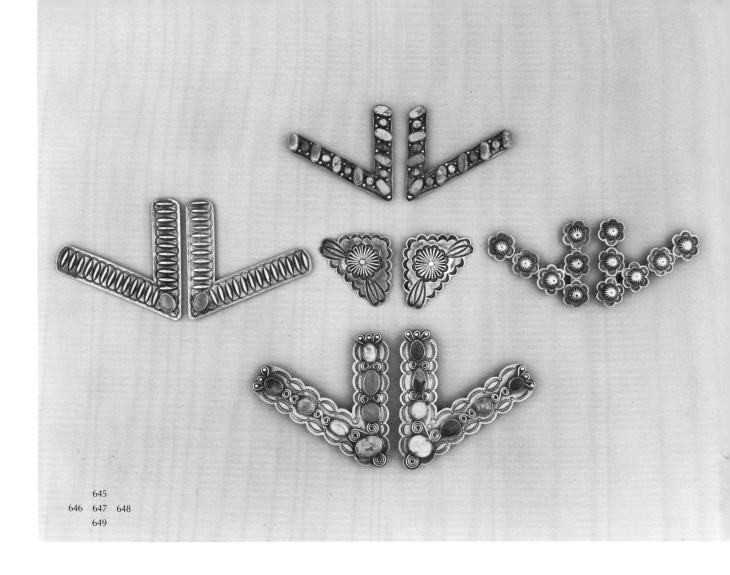

645
646 647 648
649

645 PAIR OF DRESS ORNAMENTS,
1930s
Navajo
Sheet collar points; each set with
fifteen round and elliptical Battle
Mountain turquoises; teardrop
decoration; 3¼ (8.3).
Provenance: Fred Harvey Co.,
Albuquerque, New Mexico, 1960.

646 PAIR OF DRESS ORNAMENTS,
about 1940
Navajo
Sheet collar points; each set with
single elliptical turquoise; repoussé
and stamped decoration; 3⅝ (9.2).
Provenance: unknown, 1961.
Bought as pawn.

647 PAIR OF DRESS ORNAMENTS,
about 1940
Navajo
Sheet collar points; repoussé and
stamped decoration; 2¼ (5.7).
Provenance: Hubbell's Trading
Post, Winslow, Arizona, 1953.
Bought as pawn.

648 PAIR OF DRESS ORNAMENTS,
about 1930
Navajo
Sheet collar points; each overlaid
with six buttons; stamped
decoration; 3 (7.6).
Provenance: Turpen Trading Post,
Gallup, New Mexico.
Bought as pawn.

649 PAIR OF DRESS ORNAMENTS,
1930s
Navajo
Sheet collar points; each set with
seven elliptical turquoises;
stamped, spiral wire, and teardrop
decoration; 4 (10.1).
Provenance: Turpen Trading Post,
Gallup, New Mexico, 1956.
Bought as pawn.

Not shown:

650 PAIR OF DRESS ORNAMENTS,
about 1930
Navajo
Sheet collar points; each set with
single elliptical cabochon
turquoise; repoussé and stamped
decoration; 4 (10.1).
Provenance: Taos Book Shop,
Taos, New Mexico, 1954.
Bought as pawn.

651 PAIR OF DRESS ORNAMENTS,
about 1930
Navajo
Sheet collar points; stamped and
repoussé decoration: 4¹⁄₁₆ (10.2).
Provenance: unknown, 1961.

652 PAIR OF DRESS ORNAMENTS,
about 1930
Navajo
Sheet collar points; one set with
sixteen Sleeping Beauty turquoises,
the other with seventeen of the
same; stamped decoration;
3⅝ (9.2).
Provenance: Tanner's, Scottsdale,
Arizona, 1976.

653 PAIR OF DRESS ORNAMENTS,
1930s
Navajo
Sheet collar points; each set with
one large and three small round
Sleeping Beauty turquoises;
repoussé and stamped decoration;
3¾ (9.5).
Provenance: Kachina House,
Scottsdale, Arizona, 1960.
Cf. Frank and Holbrook, p. 127.

654 PAIR OF DRESS ORNAMENTS,
about 1940
Navajo
Sheet collar points; repoussé and
stamped decoration; 2⅜ (6).
Provenance: Turpen Trading
Post, Gallup, New Mexico, 1963.
One cracked and repaired.

655 PAIR OF DRESS ORNAMENTS,
about 1940
Navajo
Sheet collar points; each set with
fifteen small round turquoises;
stamped decoration; 3½ (8.9).
Provenance: Price's All Indian
Shop, Albuquerque, New Mexico,
1961.

656 PAIR OF DRESS ORNAMENTS,
about 1940
Navajo
Sheet collar points; repoussé and
stamped decoration; 3¾ (9.5).
Provenance: unknown, 1961.
Cf. Frank and Holbrook, p. 127.

657 PAIR OF DRESS ORNAMENTS,
about 1940
Navajo
Sheet collar points overlaid with
double twisted wire and teardrops;
4 (10.2).
Provenance: Hanns Hogan,
Gallup, New Mexico, 1953.
Bought as pawn.
Cf. Heard Museum, p. 30.

658 PAIR OF DRESS ORNAMENTS,
about 1940
Navajo
Sheet collar points; repoussé and
stamped decoration; 3¾ (9.5).
Provenance: Price's All Indian
Shop, Albuquerque, New Mexico,
1961.

659 PAIR OF DRESS ORNAMENTS,
about 1945
Navajo
Dapped sheet collar points;
stamped decoration; 2¾ (7).
Provenance: Price's All Indian
Shop, Albuquerque, New Mexico,
1968.

661

660   662

663 664

660 PAIR OF DRESS ORNAMENTS,
1950s
Navajo
Scallop-edged sheet bars; repoussé
and stamped decoration; 3¼ (8.3).
Provenance: Richardson Trading
Co., Gallup, New Mexico, 1965.

661 PAIR OF DRESS ORNAMENTS,
about 1920
Navajo
Cast openwork bars; stamped
decoration; 2¾ (7).
Provenance: Fred Harvey Co.,
Santa Fe, New Mexico, 1955.
Bought as pawn.

662 PAIR OF DRESS ORNAMENTS,
about 1920–1930
Navajo
Sheet bars; stamped and repoussé
decoration; 3½ (8.9).
Provenance: Taos Book Shop,
Taos, New Mexico, 1954.
Bought as pawn.
Cf. Mera, p. 93, pl. 2.

663 PAIR OF DRESS ORNAMENTS,
about 1940
Navajo
Sheet bars; each set with two
elliptical Miami turquoises;
stamped decoration; 4¼ (10.8).
Provenance: Hubbell's Trading
Post, Winslow, Arizona, 1953.
Bought as pawn.
Probably made by Mark Chee.

664 PAIR OF DRESS ORNAMENTS,
1930s
Navajo
Sheet bars; each set with six
elliptical turquoises; twisted wire
and stamped decoration; 4½ (11.4).
Provenance: Hubbell's Trading
Post, Winslow, Arizona, 1952.
Bought as pawn.

Not shown:

665 PAIR OF DRESS ORNAMENTS,
about 1930
Navajo
Sheet bars; repoussé and stamped
decoration; 3¼ (8.3).
Provenance: Fred Harvey Co.,
Albuquerque, New Mexico, 1960.

666 PAIR OF DRESS ORNAMENTS,
about 1930
Navajo
Sheet bars; each set with ten small
round turquoises; twisted wire and
stamped decoration; 3¾ (9.5).
Provenance: Hubbell's Trading
Post, Winslow, Arizona, 1952.
Bought as pawn.

667 PAIR OF DRESS ORNAMENTS,
about 1930
Navajo
Sheet bars; repoussé and stamped
decoration; 2¾ (7).
Provenance: Chester Copman,
Santa Fe Gift Shop, Santa Fe,
New Mexico, 1957.
Bought as pawn.

668 PAIR OF DRESS ORNAMENTS,
about 1930
Navajo
Sheet bars; each set with three
small round turquoises; repoussé
and stamped decoration; 4¾ (12).
Provenance: Fenn Galleries,
Santa Fe, New Mexico, 1979.

669 PAIR OF DRESS ORNAMENTS,
1930s
Navajo
Sheet bars; repoussé decoration;
3⅝ (9.2).
Provenance: Taos Book Shop,
Taos, New Mexico, 1963.

670 PAIR OF DRESS ORNAMENTS,
about 1940
Navajo
Sheet bars; repoussé and stamped
decoration; 3⅝ (9.2).
Provenance: Richardson Trading
Co., Gallup, New Mexico, 1965.

671 672 673 674
675 676 677
678 679 680 681

671 PAIR OF DRESS ORNAMENTS,
1930s
Navajo
Elliptical buttons; each set with
single round turquoise; repoussé
decoration; 1½ (3.8).
Provenance: Fred Harvey Co.,
Albuquerque, New Mexico.

672 PAIR OF DRESS ORNAMENTS,
about 1950
Navajo
Sheet bars; repoussé decoration;
2¾ (7).
Provenance: Bruckman, Winslow,
Arizona, 1955.

673 DRESS ORNAMENT, 1940s
Navajo
Cast openwork ornament; set with
single elliptical turquoise; 1½ × 2¼
(3.8 × 5.7).
Provenance: Fred Harvey Co.,
Albuquerque, New Mexico.
Bought as pawn.

674 SET OF EIGHT BUTTONS,
about 1910
Navajo
Round repoussé fluted buttons;
½ (1.3).
Provenance: unknown.

675 SET OF TWENTY–FOUR
BUTTONS, 1930s
Navajo
Round fluted buttons; ½ (1.3).
Provenance: Hanns Hogan,
Gallup, New Mexico, 1953.

676 DRESS ORNAMENT, 1940s
Navajo
Sheet "butterfly" ornament;
stamped and repoussé decoration;
1¾ (4.4).
Provenance: unknown.

677 DRESS ORNAMENT, 1930s–1940s
Navajo
Sheet "butterfly" ornament; set
with single small round turquoise;
stamped and repoussé decoration;
1⅜ (3.5).
Provenance: Fred Harvey Co.,
Albuquerque, New Mexico, 1952.
Bought as pawn.

678 SET OF 156 BUTTONS, about 1920
Navajo
Round repoussé fluted buttons;
⅜ (1).
Provenance: Turpen Trading Post,
Gallup, New Mexico, 1961.

679 SET OF TEN DRESS ORNAMENTS,
1940s
Navajo
Sheet "butterfly" ornaments;
repoussé and stamped decoration;
1 (2.5).
Provenance: Hanns Hogan,
Gallup, New Mexico, 1953.

680 SET OF SIX DRESS ORNAMENTS,
1930s
Navajo
Sheet "butterfly" ornaments;
stamped and repoussé decoration;
1 × 2¼ (2.5 × 5.7).
Provenance: unknown.

681 GROUP OF THREE DRESS
ORNAMENTS, 1930s
Navajo
Sheet bars; repoussé decoration;
1 × 1½ (2.5 × 3.8).
Provenance: unknown.
Cf. Frank and Holbrook, p. 127.

Not shown:

682 PAIR OF BUTTONS, about 1910
Navajo
Round buttons; each set with
small round turquoise; ⅜ (1).
Provenance: unknown.

683 GROUP OF THIRTEEN BUTTONS,
about 1910
Navajo
Elliptical scallop-edged buttons;
stamped decoration; ⅝ (1.6).
Provenance: Fred Harvey Co.,
Albuquerque, New Mexico, 1953.
Cf. Frank and Holbrook, p. 195.

684 SET OF SIX BUTTONS, about 1920
Navajo
Round repoussé fluted buttons;
⅝ (1.6).
Provenance: unknown.

685 BUTTON, about 1920
Navajo
Hexagonal button; repoussé
decoration; ½ (1.3).
Provenance: unknown.

686 GROUP OF SIX BUTTONS, 1920s
Navajo
Round buttons; stamped
decoration; 1 (2.5).
Provenance: unknown.

687 GROUP OF FOUR BUTTONS,
1920s
Navajo
Round buttons; repoussé and
stamped decoration; 1 (2.5).
Provenance: unknown.

688 GROUP OF TEN BUTTONS, 1920s
Navajo
Round buttons; stamped
decoration; ¾ (1.9).
Provenance: unknown.

689 DRESS ORNAMENT, about 1930
Navajo
Sheet bar; set with three small
round turquoises; repoussé and
stamped decoration; 2⅜ (6).
Provenance: unknown.

690 SET OF THIRTY–ONE BUTTONS,
1930s
Navajo
Round fluted buttons; ½ (1.3).
Provenance: George Rummage,
Gallup, New Mexico, 1954.

691 SET OF EIGHTEEN BUTTONS,
1930s
Navajo
Round repoussé fluted buttons
with flat rim; stamped decoration;
⁹⁄₁₆ (1.4).
Provenance: unknown.

692 SET OF SEVENTEEN BUTTONS,
1930s
Navajo
Round repoussé fluted buttons;
½ (1.3).
Provenance: unknown.

693 GROUP OF FOUR BUTTONS,
1930s
Navajo
Round buttons; stamped
decoration; 1 (2.5).
Provenance: unknown.

694 PAIR OF BUTTONS, 1940s
Navajo
Round buttons; each set with
small round turquoise; stamped
decoration; ⅝ (1.6).
Provenance: unknown.
Cf. Mera, p. 91, pl. 1.

695 BUTTON, 1940s
Navajo
Round button; set with single
small round turquoise; stamped
decoration; ¾ (1.9).
Provenance: Fred Harvey Co.,
Albuquerque, New Mexico, 1956.
Bought as pawn.

696 GROUP OF TWO DRESS
ORNAMENTS, 1940s
Navajo
Cast bars; appliqué decoration;
each about 3 × ½ (7.6 × 1.3).
Provenance: Turpen Trading Post,
Gallup, New Mexico, 1953.

697 SET OF SEVEN BUTTONS, 1940s
Navajo
Round buttons; stamped
decoration; ½ (1.3).
Provenance: unknown.

698 SET OF TEN BUTTONS, 1940s
Navajo
Round repoussé fluted buttons;
½ (1.3).
Provenance: George Rummage,
Gallup, New Mexico, 1954.

699 SET OF SEVEN BUTTONS,
about 1950
Navajo
Elliptical buttons; two set with
single small round turquoises;
repoussé decoration; 1 (2.5).
Provenance: Bruckman, Winslow,
Arizona, 1954.

700 SET OF SIX BUTTONS, about 1960
Navajo
Round buttons; stamped
decoration; ½ (1.3).
Provenance: unknown.

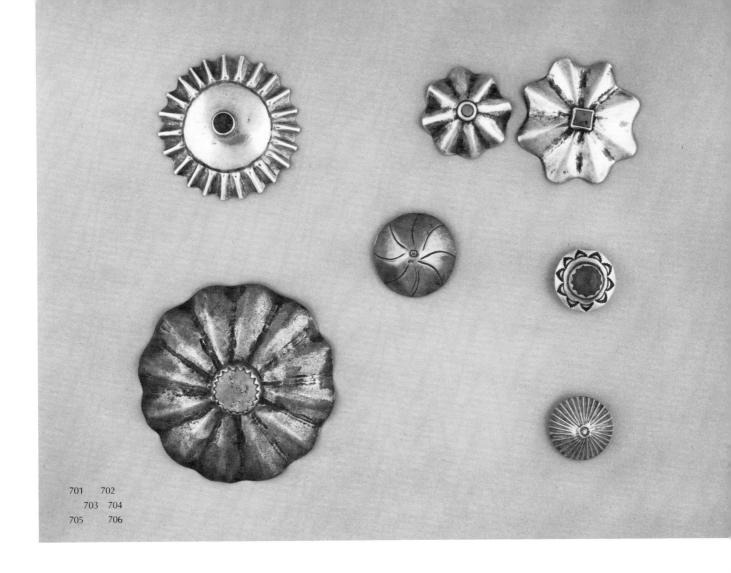

701 702
703 704
705 706

701 BUTTON, about 1910–1920
     Navajo
     Round button with fluted outer
     rim; set with small round
     turquoise; 1¾ (4.4).
     Provenance: Fred Harvey Co.,
     Albuquerque, New Mexico.

702 SET OF THREE BUTTONS,
     about 1910
     Navajo
     Round fluted buttons of graduated
     size; each set with single
     turquoise; 1 (2.5), 1½ (3.8), and
     1⅝ (4.1).
     Provenance: Fred Harvey Co.,
     Albuquerque, New Mexico.
     Bought as pawn.

703 BUTTON, about 1900
     Navajo
     Round repoussé button; chased
     and stamped decoration; 1 (2.5).
     Provenance: Fred Harvey Co.,
     Albuquerque, New Mexico.
     Bought as pawn.

704 PAIR OF BUTTONS, about 1920
     Navajo
     Round buttons; each set with
     single round cabochon turquoise
     in serrated bezel; stamped
     decoration; ¾ (1.9).
     Provenance: unknown.

705 PAIR OF BUTTONS, about 1900
     Navajo
     Round fluted buttons; each set
     with single round turquoise in
     serrated bezel; 2⅜ (6).
     Provenance: Gallup, New Mexico,
     1956.

706 BUTTON, about 1910
     Navajo
     Round repoussé fluted button;
     chased and filed decoration;
     ⅝ (1.6).
     Provenance: unknown.

Not shown:

707 PAIR OF BUTTONS, about 1920
     Navajo
     Round scallop-edged repoussé
     buttons; stamped decoration;
     1¾ (4.4).
     Provenance: Fred Harvey Co.,
     Albuquerque, New Mexico, 1956.

708 PAIR OF BUTTONS, about 1920
     Navajo
     Round repoussé fluted buttons;
     stamped decoration; 1¾ (4.4).
     Provenance: unknown.

710
722 711
721 712
720 709 713
719 714
715
718 716
717

709 PAIR OF BUTTONS, about 1940
Navajo
Round repoussé fluted buttons;
each set with single Arizona
turquoise; stamped decoration;
2⅜ (6).
Provenance: George Rummage,
Gallup, New Mexico, 1954.

710 BUTTON, about 1920
Navajo
Round repoussé button; set with
single small round turquoise;
1 (2.5).
Provenance: Hubbell's Trading
Post, Winslow, Arizona, 1953.
Bought as pawn.

711 PAIR OF BUTTONS, about 1910
Navajo
Elliptical scallop-edged buttons;
stamped decoration; 1½ (3.8).
Provenance: unknown.

712 BUTTON, about 1910
Navajo
Round repoussé fluted button; set
with small round turquoise;
stamped decoration; 1¼ (3.2).
Provenance: unknown.

713 BUTTON, 1920s
Navajo
Round scallop-edged button; set
with single small round turquoise;
repoussé and stamped decoration;
1¼ (3.2).
Provenance: Hubbell's Trading
Post, Winslow, Arizona, 1953.
Bought as pawn.

714 PAIR OF BUTTONS, about 1920
Navajo
Round repoussé buttons; each set
with single small round turquoise;
stamped decoration; 1 (2.5).
Provenance: Chief Joe Secakuku,
Winslow, Arizona, 1953.

715 SET OF THREE BUTTONS,
about 1930
Navajo
Round buttons; each with seven
round turquoises set in cluster
design on sheet mounting; ¾ (1.9).
Provenance: Hubbell's Trading
Post, Winslow, Arizona, 1953.

716 BUTTON, 1920s
Navajo
Round repoussé button; chased
and stamped decoration; ¾ (1.9).
Provenance: Hanns Hogan,
Gallup, New Mexico, 1953.

717 PAIR OF BUTTONS, 1920s–1930s
Navajo
Round buttons; each set with
small round turquoise; stamped
decoration; 1¼ (3.2).
Provenance: George Rummage,
Gallup, New Mexico, 1954.

718 PAIR OF BUTTONS, 1920s
Navajo
Round buttons; each set with
round turquoise; stamped
decoration; 1¼ (3.1).
Provenance: George Rummage,
Gallup, New Mexico, 1956.

719 BUTTON, about 1920
Navajo
Elliptical button; set with elliptical
turquoise; stamped decoration;
1½ (3.8).
Provenance: Hanns Hogan,
Gallup, New Mexico, 1953.

720 PAIR OF BUTTONS, 1920s
Navajo
Round scallop-edged buttons;
repoussé and stamped decoration;
1½ (3.8).
Provenance: Fred Harvey Co.,
Albuquerque, New Mexico.
Bought as pawn.

721 SET OF SIX BUTTONS, 1930s
Navajo
Round scallop-edged buttons;
repoussé decoration; 1 (2.5).
Provenance: Hanns Hogan,
Gallup, New Mexico, 1953.
Bought as pawn.

722 PAIR OF BUTTONS, about 1920
Navajo
Round buttons; stamped
decoration; 1⅜ (3.5).
Provenance: Fred Harvey Co.,
Albuquerque, New Mexico.

Not shown:

723 GROUP OF FIVE BUTTONS, 1920
Navajo
Round repoussé buttons; stamped
decoration; 1¼ (3.2).
Provenance: Hubbell's Trading
Post, Winslow, Arizona, 1953.

724 GROUP OF FOUR BUTTONS,
1930s
Navajo
Round buttons; stamped
decoration; ⅝ (1.6).
Provenance: Fred Harvey Co.,
Albuquerque, New Mexico.
Bought as pawn.

725 SET OF THREE BUTTONS, 1930s
Navajo
Round buttons; each set with
eleven round turquoises; teardrop
and twisted wire decoration;
1 (2.5).
Provenance: Hubbell's Trading
Post, Winslow, Arizona, 1953.

726 SET OF FIVE BUTTONS, 1930s
Navajo
Round buttons; stamped
decoration; ¾ (1.9).
Provenance: unknown.

727 PAIR OF BUTTONS, 1930s
Navajo
Round scallop-edged repoussé
buttons; stamped decoration;
1½ (3.8).
Provenance: Eleanor Beddell,
Santa Fe, New Mexico, 1957.

728 PAIR OF BUTTONS, 1940s
Navajo
Round scallop-edged repoussé
buttons; each set with single
turquoise; stamped decoration;
2¼ (5.7).
Provenance: Irma Bailey,
Albuquerque, New Mexico, 1969.

729   730

731

732

733   734   735

729 PAIR OF BUTTONS, about 1960
Cochiti Pueblo
Made by Joe Quintana; maker's
mark: JHQ
Round buttons; stamped
decoration; 1¾ (4.4).
Provenance: unknown.

730 PAIR OF BUTTONS, about 1950
Navajo
Cast openwork buttons; each set
with single elliptical turquoise;
2 (5.1).
Provenance: Fred Harvey Co.,
Albuquerque, New Mexico, 1962.
Bought as pawn.

731 SET OF NINE BUTTONS, 1940s
Navajo
Coin buttons (three quarters, six
dimes); ¾ (1.4) and ⅜ (1).
Provenance: unknown.

732 BUTTON, 1940s
Navajo
Rectangular button; filed and
stamped decoration; 1 (2.5).
Provenance: unknown.

733 BUTTON, 1940s
Navajo
Round scallop-edged button; set
with small round turquoise;
stamped decoration; ¾ (1.9).
Provenance: unknown.

734 BUTTON, 1940s
Navajo
Cast openwork button; set with
small round turquoise; ¾ (1.9).
Provenance: unknown.

735 SET OF THREE BUTTONS, 1950s
Hopi
Round buttons; overlay
decoration; ¾ (1.9).
Provenance: unknown.

162

Not shown:

736 SET OF THREE BUTTONS, 1940s
Navajo
Cast buttons; each set with
single round turquoise; 1½ (3.8).
Provenance: unknown.

737 SET OF SIX BUTTONS, about 1950
Navajo
Cast openwork buttons; ¾ (4.4).
Provenance: unknown.

738 SET OF FIFTEEN BUTTONS,
about 1950
Navajo
Round buttons; stamped
decoration; 1⅛ (2.9).
Provenance: unknown.

739 GROUP OF NINETEEN
BUTTONS, about 1950
Navajo
Round repoussé buttons; stamped
decoration; from ½ (1.3) to
1½ (3.8).
Provenance: Santa Fe Indian
School, Santa Fe, New Mexico,
1954.

740 SET OF SIX BUTTONS, about 1950
Navajo
Round buttons; stamped
decoration; 1 (2.5).
Provenance: unknown.

741 PAIR OF BUTTONS, about 1950
Navajo
Round buttons; chased and
stamped decoration; 1¼ (3.2).
Provenance: unknown.

742 BUTTON, about 1950
Navajo
Round scallop-edged button; set
with single round turquoise;
stamped and filed decoration;
1½ (3.8).
Provenance: unknown.

743 GROUP OF TWO BUTTONS,
about 1950
Navajo
Round scallop-edged buttons;
stamped decoration; ¾ (1.9).
Provenance: unknown.

744 GROUP OF TWO BUTTONS,
about 1950
Navajo
Round scalloped-edged buttons;
each set with small round
turquoise; 1 (2.5).
Provenance: unknown.

745 BUTTON, about 1950
Navajo
Round fluted button; set with
small round turquoise in serrated
bezel; ¾ (1.9).
Provenance: Fred Harvey Co.,
Albuquerque, New Mexico.

746 SET OF THREE BUTTONS, about
1950
Navajo
Cast openwork buttons; each set
with elliptical cabochon
turquoise; 1¼ (2.9).
Provenance: unknown.

747 PAIR OF BUTTONS, about 1950
Navajo
Cast openwork buttons; each set
with single square turquoise;
1⅝ (4.1).
Provenance: Price's All Indian
Shop, Albuquerque, New Mexico.

748 PAIR OF BUTTONS, about 1950
Navajo
Round die-fluted buttons; each
set with single turquoise;
1¾ (4.4).
Provenance: George Rummage,
Gallup, New Mexico, 1954.

749 BUTTON, 1950s
Navajo
Cast openwork button; set with
small round turquoise; ½ (1.3).
Provenance: unknown.

750 PAIR OF BUTTONS, 1950s
Navajo
Round buttons; stamped
decoration; ⅝ (1.6).
Provenance: Fred Harvey Co.,
Albuquerque, New Mexico.

751 PAIR OF BUTTONS, about 1950
Navajo
Round buttons; repoussé and
stamped decoration; ⅝ (1.6).
Provenance: unknown.

752 SET OF FIVE BUTTONS, 1950s
Navajo
Round scallop-edged buttons;
each set with small round
turquoise; ⅜ (1).
Provenance: unknown.

753
754 754
755
756

753 PIN, 1930s–1940s
      Hopi
      Pin in the form of a butterfly;
      set with twelve small round Lone
      Mountain turquoises; stamped
      decoration; 2¾ (7).
      Provenance: unknown.

754 PAIR OF PINS, 1940s
      Navajo
      Bar pin; channel-set with three
      clusters of seven small round
      turquoises each; teardrop and
      repoussé decoration; ½ × 2¼
      (1.3 × 5.7).
      Provenance: unknown.
      Bought as pawn.

755 PIN, about 1930
      Navajo
      Sheet mounting; set with three
      large elliptical turquoises in
      serrated bezels; three "rays" on
      each side, set with round
      cabochon turquoises; teardrop,
      bent wire, and twisted wire
      decoration; 1½ × 3⅜ (3.8 × 8.6).
      Provenance: unknown.

756 PIN, about 1935
      Navajo
      Sheet mounting; set with large
      turquoises; teardrop, twisted wire,
      and bent wire decoration;
      2¼ × 3¾ (5.7 × 9.5).
      Provenance: unknown.

Not shown:

757 PIN, about 1935
Navajo
Cast openwork pin; set with large
elliptical turquoise in serrated
bezel; 2¼ × 3 (5.7 × 7.6).
Provenance: unknown.

758 PIN, about 1935
Navajo
Bar pin; repoussé and stamped
decoration; 1 × 3¹⁵⁄₁₆ (2.5 × 8.4).
Provenance: unknown.

759 PIN, about 1935
Zuni
Sheet pin; set with eight small
elliptical turquoises in serrated
bezels; twisted wire and teardrop
decoration; ⅜ × 2 (1 × 5.1).
Provenance: unknown.

760 PIN, 1930s
Zuni
Bar pin; set with twelve small
round Miami turquoises;
flattened twisted wire and
teardrop decoration; ¼ × 2¾
(0.6 × 7).
Provenance: unknown.

761 PAIR OF PINS, 1930s
Hopi
Sheet pins in the shape of a
butterfly; wire and stamped
decoration; 2⅛ (5.4).
Provenance: unknown.

762 PIN, about 1940
Navajo
Sheet cross; set with nine round
Lone Mountain turquoises;
2⅜ (6).
Provenance: Chief Joe Secakuku,
Winslow, Arizona, 1954.

763 PIN, about 1940
Navajo
Cast openwork pin; set with
single rectangular turquoise;
1¾ × 4¾ (4.4 ×12.1).
Provenance: unknown.

764 PAIR OF PINS, 1940s
Navajo
Bar pin; channel-set with two
clusters of seven small round
turquoises each; teardrop and
repoussé decoration; 3 (7.6).
Provenance: Turpen Trading Post,
Gallup, New Mexico, 1952.
Similar to no. 754.

765
766 767 768

765 PIN, about 1950
Cochiti Pueblo
Made by Joe Quintana; maker's
mark: JHQ
Sheet pin in "butterfly" shape;
set with single rectangular
Number 8 spiderweb turquoise;
stamped decoration; ¾ × 2¼
(1.9 × 5.7).
Provenance: unknown.

766 PIN, 1950s
Hopi
Made by Clarence Lomayestwa;
maker's mark: ↓
Hopi Silvercraft Guild mark.
Round pin; overlay decoration;
2 (5.1).
Provenance: unknown.

767 PIN, 1950s
Zuni
Round pin; set with fifty-eight
round and oval Lone Mountain
turquoises in a cluster; teardrop
decoration; 2¼ (5.7).
Provenance: unknown.

768 PIN, 1970s
Navajo
Cast pin in the form of a winged
creature; set with two elliptical
turquoises; 2¾ × 1¹¹⁄₁₆ (7 × 4.3).
Provenance: unknown.

Not shown:

769 PIN, about 1940
Navajo
Cast openwork pin; 1 × 2¼
(2.5 × 5.7).
Provenance: Tom Moore, Gallup,
New Mexico, 1953.

770 PIN, 1940s
Navajo
Eliptical pin; set with elliptical
petrified wood, surrounded by
sixteen round Blue Gem and
Lone Mountain turquoises;
twisted wire and appliqué decoration; 1½ × 2⅝ (3.8 × 6.6).
Provenance: unknown.

771 PIN, 1940s
Navajo
Pin in the shape of an insect; set
with single elliptical turquoise;
twisted wire and stamped decoration; 1¾ × 1½ (4.4 × 3.8).
Provenance: unknown.

772 PIN, 1950
Navajo
Carinated and double twisted
wires in the form of a naja;
repoussé decoration at terminals;
2⅛ (5.4).
Provenance: unknown.

773 PIN, about 1950
Navajo
Sheet pin of sunburst form with
thirteen rays; set with round
Number 8 turquoise in center;
bead wire decoration; 3¼ (8.3).
Provenance: Tom Moore, Gallup,
New Mexico.

774 PIN, 1950s
Navajo
Sheet pin with oval pendant;
both set with triangular Miami
turquoise; stamped decoration;
1⅝ × 1½ (4.1 × 3.8).
Provenance: unknown.
Decoration similar to no. 491.

775 PIN, 1960
Navajo
Cast pin in the form of a naja;
set with four turquoises in
serrated bezels; stamped decoration; 3½ × 2¹⁄₁₆ (8.9 × 5.2).
Provenance: unknown.

776 PIN, 1960s
Navajo
Made by Johnny Pablo.
Sheet pin in the form of knife-
wing god; stamped decoration;
1¼ × 1¾ (3.2 × 4.4).
Provenance: Price's All Indian
Shop, Albuquerque, New Mexico,
1970.

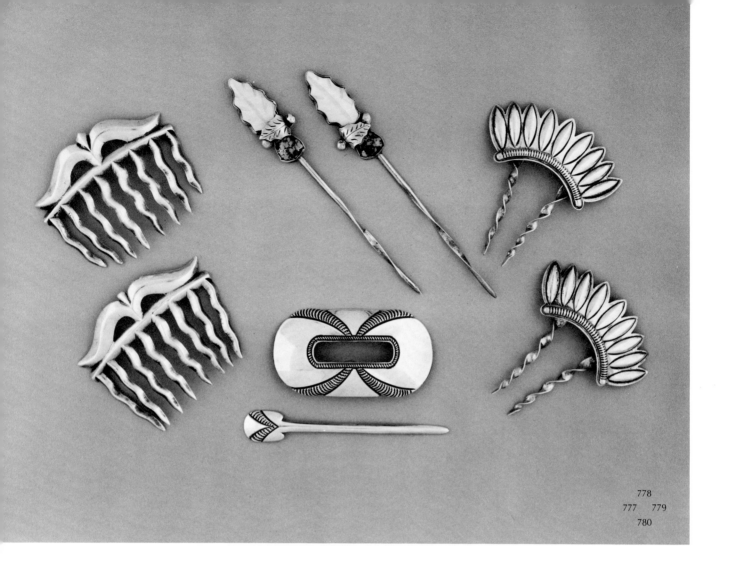

778
777   779
780

777 PAIR OF HAIR ORNAMENTS,
     about 1950
     Navajo
     Cast openwork combs; 2½ × 2¾
     (6.4 × 7).
     Provenance: unknown.

778 PAIR OF HAIR ORNAMENTS,
     about 1960
     Probably Zuni
     Maker's mark: R. PLATERO
     Stamped: HANDMADE
     Half-round wire pins; each set
     with abalone carved in the form
     of a leaf and single Persian
     turquoise of irregular shape;
     teardrop and appliqué decoration;
     5½ (14).
     Provenance: unknown.

779 PAIR OF HAIR ORNAMENTS,
     about 1950
     Navajo
     Double sheet prongs on curved
     sheet mounting; repoussé
     decoration; 3 (7.6).
     Provenance: unknown.

780 HAIR ORNAMENT, about 1950
     Navajo
     Elliptical sheet barrette; stamped
     and repoussé decoration;
     matching pin; 3 × 1¾ (7.6 × 4.4).
     Provenance: unknown.

Not shown:

781 PAIR OF HAIR ORNAMENTS,
     about 1935
     Navajo
     Two twisted half-round wire
     prongs on sheet mounting in
     crescent shape; stamped and
     filed decoration; 4⅝ (11.7).
     Provenance: unknown.

782 PAIR OF HAIR ORNAMENTS,
     about 1940
     Navajo
     Two twisted sheet prongs on
     sheet mounting in crescent shape;
     stamped and filed decoration;
     4¼ (10.8).
     Provenance: unknown.

783 PAIR OF HAIR ORNAMENTS,
     about 1950
     Navajo
     Two twisted sheet prongs on

sheet mounting in crescent form;
stamped and filed decoration;
3⅛ (7.9).
Provenance: unknown.

784 HAIR ORNAMENT, about 1950
     Navajo
     Dapped sheet band; stamped
     decoration; 14½ (37.9).
     Provenance: unknown.

785 HAIR ORNAMENT, 1950s
     Navajo
     Triple band of square wire; set
     with four elliptical turquoises at
     apex (one on side missing);
     12 (30.5).
     Provenance: unknown.

786 HAIR ORNAMENT, about
     1955–1960
     Navajo
     Sheet barette in crescent form;
     set with six oval Lone Mountain
     turquoises; appliqué decoration;
     matching pin; 3⅜ (8.6).
     Provenance: Fred Harvey Co.,
     Albuquerque, New Mexico.
     Bought as pawn.

787 788

787 HATBAND, 1930–1940
Navajo
Sheet band; clasp set with one
elliptical and five small round
turquoises (one missing); stamped
decoration; 7⅜ (18.8).
Provenance: Turpen Trading Post,
Gallup, New Mexico, about 1953.

788 HATBAND, 1940s
Navajo
Sheet band; clasp set with three
small round turquoises; twisted
wire, bead wire, and stamped
decoration; 7½ (19.1).
Provenance: Turpen Trading Post,
Gallup, New Mexico.

Earrings

The use of earrings in the Southwest dates to prehistoric times. Early earrings were simple drilled stones that were strung on thongs and tied into a pierced earlobe, or small strings of turquoise beads (jaclas) worn in the same manner. The Spanish introduced glass earrings, and these were succeeded by Indian-made metal earrings, at first of brass and then of silver wire. The wire hoops were often threaded with one or two spherical silver beads or with a single squash blossom bead. The hoop form was followed by a silver plaque set with one or many turquoises—the type that predominates today. Most earrings made in this style after the turn of the century were intended for the tourist market. Zuni smiths typically add several dangles of wire at the lower edge of the plaque.

The measurement given for earrings is length.

J.B.W.
L.L.

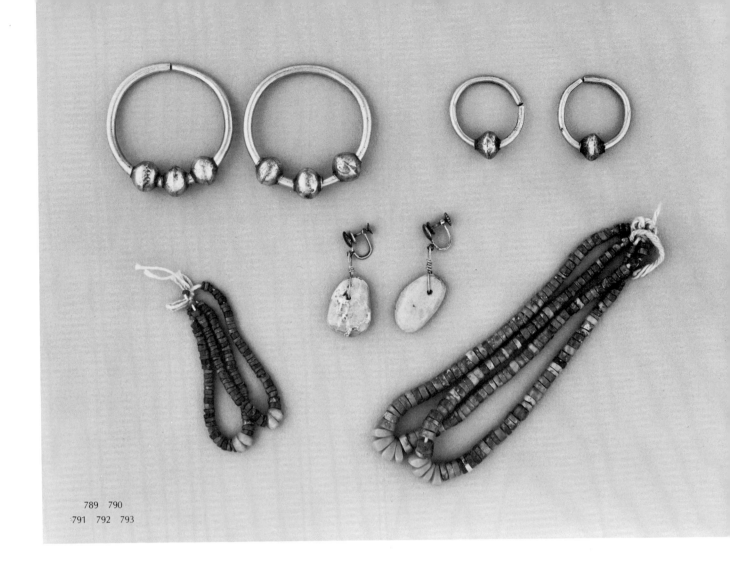

789 790
791 792 793

789 PAIR OF EARRINGS, possibly
     around 1910 or earlier
     Navajo
     Wire hoop with three spherical
     beads; 1⅝ (4.1).
     Provenance: W. S. Dutton,
     Santa Fe, New Mexico.

790 PAIR OF EARRINGS, about 1910
     or earlier
     Navajo
     Wire hoop with single spherical
     bead; 1 (2.5).
     Provenance: unknown.

791 PAIR OF CHILD'S EARRINGS,
     about 1850
     Pueblo
     Jacla of graduated discoidal
     turquoise beads on a string with
     white shell beads at center;
     2½ (6.4).
     Provenance: Hubbell's Trading
     Post, Winslow, Arizona, 1953.

792 PAIR OF EARRINGS, about 1900
     Navajo
     Turquoise nugget pendant on
     modern earring clasp; 2 (5.1).
     Provenance: unknown.

793 PAIR OF EARRINGS, about 1900
     Pueblo
     Jacla of graduated discoidal
     turquoise beads on a string with
     red plastic beads at center;
     5 (12.7).
     Provenance: Turpen Trading Post,
     Gallup, New Mexico, 1952.
     Bought as pawn.
     Red plastic beads are a later
     addition.

794 796
795
797 798

794 PAIR OF EARRINGS, about 1940
Navajo
Oval turquoises on sheet
mounting; four wire dangles;
teardrop and twisted wire
decoration; 3 (7.6).
Provenance: Gallup, New Mexico,
1955.

795 SINGLE EARRING, 1930s
Navajo
Oval turquoise on sheet
mounting; bead wire decoration;
1⅝ (4.1).
Provenance: Hotevilla, Arizona,
1952.

796 PAIR OF EARRINGS, about 1940
Navajo
Elliptical turquoises on sheet
mounting; five oval turquoises on
bar suspended; two wire dangles;
bead wire decoration; 2 (5.1).
Provenance: unknown.

797 PAIR OF EARRINGS, about 1930
Zuni
Sheet mounting set with one
elliptical and twelve round
turquoises; dangles missing;
1⅜ (3.5).
Provenance: Hubbell's Trading
Post, Winslow, Arizona, 1953.
Bought as pawn.

798 PAIR OF EARRINGS, about 1935
Zuni
Elliptical Battle Mountain
turquoise with triangular
turquoise as pendant; twisted
wire decoration; 1¾ (4.4).
Provenance: Turpen Trading Post,
Gallup, New Mexico, 1952.
Bought as pawn.

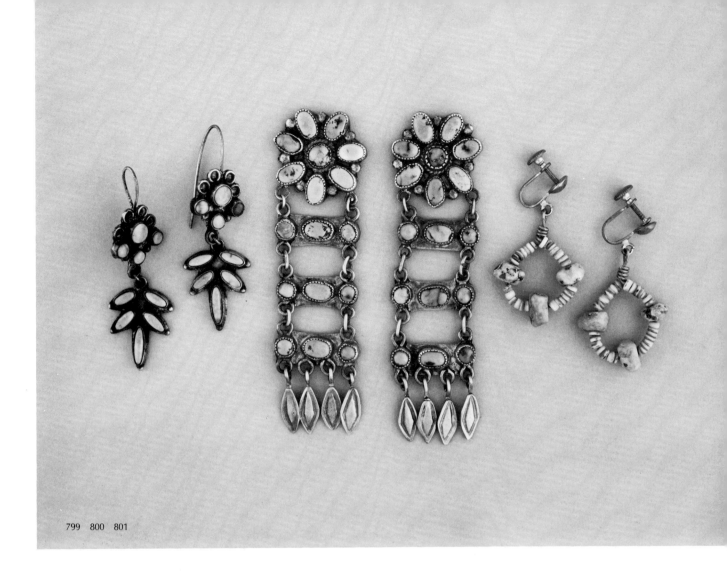

799 800 801

799 PAIR OF EARRINGS, about 1950
Zuni
Half-clusters of four small round
turquoises; cluster of elliptical
turquoises in leaf shape as
pendant; 2¼ (5.7).
Provenance: unknown.

800 PAIR OF EARRINGS, about 1940
Zuni
Cluster of round and elliptical
turquoises in serrated bezels;
three bars set with turquoise as
pendants; sheet dangles; stamped
decoration; 3½ (8.9).
Provenance: Asa Glascock,
Gallup, New Mexico, 1952.

801 PAIR OF EARRINGS, 1950s
Pueblo
Loop of discoidal shell beads
with three turquoise beads
interspersed; 1¾ (4.4).
Provenance: unknown.

Not shown:

802 PAIR OF EARRINGS, about 1940
     Zuni
     Single round turquoise with
     crescent sheet pendant set with
     seven round turquoises; nine wire
     dangles; twisted wire decoration;
     2½ (6.4).
     Provenance: Asa Glascock,
     Gallup, New Mexico, 1953.

803 PAIR OF EARRINGS, 1940
     Navajo
     Round repoussé plaque; wire
     dangles; spiral wire decoration;
     2 (5.1).
     Provenance: unknown.

804 PAIR OF EARRINGS, 1940s
     Navajo
     Undrilled flattened bead; three
     wire dangles; stamped decoration;
     2 (5.1).
     Provenance: Turpen Trading Post,
     Gallup, New Mexico.
     Bought as pawn.

805 PAIR OF EARRINGS, 1940s
     Zuni
     Repoussé ornament with plaque
     with three turquoises as pendants;
     three wire dangles; 1⅝ (4.1).
     Provenance: Hanns Hogan,
     Gallup, New Mexico, 1953.
     Bought as pawn.

806 PAIR OF EARRINGS, 1940s
     Navajo
     Wire hoop with spherical bead;
     1½ (3.8).
     Provenance: unknown.

807 PAIR OF EARRINGS, 1940s
     Zuni
     Single round turquoise and two
     linked elliptical plaques, each set
     with three turquoises; three wire
     dangles; 2 (5.1).
     Provenance: unknown.

808 PAIR OF EARRINGS, 1940s
     Zuni
     Elliptical Nevada turquoise with
     three wire dangles, each set with
     small oval turquoise; 1⅝ (4.1).
     Provenance: Ramah, New
     Mexico, 1953.

809 PAIR OF EARRINGS, about 1950
     Zuni
     Wire oval set with four small
     oval turquoises; four wire
     dangles; 2 (5.1).
     Provenance: unknown.

810 PAIR OF EARRINGS, about 1950
     Zuni
     Two triangular turquoises on sheet
     mountings, linked together; three
     sheet dangles; twisted wire, bent
     wire, and stamped decoration;
     2⅜ (6).
     Provenance: unknown.

811 PAIR OF EARRINGS, about 1950
     Zuni
     Small round turquoise with
     half-cluster of one round and
     three oval turquoises as pendant;
     wire dangles; twisted wire
     decoration; 2⅝ (6.7).
     Provenance: unknown.

812 PAIR OF EARRINGS, about 1950
     Zuni
     Two round turquoises on sheet
     mountings, linked together; wire
     dangles; 2⅜ (6).
     Provenance: Eric Kohlberg,
     Denver, Colorado, 1955.
     Bought as pawn.

813 PAIR OF EARRINGS, about 1950
     Zuni
     Six small round turquoises set on
     triangular plaque; wire dangles;
     1¾ (4.4).
     Provenance: Hubbell's Trading
     Post, Winslow, Arizona, 1953.

814 PAIR OF EARRINGS, about 1950
     Zuni
     Three elliptical turquoises on
     sheet mounting; wire dangles;
     2 (5.1).
     Provenance: Hotevilla, Arizona,
     1952.

815 PAIR OF EARRINGS, about 1950
     Zuni
     Sheet mounting in modified
     squash blossom form set with one
     oval and five small elliptical
     turquoises; 2 (5.1).
     Provenance: Packard's Trading
     Post, Santa Fe, New Mexico,
     1950s.

816 PAIR OF EARRINGS, about 1950
     Zuni
     Single round turquoise with larger
     oval turquoise as pendant;
     twisted wire decoration; 2¼ (5.7).
     Provenance: unknown.

817 PAIR OF EARRINGS, about 1950
     Zuni
     Four elliptical turquoises in
     cluster; five wire dangles;
     1⅝ (4.1).
     Provenance: unknown.

818 PAIR OF EARRINGS, 1950
     Zuni
     Cluster of round and oval
     turquoises; two bars set with
     turquoises as pendants; six wire
     dangles; twisted wire decoration;
     2⅝ (6.7).
     Provenance: Asa Glascock,
     Gallup, New Mexico, 1953.

819 PAIR OF EARRINGS, about 1960
     Zuni
     Half-cluster of five small
     round turquoises with oval
     mounting and nine small
     turquoises as pendant; three
     wire dangles; 2¼ (5.7).
     Provenance: Nettie Wheeler,
     Muskogee, Oklahoma, 1968.

Rings

Metal finger rings, first brought to the South-west by the Spanish, continued to be supplied as commercial goods until the Navajo began making their own rings of silver, probably in the 1860s. Most of the rings shown in photographs from Bosque Redondo are simple bands or bands widened at the front. About 1880 the Navajo began to set rings with a single small flat stone—turquoise, garnet, or even glass—and to apply stamped decoration. Those early rings are not represented in the Doneghy collection.

After the turn of the century larger stones came into use—now almost always turquoise and often cut in cabochon form. To support the larger stones, the band was usually split into two or more splayed strips. By about 1930, Zuni-style turquoise cluster rings had become popular with Navajo as well as Zuni smiths. The two most prevalent ring forms remain the large single turquoise and the turquoise cluster, both of which are set on split bands.

Height is given first, then width; both measurements include the stone.

J.B.W.
L.L.

820 821 822 823
824 825
826 827 828

820 RING, 1930s
Navajo
Split shank; set with large
rectangular Blue Gem turquoise
surrounded by smaller oval
turquoises; teardrop decoration;
1¾ × 1 (4.4 × 2.5).
Provenance: Turpen Trading Post,
Gallup, New Mexico, 1954.
Bought as pawn.

821 RING, about 1920
Navajo
Three wires; set with rectangular
cabochon turquoise in serrated
bezel; teardrop decoration;
1 × 1¼ (2.5 × 3.2).
Provenance: Chester Copman,
Santa Fe Gift Shop, Santa Fe,
New Mexico, 1956.

822 RING, 1930s
Hopi
Split shank; set with drilled oval
turquoise; bead wire decoration;
1¼ × 1 (3.2 × 2.5).
Provenance: Chief Joe Secakuku,
Winslow, Arizona, 1955.

823 RING, 1930s
Navajo
Cast band; set with large
elliptical turquoise in serrated
bezel, surrounded by smaller
turquoises; teardrop decoration;
1¾ × 1⅛ (4.4 × 2.9).
Provenance: Nettie Wheeler,
Muskogee, Oklahoma.

824 RING, 1930s
Navajo
Heavy sheet band; set with
square turquoise in four
flattened prongs; appliqué and
stamped decoration; ⅝ × 1
(1.6 × 2.5).
Provenance: unknown.

825 RING, 1930s
Navajo
Split band; set with elliptical
turquoise on sheet mounting;
twisted and spiral wire decoration;
1⅞ × ¾ (4.8 × 1.9).
Provenance: George Rummage,
Gallup, New Mexico, 1956.
Bought as pawn.

826 RING, 1930s–1940s
Navajo
Sheet band; set with elliptical
turquoise; stamped decoration;
⁹⁄₁₆ × 1 (1.4 × 2.5).
Provenance: unknown.

827 RING, 1930s–1940s
Navajo
Split shank; set with rectangular
turquoise in serrated bezel;
stamped, appliqué, and twisted
wire decoration; ⅞ × 1⅛
(2.2 × 2.9).
Provenance: Chief Joe Secakuku,
Winslow, Arizona, 1955.

828 RING, 1930s
Navajo
Three round wires; set with
elliptical turquoise; teardrop
decoration; ½ × ⅞ (1.3 × 2.2).
Provenance: unknown.

Not shown:

829 RING, 1920s–1930s
Navajo
Split shank; set with triangular
turquoise; 1¼ × 1 (3.2 × 2.5).
Provenance: unknown.

830 RING, 1920s–1930s
Navajo
Split shank; set with oval
turquoise; twisted wire and
teardrop decoration; ⅝ × 1
(1.6 × 2.5).
Provenance: unknown.

831 RING, 1920s–1930s
Navajo
Split shank; set with elliptical
cabochon turquoise surrounded
by twelve small turquoises;
teardrop and bead wire
decoration; 1 × 1¼ (2.5 × 2.9).
Provenance: unknown.

832 RING, about 1930
Hopi
Split shank; set with large oval
turquoise; bead wire and teardrop
decoration; 1¼ × 1 (3.2 × 2.5).
Provenance: Chief Joe Secakuku,
Winslow, Arizona, 1955.

833 RING, 1930s
Navajo
Split shank; set with elliptical
turquoise; appliqué, twisted wire,
and looped wire decoration;
¾ × ¾ (1.9 × 1.9).
Provenance: Chief Joe Secakuku,
Winslow, Arizona, 1953.

834 RING, 1930s
Navajo
Split band; set with one elliptical
and two round turquoises in
serrated bezels; twisted wire and
teardrop decoration; 1¾ × 1
(4.4 × 2.5).
Provenance: Dressman, Santa Fe,
New Mexico, 1952.

835 RING, 1930s
Navajo
Split shank; set with elliptical
turquoise; twisted wire and
stamped decoration; ⅞ × ¾
(2.2 × 1.9).
Provenance: Hagberg's, Gallup,
New Mexico, 1956.

836 RING, 1930s
Navajo
Split shank; set with large oval
turquoise in scalloped bezel;
1¾ × 1⅛ (4.4 × 2.9).
Provenance: unknown.

837 RING, 1930s
Navajo
Split band; set with elliptical
drilled turquoise in serrated
bezel; twisted wire, teardrop, and
appliqué decoration; 1¼ × 1⅛
(3.2 × 2.9).
Provenance: Tesuque Trading
Post, Santa Fe, New Mexico, 1954.

838 RING, 1930s
Navajo
Split shank; set with triangular
turquoise; teardrop and twisted
wire decoration; ¾ × ⅞
(1.9 × 2.2).
Provenance: unknown.
Bought as pawn.

839 RING, 1930s
Navajo
Split shank; set with nine round
turquoises on sheet mounting;
teardrop decoration; 1 × ⅞
(2.5 × 2.2).
Provenance: unknown.
Bought as pawn.

840 RING, 1930s
Navajo
Split shank; set with triangular
turquoise; twisted wire and spiral
wire decoration; ½ × ⅞
(1.3 × 2.2).
Provenance: unknown.
Bought as pawn.

841 RING, 1930s–1940s
Navajo
Split shank; set with three round
flat turquoises on sheet mounting;
teardrop decoration; 1¹³⁄₁₆ × 1⅛
(4.6 × 2.9).
Provenance: unknown.

842 RING, 1930s–1940s
Zuni
Band of five twisted wires; set
with two heart-shaped turquoises
surrounded by twenty-three small
oval turquoises; teardrop
decoration; 1¾ × 1 (4.4 × 2.5).
Provenance: unknown.
Bought as pawn.

843 RING, about 1940
Zuni
Sheet band; set with seven
turquoises in serrated bezels;
teardrop decoration; ³⁄₁₆ × ⅞
(0.5 × 2.2).
Provenance: unknown.

844 845 846 847
848 849 850 851

844 RING, 1940s
Navajo
Split shank; set with elliptical
turquoise; twisted wire
decoration; 1¾ × 1 (4.4 × 2.5).
Provenance: Chief Joe Secakuku,
Winslow, Arizona, 1955.

845 RING, 1940s
Navajo
Split shank; set with elliptical
spiderweb turquoise; teardrop
and twisted wire decoration;
1¼ × 1⅛ (3.2 × 2.9).
Provenance: Tesuque Trading
Post, Santa Fe, New Mexico, 1954.

846 RING, 1940s
Navajo
Split shank; set with square
turquoise; twisted wire and
appliqué decoration; ⅞ × 1
(2.2 × 2.5).
Provenance: Chief Joe Secakuku,
Winslow, Arizona.

847 RING, 1950s
Navajo
Split shank; set with three square
turquoises with one square
turquoise on either side; filed
decoration; 1¾ × ⅞ (4.4 × 2.2).
Provenance: Chief Joe Secakuku,
Winslow, Arizona, 1959.

848 CHILD'S RING, about 1950
Navajo
Split shank; set with small
elliptical turquoise; bent wire
decoration; ⅜ × ⅝ (1 × 1.6).
Provenance: Turpen Trading Post,
Gallup, New Mexico, 1956.

849 CHILD'S RING, about 1950
Navajo
Sheet band; set with round
turquoise on sheet mounting;
bead wire and bent wire
decoration; ⅝ × ⅝ (1.6 × 1.6).
Provenance: Turpen Trading Post,
Gallup, New Mexico, 1956.

850 RING, 1960s
Zuni
Sheet band; set with small round
turquoise, five pear-shaped
turquoises in serrated bezels on
either side; teardrop decoration;
⅜ × 1 (1 × 2.5).
Provenance: unknown.

851 CHILD'S RING, about 1950
Navajo
Split shank; set with small round
turquoise; twisted wire
decoration; ³⁄₁₆ × ⅝ (0.5 × 1.6).
Provenance: Turpen Trading Post,
Gallup, New Mexico, 1956.

Not shown:

852 RING, 1940s
Hopi
Split shank; plaque set with eight
round flat turquoises; teardrop
and wire decoration; 1¼ × 1
(2.9 × 2.5).
Provenance: Chief Joe Secakuku,
Winslow, Arizona, 1953.

853 RING, 1940s
Navajo
Split shank; set with large oval
turquoise; square wire and bead
wire decoration; 1¼ × 1
(3.2 × 2.5).
Provenance: Turpen Trading Post,
Gallup, New Mexico, 1953.

854 RING, 1940s
Zuni
Split shank; set with large cluster
of twenty-six oval and round
turquoises in serrated bezels;
teardrop and twisted wire
decoration; 1¾ × ¾ (4.4 × 1.9).
Provenance: unknown.

855 RING, about 1950
Navajo
Split shank; set with round
turquoise surrounded by eight
smaller round turquoises; twisted
wire and teardrop decoration;
1½ × 1¼ (3.8 × 3.2).
Provenance: Chief Joe Secakuku,
Winslow, Arizona, 1959.

856 RING, about 1950
Zuni
Split shank; set with seven small
round turquoises; teardrop and
stamped decoration; ½ × ¾
(1.3 × 1.9).
Provenance: unknown.

857 RING, about 1950
Zuni
Split shank; set with single
turquoise carved in leaf shape;
1¼ × 1⅛ (3.2 × 2.9).
Provenance: Bruckman, Winslow,
Arizona, 1956.

858 RING, about 1950
Zuni
Split shank; set with elliptical
turquoise; stone and bezel filed
into six sections; ⅞ × 1
(2.2 × 2.5).
Provenance: Tesuque Trading
Post, Santa Fe, New Mexico, 1954.

859 RING, 1950
Navajo
Split shank; set with three
elliptical turquoises; appliqué

and stamped decoration;
¹³⁄₁₆ × ¾ (2.1 × 1.9).
Provenance: unknown.
Bought as pawn.

860 RING, about 1950
Navajo
Split shank; set with oval
turquoise surrounded by fourteen
small oval turquoises; twisted
wire and teardrop decoration;
1⅜ × 1 (3.5 × 2.5).
Provenance: unknown.
Bought as pawn.

861 RING, about 1950
Navajo
Split shank; set with large
elliptical turquoise surrounded by
seventeen smaller oval turquoises;
twisted wire decoration;
1¾ × 1 (4.4 × 2.5).
Provenance: Chief Joe Secakuku,
Winslow, Arizona, 1955.

862 RING, about 1950
Navajo
Split shank; set with elliptical
turquoise flanked by three small
round turquoises, two half-round
turquoises on top and bottom;
1 × 1 (2.5 × 2.5).
Provenance: Turpen Trading Post,
Gallup, New Mexico.

863 RING, about 1950
Navajo
Split shank; set with round
cabochon turquoise; twisted wire
decoration; 1⅛ × 1¼ (2.9 × 3.2).
Provenance: Turpen Trading Post,
Gallup, New Mexico, 1953.

864 RING, 1950s
Zuni
Sheet band; set with thirteen
round turquoises; twisted wire
decoration; ⅛ × ⅞ (0.3 × 2.2).
Provenance: unknown.

865 CHILD'S RING, 1950s
Zuni
Half-round wire; set with three
tiny turquoises in serrated bezels;
teardrop decoration; ⅛ × ⅝
(0.3 × 1.6).
Provenance: Turpen Trading Post,
Gallup, New Mexico.

866 RING, 1950s
Navajo
Split shank; set with single
pear-shaped cabochon turquoise;
twisted wire decoration; ¾ × 1¼
(1.9 × 3.2).
Provenance: unknown.

867 RING, 1950s
Navajo
Split shank; rectangular plaque
set with three round cabochon
turquoises; teardrop decoration;
1¾ × ¾ (4.4 × 1.9).
Provenance: unknown.

868 RING, 1950s
Navajo
Split shank; rectangular plaque
set with six round turquoises;
bezel wire and teardrop decoration; ¹³⁄₁₆ × ¾ (2.1 × 1.9).
Provenance: unknown.

869 RING, 1950s
Navajo
Three square wires; set with
round cabochon turquoise;
¾ × 1 (1.9 × 2.5).
Provenance: Hubbell's Trading
Post, Winslow, Arizona, 1953.

870 RING, 1950s
Navajo
Split shank; set with elliptical
turquoise surrounded by fourteen
oval turquoises; twisted wire
decoration; 1⅛ × 1 (2.9 × 2.5).
Provenance: Turpen Trading Post,
Gallup, New Mexico.

871 RING, 1950s
Navajo
Split shank; set with three round
and two triangular turquoises on
lozenge-shaped plate; teardrop
decoration; 1¹⁄₁₆ × ¾ (2.7 × 1.4).
Provenance: unknown.

872 RING, 1950s
Hopi
Hopi Silvercraft Guild mark.
Split shank; sheet mounting with
overlay; twisted wire and appliqué
decoration; ⅞ × ⅞ (2.2 × 2.2).
Provenance: unknown.

873 RING, about 1960
Navajo
Split shank; set with elliptical
turquoise; twisted wire
decoration; ⅝ × 1 (1.6 × 2.5).
Provenance: unknown.

874 RING, about 1960
Navajo
Split shank; set with elliptical
turquoise on sheet mounting;
teardrop and faceted teardrop
decoration; 1 × 1 (2.5 × 2.5).
Provenance: Peggy Evans,
Albuquerque, New Mexico, 1961.

Bridle

The introduction of the horse by white
conquerors into Indian cultures produced
vast social and economic changes, perhaps
nowhere more than among the Navajo. In
gaining mobility and increased military and
hunting capabilities, they also gained a means
of displaying wealth. The Spanish, following
the Moors, had long decorated their prized
horses with silver-mounted bridles. The Navajo
readily adopted the type, and silver-covered
headstalls were included in the repertoire of
early Navajo smiths. The bridle proper was
made of buckskin, often braided, and was
then sheathed in silver to cover portions of
the leather. Typically, the sidepieces were
each ornamented with a round concha and a
curved, tapering silver strap end, while the
browband carried a silver plaque from which
hung a pendant, usually a naja. It was from
Spanish bridles like this that the Navajo
adapted the naja for use on necklaces. Early
bridles were filed or chased; as time passed,
the decoration became more elaborate. Cars
and trucks have now largely replaced the
horse as a means of transportation and a
source of prestige, but a few bridles are
still made for collectors.

L.L.
J.S.

875 BRIDLE, 1960s
Navajo
Leather bands with sheet
mountings; center mounting set
with three oval turquoises;
carinated wire naja with turquoise
center pendant; two conchas at
sides, each set with oval
turquoise; stamped decoration;
14½ × 14⅞ (68 × 77).
Provenance: Packard's Trading
Post, Santa Fe, New Mexico, 1973.

Collector's Afterword

Virginia Doneghy

I do not remember exactly when I made my first trip to the Southwest, but I know it was in the late 1930s. I had been to California and wanted to see Santa Fe before returning to Minnesota. I also wanted to see El Paso, "the heart of the great American desert." In El Paso I saw by chance a notice of the Fiesta of San Jeronimo which was being held in Taos and decided to bypass Santa Fe for the moment and head directly to Taos. It was from the bus window, when we stopped briefly at La Fonda, a Harvey hotel in Santa Fe, that I caught a glimpse of what seemed to me the most beautiful necklace I had ever seen. It was in the window of the gift shop at the hotel, and I will never forget how beautiful and unexpected it was.

At the Martin Hotel in Taos I met Mr. Bragg, a man who taught in the Indian School Service and during the summer was working at the hotel and also conducting tourist parties. He turned out to be from my home county of Macon in Missouri, and the kindnesses he showed me are too numerous to mention. He drove me out to the Indian pueblo several times, telling me what I could and could not do. He introduced me to people and took me into Indian homes.

When the Fiesta was over and I had arrived in Santa Fe, the necklace was still in the window. It was as beautiful on close inspection as it had been from the bus. It was quite long, had earrings to match, and cost $75. It might as well have been $7,500. But I began then what I have continued to do—I looked and looked and looked. And at Mr. Frank Patania's on the Plaza I found a mate, obviously by the same silversmith, much shorter, no earrings, for $25, and that was my first purchase.

I did not go out each year, but most years. I now remember certain things that interested me very much that I did not buy, for I *had* a necklace—it never occurred to me to buy another. But things gradually changed, and I began to yield to temptation.

For me and for many other tourists, the Santa Fe Railroad station in Albuquerque was the gate to the Indian country. And inside the gate was the beautiful Alvarado Hotel, where I met Mr. Mark R. Boyd and Mr. Robert G. Evans. Mr. Boyd was the director of the Fred Harvey retail department. He had spent twenty years at the Grand Canyon and knew and loved the Hopi. In Albuquerque he was in a position to meet people of all kinds, for everybody came by train. He told me many things, since he was widely read on Southwest Indian matters and I was not, and he had many Indian friends. Mr. Evans was the reservation buyer, having taken over those responsibilities from the great Mr. Schweizer. He had no hesitancy in telling me where my taste was wrong, a fact I greatly appreciated.

Eventually I established what I called "my route," but on those very early visits I was wedded to the Alvarado Hotel and Gift Shop in Albuquerque and El Navajo in Gallup (in the neighborhood where the Turpen Trading Post was then located). Mr. Boyd and Mr. Evans at the former and Mr. Tobe Turpen, Jr., at the latter were really my guardian angels, but I did not know it nor did they. Three experts and an ignoramus in their midst, but an ignoramus who was fascinated and wanted to learn.

The procedure at both stores was the same. Shops in those days did not bother about tissue paper, cotton, fancy boxes, and colored ribbons. The stock in trade was brown paper bags. At each store behind the counter or in the office a series of bags was lined up— one for rings, one for bracelets, one for pins, and so on. When after a day or two or three the final day of reckoning came, I would select and discard (often with advice), and then wait until the next year. This was *it* and it was heaven.

I cannot begin to record the many dealers to whom I am indebted, and so I will only mention the few with whom I had most dealings. Mr. George Rummage of Gallup; Frances Quarles in Taos, and after her death Brice and Judy Sewell; and Miss Morrill and Miss Janssen of the Taos Book Shop. Al Packard in Santa Fe always had something I wanted, and as the years went on I perhaps depended on him more than anyone. When the Harvey shop in Albuquerque closed, Price's All Indian Shop became my headquarters there. Mr. Eric Kohlberg in Denver had a fine shop, and many small shops everywhere yielded treasures.

My collection has emerged from a world which no longer exists. Practically nothing in it could be found or duplicated today. Craftsmanship and aesthetic quality have deteriorated over the years. There is practically nothing old left to buy. If I were making my first visit to the Southwest today, I would never become a collector. But since I am interested in crafts, each year I try to buy something new which I consider good. This is easier said than done, and belts and bracelets (plain band) are what most frequently fill the bill. My emphasis has been on Navajo, and my taste is traditional. The old Hopi (unlike the new) cannot be distinguished from Navajo, but I got all my old Hopi pieces from a Hopi dealer, Chief Joe Secakuku of the

Second Mesa, who always told me where the Hopi articles came from. It was he who said the only way to know whether it was Navajo or Hopi was to know where it came from. My collection is also largely pawned, and thus, rightly or wrongly, I feel exhibits Indian taste as well as my own.

My modus operandi has been to look, look, look, to read, and above all to listen. I have full and complete notes. For almost every piece, I have recorded the description in sufficient detail to identify it. I have the date and place of purchase, the dealer's name, the price I paid, and the appraised value. In addition, I have noted dealers' opinions, my own observations and opinions, whether or not I have encountered the same piece in more than one shop, whether I paid too much, discrepancies in price, and so on. I have practically all my bills, my canceled checks with the number of the item noted on them, and all my pawn tickets. I have never listed a thing as being pawned unless I was so told by the dealer or had the pawn ticket in my own hands. Likewise I have never felt competent to attribute a date, but when Mr. Packard, Mr. Tom Bahti, Mr. Tobe Turpen, Jr., and Mr. Evans did so, I accepted their judgment.

Not all of my pieces are equally "fine." I have bought the best when I could, but I have considered it important to get examples of what the poor and everyday Indian treasured as well as what the well-to-do would wear. It is important to see how the same motif and design were executed with poor tools as well as with good ones, and how a less skillful craftsman tried to keep up with his more affluent kinsmen.

Only on several trips to the Hopi Snake Dance did I really get into the reservation, a fact which I regret. I was dependent on public transportation, including the mail buses, and claim I have helped deliver more baby chicks than any other woman tourist. On the mail buses as time went on I got to know the drivers, and more than once they went out of their way for me to see something interesting. By modern standards I did things the hard way, but I certainly enjoyed it.

Glossary

Annealing—A process of tempering metal by heating and rapid cooling; in Southwest silverwork, heating and softening coins just enough to work the metal into the desired shape. See *Sintering*.

Appliqué—A small decorative element soldered to a silver object.

Bent wire—Decorative appliqué consisting of short sections of fine round wire bent into circles or half-circles.

Bezel—A thin strip of silver rimming a stone and holding it to the backing. The upper edge is often serrated or scalloped, so that the bezel can be bent inward more tightly around the stone.

Boss—A raised ornament, either solid or repoussé. See *Repoussé*.

"Bruised heart"—An ornamental device frequently found at the lower terminal of Southwest metal crosses. It is heart-shaped, with a slight indentation on one side. The origin of the motif is unclear.

"Butterfly"—A characteristic Navajo design configuration consisting of a center element flanked by two radiating "wings." Most explicit in dress and belt ornaments, it also frequently governs the arrangement of stones on bracelets and rings. The association with butterflies was made by Euro-American traders; the form does not carry this connotation among the Navajo.

Cabochon—A style of gem cutting in which the stone is polished into a high round shape and not faceted.

Casting—Formation of an object in a mold. Among the Navajo simple casting of ingots began in the 1870s; by the 1880s more elaborate casting was done in molds made of tufa, a light, porous rock found on the reservation. Tufa casts are still made, but modern smiths also cast in oiled sand or in centrifugal casting machines (spin-casting) that permit them to produce many identical pieces.

Chalcedony—Bluish gray or greenish gray quartz, sometimes polished and set in Southwest Indian jewelry.

Channelwork—Inlaying or setting of multiple stones, usually turquoises, separated by thin silver strips. The effect is similar to that of cloisonné enameling.

Chasing—Decoration of a silver surface by means of a chisel and hammer.

Chrysocolla—A blue or green mineral sometimes substituted for turquoise in Southwest Indian jewelry.

Concha (Spanish "shell")—A small silver plate, usually elliptical or round in outline and characteristically decorated with a radiating center device and a scalloped edge. It is used in multiples to decorate belts.

"Cornflower"—A variant of the squash blossom motif in which the bead and projecting decoration are flattened and reduced to three petallike elements. Also called "corntassel" and "fleur-de-lis." See *Squash blossom*.

Crimped wire—Bezel wire bent into a zigzag pattern and used as a decorative appliqué.

Dapping—Shaping a silver object by forcing it into a round-bottomed trough.

Gadrooning—Repoussé surface decoration consisting of a series of curved convex ridges.

Hopi Silvercraft Guild—A cooperative organization formed in 1949 to support production and marketing of Hopi-made silver goods. In addition to their own mark, members mark their work with the guild's sun stamp:

Hubbell glass—Glass beads imported from Italy from about 1900 on and sold at trading posts, in particular that of Lorenzo Hubbell at Ganado, Arizona, as substitutes for turquoise.

Ingot—A silver slug formed by melting metal and casting it in a small trough mold.

Jacla—A small loop of discoidal turquoise or turquoise and shell beads, usually no more than four inches long. Formerly tied into pierced earlobes as earrings, jaclas are now principally worn as pendants on stone and shell bead necklaces.

Ketoh—A wide leather band worn by archers on the left wrist as protection from the snap of the bowstring. In the early period of silverwork the Navajo began to decorate these bands with silver plaques, and later they also used cast ornaments for this purpose.

Looped wire—Round wire formed with pliers into a series of scrolls and used as appliqué ornament or as a bracelet structure.

Malachite—A deep green mineral containing copper, occasionally set in Southwest silver jewelry.

Naja (Navajo *najahe*, "crescent")—A crescent-shaped silver ornament used as a forehead pendant on horse bridles and also as a necklace pendant. It is probably derived from Spanish saddlery decoration, which in turn has Near Eastern sources. Many variant types exist.

Navajo Arts and Crafts Guild—A cooperative formed in 1941 to produce and market Navajo-made silver, textiles, and other goods. Some pieces made under its auspices bear the guild label or stamp:

"Needlepoint"—A style of cutting and setting tiny elongated turquoises in parallel or concentric rows. Practiced chiefly by Zuni smiths.

Overlay—A technique developed by Hopi smiths in the late 1930s for surface decoration. A silver sheet with cutout designs is soldered to a backing sheet, and the indented areas are blackened by oxidization to emphasize the contrast.

"Oxbow"—A decorative element surmounting a naja. In occasional use since the 1930s, it is essentially a double bicurve design.

"Pumpkin seed"—Seed-shaped or leaf-shaped variant of the squash blossom motif. See *Squash blossom.*

Repoussé—Relief decoration of a flat surface by raising a pattern from the reverse side.

Rowwork—Arrangement of small turquoises in one or more closely set rows. Typical of Zuni style.

Sheet—Silver formed into a flat surface of even thickness. Early smiths produced this necessary material by hammering heated metal; since 1929 commercially produced sheet in various gauges has been available.

Silver—Nineteenth-century smiths obtained their metal by melting U.S. or Mexican coins, both currencies consisting of an alloy of about one part copper to nine parts silver. When laws against defacing coinage were enforced, smiths began to rely on ingots of sterling (a purer alloy) provided by traders.

Sintering—Forming materials into a solid mass by means of heat but without melting. In glass-working, the process is used to join chips of different colors, creating a speckled appearance. See *Annealing.*

Spiny oyster—A Pacific bivalve with a mottled red and white shell that was traded inland to the Southwest in prehistoric and historic times.

Spiral wire—Fine round wire formed into small flat spirals and applied as a decorative element. Used primarily in the 1930s.

Split band, split shank—A basic structure for bracelets or rings. A strip of sheet metal is cut horizontally one or more times, with the ends left intact, and the thin strips are then pulled apart to widen the piece.

Squash blossom—An elaborate bead form consisting of a conical "blossom" attached to a spherical bead. Squash blossoms are frequently used in combination with plain beads on Navajo and other Southwest necklaces. The form is derived from Spanish trouser buttons in the shape of pomegranates. The term is of Euro-American origin; the Navajo word for the type means roughly "bead that spreads out."

Stamping—Decoration of a silver surface by striking it with a small metal die bearing a raised pattern.

Teardrop—A scrap of silver heated until it forms a globule, and then used as an appliqué ornament. Also known as "raindrop" and "shot."

Turquoise—A mineral whose characteristic blue or green color is imparted by copper aluminum phosphate. In the American Southwest, turquoise was worked into beads and other ornaments in prehistoric times. Turquoise mines produce stones of varying appearance and grade; the source of top-grade turquoise can often be identified from the stone's distinctive coloration and the pattern of its matrix (the brownish or blackish mineral in which the turquoise is formed). Low-grade turquoise is pale and chalky, but it can be treated to resemble the harder stone. Much recently produced turquoise is stabilized by an acrylic coating.

Variscite—A greenish mineral related to turquoise and occasionally substituted for it.

Wire—Early Southwest metal bracelets were made of commercially produced copper or brass wire acquired through trade. With the beginning of indigenous silverwork, smiths manufactured silver wire by hammering; later on, they used a draw-plate. Carinated, or triangular, wire was fabricated early, and so was square wire, which was twisted to form the basis of bracelets.

Early in the twentieth century, round, square, and carinated silver wire became available commercially. Double twisted wire—two round wires held parallel and then twisted about each other—came into use in the 1920s.

Commercially produced bead wire, a decorative element duplicating a row of tiny teardrops, was common in the 1930s.

Bibliography

Adair, John. *The Navajo and Pueblo Silversmiths.* Norman: University of Oklahoma Press, 1944.

Ashton, Sharon, and Robert Ashton. *The C. G. Wallace Collection of American Indian Art.* Sale 3806. New York: Sotheby Parke Bernet, 1975.

Bedinger, Margery. *Indian Silver: Navaho and Pueblo Jewelers.* Albuquerque: University of New Mexico Press, 1973.

————. *Navaho Indian Silver-Work.* Old West Series of Pamphlets, no. 8. Denver: John Vanmale, 1936.

Berlant, Anthony, and Mary H. Kahlenberg. *Walk in Beauty: The Navajo and Their Blankets.* Boston: New York Graphic Society, 1977.

Bunzel, Ruth L. *The Pueblo Potter: A Study of Creative Imagination in Primitive Art.* Columbia University Contributions to Anthropology, vol. 8. New York: Columbia University Press, 1929.

Dittert, Alfred E., Jr., and Fred Plog. *Generations in Clay: Pueblo Pottery of the American Southwest.* Flagstaff, Ariz.: Northland Press, in cooperation with the American Federation of Arts, 1980.

Ellison, Rosemary. *Contemporary Southern Plains Indian Metalwork.* Anadarko: Oklahoma Indian Arts and Crafts Cooperative, 1976.

Frank, Larry, and Millard J. Holbrook II. *Indian Silver Jewelry of the Southwest, 1868–1930.* Boston: New York Graphic Society, 1978.

Frisbie, Charlotte Johnson. *Kinaaldá: A Study of the Navaho Girl's Puberty Ceremony.* Middletown, Conn.: Wesleyan University Press, 1967.

Frisbie, Charlotte J., ed. *Southwestern Indian Ritual Drama.* School of American Research Advanced Seminar Series. Albuquerque: University of New Mexico Press, 1980.

Gilpin, Laura. *The Enduring Navaho.* Austin: University of Texas Press, 1968.

Hatcher, Evelyn Payne. *Visual Metaphors: A Formal Analysis of Navajo Art.* American Ethnological Society Monograph 58. St. Paul, Minn.: West Publishing Company, 1974.

Heard Museum. *White Metal Universe: Navajo Silver from the Fred Harvey Collection.* Phoenix, 1981.

Hill, W. W. *The Agricultural and Hunting Methods of the Navaho Indians.* Yale University Publications in Anthropology, no. 18. New Haven, Conn.: Yale University Press, 1938.

Jett, Stephen C., and Virginia E. Spencer. *Navajo Architecture.* Tucson: University of Arizona Press, 1981.

Kahlenberg, Mary Hunt, and Anthony Berlant. *The Navajo Blanket.* Los Angeles: Praeger Publishers, in association with the Los Angeles County Museum of Art, 1972.

Kelly, Lawrence C. *Navajo Roundup.* Boulder, Colo.: Pruett Publishing Company, 1970.

King, Dale Stuart. *Indian Silverwork of the Southwest.* Vol. 2. Tucson: Dale Stuart King, 1976.

Kluckhohn, Clyde, and Dorothea Leighton. *The Navaho.* Rev. ed. Cambridge, Mass.: Harvard University Press, 1974.

Lund, Marsha Mayer. *Indian Jewelry: Fact and Fantasy.* Boulder, Colo.: Paladin Press, 1976.

Matthews, Washington. *Navaho Legends Collected and Translated.* Memoirs of the American Folk-Lore Society, vol. 5. Boston: Houghton, Mifflin and Company, published for the American Folk-Lore Society, 1897.

————. "Navajo Silversmiths." In Bureau of American Ethnology, Annual Report no. 2, 1880–81, pp. 167–178. Washington, D.C.: Government Printing Office, 1883.

Mills, George. *Navaho Art and Culture.* Colorado Springs, Colo.: Taylor Museum, 1959.

Mindeleff, Cosmos. "Navaho Houses." In Bureau of American Ethnology, Annual Report no. 2, 1895–96. Part 2, pp. 475–517. Washington, D.C.: Government Printing Office, 1898.

Newcomb, Franc Johnson. *Hosteen Klah: Navaho Medicine Man and Sand Painter.* Norman: University of Oklahoma Press, 1964.

Reichard, Gladys A. *Navaho Religion: A Study of Symbolism.* 2d ed. Bollingen Series 18. Princeton, N.J.: Princeton University Press, 1963.

Webb, William. *Dwellers at the Source.* New York: Grossman Publishers, 1973.

Witherspoon, Gary. *Language and Art in the Navajo Universe.* Ann Arbor: University of Michigan Press, 1977.

Woodward, Arthur. *Navajo Silver: A Brief History of Navajo Silversmithing.* Flagstaff, Ariz.: Northland Press, 1971.

Worth, Sol, and John Adair. *Through Navajo Eyes: An Exploration in Film Communication and Anthropology.* Bloomington: Indiana University Press, 1973.

Wright, Margaret Nickelson. *Hopi Silver: The History and Hallmarks of Hopi Silversmithing.* Flagstaff, Ariz.: Northland Press, 1973.

Wyman, Leland C. *Blessingway.* Tucson: University of Arizona Press, 1970.

Wyman, Leland C., ed. *Beautyway: A Navaho Ceremonial.* Bollingen Series 53. New York: Pantheon Books, 1957.

Exhibition Staff

Samuel Sachs II, *Director*
Timothy Fiske, *Associate Director*
Michael Conforti, *Chairman, Curatorial Division;*
   Bell Memorial Curator of Decorative Arts and Sculpture
Louise Lincoln, *Curator in charge of exhibition;*
   Assistant Curator, African, Oceanic, and New World Cultures
Marcy Dahlquist, *Chairman, Communications Division*
Harold Peterson, *Librarian; Editor in Chief*
Elisabeth Sövik, *Associate Editor*
Ruth Dean, *Designer*
Anne Knauff, *Design Assistant*
Leland Randall, *Design Assistant*
Gary Mortensen, *Photographer*
Petronella Ytsma, *Assistant Photographer*
Marilyn Bjorklund, *Registrar*
Karen Duncan, *Assistant Registrar*
Todd Maitland, *Cataloguer, Registrar's Office*
Claire Ouellette, *Secretary, Registrar's Office*
Russell Belk, *Chief, Works of Art Crew*
Roxy Ballard, John Black, Craig Howell, Tom Jance, Theo Manzavrakos,
   David Marquis, Cathy Newton, Tim Stanko, *Works of Art Crew*
John Olson, *Lighting Technician*
Esther Nelson, *Maintenance Technician*
Kathryn C. Johnson, *Chairman, Education Division*
John Terry Zeller, *Coordinator, School Services*
Jane Hancock, *Supervisor, Audiovisual Department*
Robert Doyle, *Audiovisual Producer*
Lisa Nebenzahl, *Audiovisual Producer*
Judith Yellin, *Slide Librarian*
Diane Levy, *Supervisor, Tours and Docent Training*
Theodore A. Park, *Tours Associate*
Barbara Sarbach, *Tour Scheduler*
Emma Decent, *Tour Scheduler*
Emily Schmit Laskin, *Supervisor, Public Programs*
Mary Huber, *Circulating Materials Assistant*
Robert Booker, *Supervisor, Arts Resource and Information Center*
James Stave, *Administrative Assistant, Exhibitions*
Melissa Moore, *Publication and Production Coordinator*
Gordon Cable, *Chief of Security*